The Everywhere Millionaire

The Everywhere Millionaire

WHO IS REALLY RICH IN AMERICA
AND HOW THEY GOT THERE

Owen Zidar and Eric Zwick

Henry Holt and Company New York

Henry Holt and Company
Publishers since 1866
120 Broadway
New York, New York 10271
www.henryholt.com

Henry Holt® and ® are registered trademarks of Macmillan Publishing Group, LLC.
EU Representative: Macmillan Publishers Ireland Ltd., 1st Floor, The Liffey Trust Centre,
117–126 Sheriff Street Upper, Dublin 1, D01 YC43

Distributed in Canada by Raincoast Book Distribution Limited

Library of Congress Cataloging-in-Publication data is available.

ISBN 9781250378507

First Edition 2026

Designed by Kelly S. Too

Printed in the United States of America

10 9 8 7 6 5 4 3 2 1

The names and identifying details of some individuals discussed in this book have been changed.

To our parents.

CONTENTS

Prologue

The Wedding of the Century

This is now my royal wedding.

—Lauren Zigman, a wedding planner describing Madelaine Brockway's wedding

In November 2023, Bob and Paula Brockway of Coral Gables, Florida, hosted a wedding for their daughter, Madelaine. The festivities cost upward of $60 million and drew millions of viewers on social media, turning the event into a viral sensation dubbed the "wedding of the century."

Weeks before the nuptials, the twenty-six-year-old bride flew with friends for a four-day bachelorette jaunt in Canyon Point, Utah. They stayed at the Amangiri, which, at the time, charged $3,150 per night for a basic room. The group partied to a different theme each night—from "Pretty in Pink" to "Aliens Among Us" to "Golden Hour" to a final evening when Brockway and her girlfriends donned eighteenth-century powdered wigs, petticoats, and elaborate makeup for a French royalty–themed soirée.

Then came the wedding celebration, for which guests were flown by private jet to Paris. The five days of festivities included a private lunch in the Chanel Haute Couture Suite, a rehearsal dinner at the Paris Opera House, fireworks at the Eiffel Tower, a party under the Arc de Triomphe, and a night at the Palace of Versailles.

The Brockways rented out the entire grounds of Versailles. Guests dined in the palace in the style of the lost monarchy, served by waiters dressed in period costume. More than fifty hair and makeup artists styled the guests for the dinner. Guests wandered through the palace, snapping selfies in the Hall of Mirrors, where the Allies and Germany signed the treaty that formally ended World War I.

The bride and groom exchanged vows at the historic Château de Villette in Condécourt, an estate thirty miles northwest of the city designed by the same architect as Versailles. Known as "Little Versailles," the estate has hosted luminaries over the years, including Thomas Jefferson, Benjamin Franklin, and Tom Cruise. Author Dan Brown drew inspiration when he visited while working on *The Da Vinci Code.*

At the wedding reception, Adam Levine of Maroon 5 performed "She Will Be Loved" for the couple's first dance as the illuminated Eiffel Tower gleamed in the distance.

Who's got $60 million to drop on such an extravaganza for their daughter? You might think Bob and Paula Brockway made their money as investment bankers from Wall Street. Or tech executives from Silicon Valley.

Actually, they're car dealers.

The Everywhere Millionaire

Introduction

Who are the rich in America?

Perhaps the most popular measure of wealth in America is the Forbes 400, which lists the nation's richest people. In 2025, the top of the list features familiar names like Musk, Bezos, Gates, and Zuckerberg. Below them are family dynasties like the Waltons and Kochs, finance titans like Ken Griffin and Warren Buffett, entertainment bigwigs like George Lucas and Steven Spielberg, and sports team owners like Jerry Jones (Dallas Cowboys) and Robert Kraft (New England Patriots).

About three-quarters of the Forbes 400 are owners of public companies or tycoons in finance, tech, and real estate. TV paints a similar picture with shows like *Billions* and *Succession*—the former about a hedge fund manager set in New York and Connecticut, the latter about a media patriarch and his family dynasty set in New York.

Yet these titans (fictional or otherwise) are but a sliver of the nation's truly rich. Wealth in America is more abundant, and closer to home, than most people think.

The Brockways, whose vast wealth came from a family car dealership, are hardly unique. In nearly every city and town, so-called small business owners have built extraordinary fortunes running ordinary businesses.

Some are entrepreneurs who launched their own ventures, working long hours and reinvesting the profits to stay afloat and grow. Others inherited a family firm, continuing and building upon the success of prior generations.

Pop culture portrays the rich as an elite few, akin to the Rockefellers and Carnegies in the nineteenth-century Gilded Age. In reality, rich private business owners are now so plentiful that we're living in America's first Age of Millionaires.

* * *

What do we mean by rich?

We define the rich as households with at least $5 million in wealth, which means they are in the top 4 percent in household wealth in America as of 2022. Wealth combines both liquid holdings (bank accounts, stocks, etc.) and illiquid holdings (businesses, real estate, etc.) and subtracts debt (mortgages, student and car loans, etc.).

Nearly five million households clear that threshold, including more than two million decamillionaires (at least $10 million), and around sixty-five thousand centimillionaires (at least $100 million). Most of them own a private business—as do three-quarters of decamillionaires and nearly all centimillionaires.

We define Main Street Millionaires as the rich owners of private businesses. As of this writing, they number about three million. Their average wealth is around $25 million.

Collectively, Main Street Millionaires have more than thirteen times the wealth of the Forbes 400. For every member of the Forbes 400, more than four thousand private business owners each have at least $10 million in net worth. For every large public company CEO, more than one thousand private business owners each have at least $25 million in wealth. Far more than a few high-profile billionaires on the coasts, these are the real rich in America.

These successful business owners are growing not just in number but in the size of their wealth. The number of decamillionaire business owners has more than doubled since the early 1990s (even after adjust-

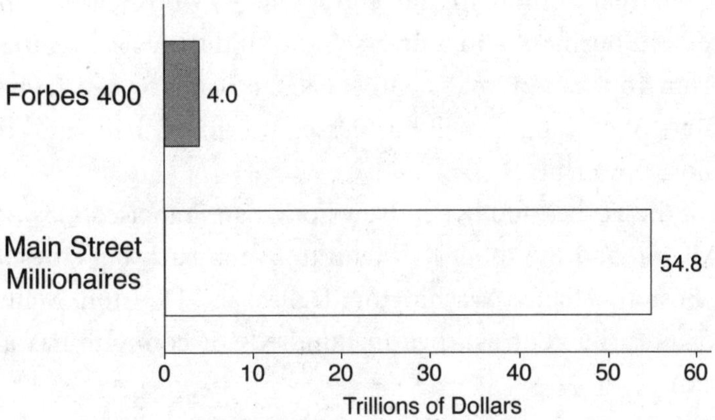

ing for inflation), and the number of centimillionaire business owners has nearly quadrupled.

As many business owners reinvested in their firms, benefited from economic growth, and enjoyed lower interest rates and taxes than those of earlier decades, their business valuations and collective wealth boomed far more than that of the Forbes 400. (These same forces drove impressive growth among the Forbes 400 as well, but they remain a tiny share of the rich in America when compared to Main Street Millionaires.)

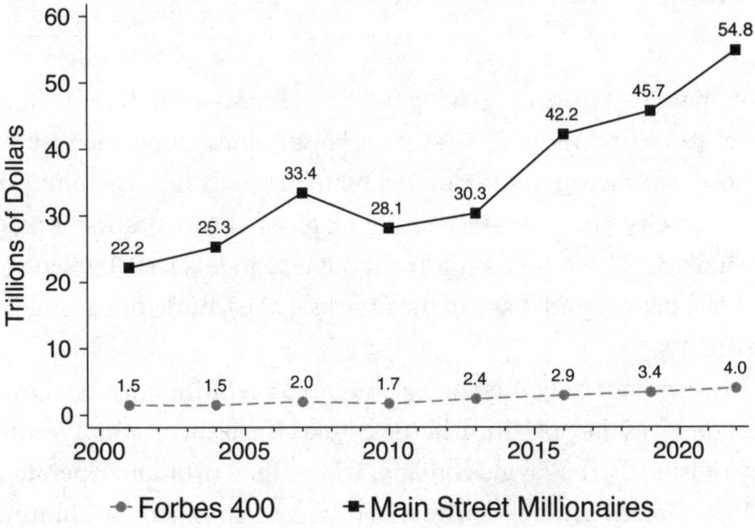

Main Street Millionaires are entrepreneurs who created, inherited, or acquired businesses in a diverse set of industries across the country. From Topeka to Omaha, Great Falls to Baton Rouge, owners and operators of so-called small businesses are richer than you'd think—and more powerful.

Half the Forbes 400 live in New York, San Francisco, Los Angeles, and Miami, and the other half tend to live in such big cities as Chicago, Boston, Atlanta, Washington, Dallas, and Houston. Main Street Millionaires, by contrast, live in hundreds of communities all over America.

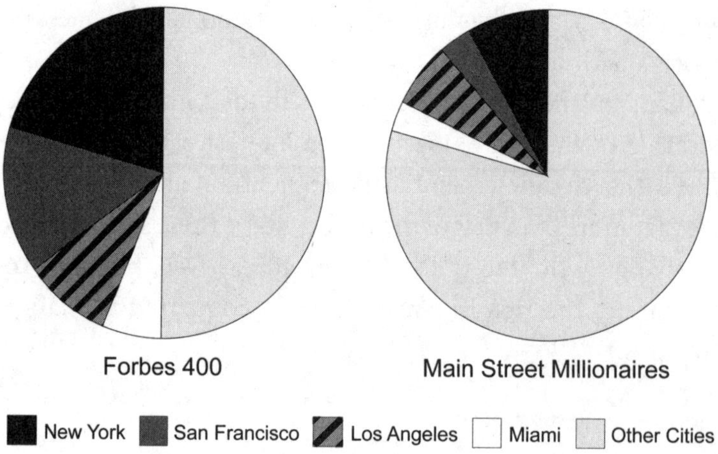

Suppose that instead of flying from San Francisco to New York, you drove. You'd find more 5,000-square-foot homes along the way than in those two metropolitan areas combined. You'd find them in every town and city you pass—especially in glitzy resort destinations like Aspen, Park City, and Jackson Hole, but also in less well-known spots like Mackinaw Island, Lake of the Ozarks, Lake Minnetonka, and Lake Martin.

These are not only the homes of Main Street Millionaires; they are often their second or third homes. Take Kurt and Kathi Westman. They're from Fort Wayne, Indiana, where they own and operate Al-Fe Heat Treating, one of America's largest commercial aluminum heat-treating companies. They vacation in the Florida Keys, where they have owned a $42 million, 11,000-square-foot oceanfront home.

You probably know a Main Street Millionaire, even if you don't realize it. They're coaching your child's soccer team, sitting next to you at community fundraisers, or chatting with you at neighborhood barbecues. They might be the dentist who expanded his office to a regional network of practices, the commercial HVAC contractor whose trucks you see around town, or the owner of that local restaurant chain that keeps opening new locations. They're hiding in plain sight, as ordinary people who run businesses woven into the fabric of everyday life.

How did we discover them?

* * *

This book began with an investigation that was impossible until recently.

For decades, explorers attempting to map America's wealth suffered a massive blind spot with most of American wealth blacked out. We knew about public company CEOs from SEC filings and billionaires from *Forbes* lists, but not private business owners whose fortunes were almost invisible. Their tax returns are confidential, their firms are unlisted, and no database connected owners to their companies, employees, or wealth.

That changed in 2014, when the Treasury Department asked us to help figure out how much business owners were paying in taxes. To do so, we built the first database that connects the data on tax forms to individual businesses, their owners, and their employees. We could link business owners to their businesses and those businesses to their employees. (The names of the individuals and businesses who submitted these forms is confidential information stored in a distinct database from the de-identified and anonymized data we analyzed.)

That data proved a gold mine. With it, we discovered a hidden world of rich business owners. For the first time, we could fill out the full map of American enterprise—from small firms to the richest Americans—and see who owned what, how much they earned, where they lived, and how they built their fortunes.

These data enabled us to learn about private business owners all the way up the income scale, including in the top 10 percent, 1 percent, 0.1 percent, and above. What we found changed how we think about inequality: One of the most common explanations for why someone made it to the top was that he or she owned a large stake in a mundane business.

We tracked the journey of all the nation's entrepreneurs from childhood through the years after they started and built their businesses. We pinpointed the key factors that enable them to thrive.

After a decade of work, we have painted the most comprehensive portrait to date of who the rich really are in today's America, how they got rich, and how they are shaping our economic, financial, and political life.

* * *

Through our work, we discovered something that has driven the wealth of Main Street Millionaires and fundamentally transformed the landscape of American business—the explosive growth over the last forty years in the number of "pass-through" businesses.

In the tax code, pass-throughs are sole proprietorships, partnerships, limited liability companies, and S corporations. In plain English, they are doctors, dentists, accountants, lawyers, car dealers, real estate developers, restaurateurs, architects, building equipment contractors, consultants, computer system designers, and other professionals who organize their businesses as pass-throughs.

What's behind the explosive growth in pass-throughs?

Largely, the tax code. Pass-throughs do not pay corporate or dividend taxes. Instead, their profits (and losses) pass through to their owners' individual income taxes. In recent decades, lower tax rates for pass-throughs have driven business owners to adopt that structure.

Until the 1980s, traditional C corporations (like General Motors and IBM), which face corporate taxes, reigned over the economy. Now, pass-throughs are America's dominant form of business. They reside in every region and operate in most business sectors.

Pass-throughs are hugely important in driving the wealth of Main Street Millionaires. In recent years, around 70 cents of every $1 of pass-through earnings go to those in the top 1 percent in income. Over 69 percent of the top 1 percent, and over 84 percent of the top 0.1 percent, earn some pass-through income. More than 1.1 million pass-through owners have yearly income over $500,000, 150,000 have income over $2.2 million, and 15,000 have income over $10.5 million.

Nontax factors also drove the growing wealth of Main Street Millionaires. Among them were falling interest rates, rising globalization, better technology, and deregulation, which delivered lower borrowing costs, higher business valuations, and access to bigger markets for many Main Street businesses.

* * *

In this book, we tell the stories of dozens of Main Street Millionaires, with information that we gathered from interviews and secondary sources.

How did we find them?

After learning that pass-throughs dominate the business world, we set out to identify the most lucrative ones and the people behind them. To do that, we looked, for instance, at industry publications that ranked top earners. We interviewed industry experts and combed through databases such as Dun and Bradstreet, which collects reams of information about businesses and their leaders. We also tapped our own networks. The more people we told about our quest to find rich private business owners, the more leads we gathered.

Once we identified the top earners in an industry, we learned more about them through public information, including newspaper and magazine profiles, registries of private jet and yacht owners, and property records for homes. That's how we learned about Bob and Paula Brockway and their daughter's "wedding of the century." We interviewed dozens of multimillionaire private business owners who were willing to share their stories, and we collected more stories than we could write about.

Though we can't be sure that every single Main Street Millionaire is a pass-through business owner, the explosive growth in pass-throughs and the concentration of pass-through income at the top tell us that the vast majority of them are, or have been, pass-through owners.

* * *

This book recasts fundamental popular notions about wealth in today's America.

Part I introduces many of the Main Street Millionaires who are accumulating vast fortunes.

Part II traces where they came from and how they grew rich, revealing what their experiences say about the state of the American Dream and the many paths to prosperity.

Part III uncovers the political power of Main Street Millionaires—how they use their wealth and influence to shape politics and policy at the national, state, and local levels.

The story of Main Street Millionaires is largely unknown and hugely important. We sometimes call them the Stealthy Wealthy because they fly under the radar. Or, as a colleague put it, "Private business owners are the dark matter of wealth in America." We want to make the rich visible and correct misconceptions about who they really are.

We seek neither to glorify nor vilify business owners. Some create jobs and help expand the economy, while others just line their own pockets. Regardless, understanding their rise is essential to understanding modern affluence and influence.

Across these pages, some stories may inspire you to pursue paths to prosperity that you had never considered. Others may raise questions about whether wealth is distributed and wielded fairly.

Either way, you'll be better able to spot Main Street Millionaires in your own community, understand how they built their fortunes, and recognize how they are reshaping our everyday lives.

PART I

Who Is Really Rich in America?

1

The Rise of Pass-Throughs

We should continue to improve the pass-through provisions at every step.
—Rep. Kevin Brady (R-TX), chairman, House Ways and Means Committee, December 9, 2017, in private correspondence during Congress's debate over President Trump's tax cuts that year

When Ronald Reagan was starring in low-budget B movies from the late 1930s to the early '60s, he never wanted to make too many movies in any one year. If he earned too much, he'd find himself in the top individual income tax bracket, which meant that he'd take home as little as nine cents for every dollar he earned. That experience drove his desire to cut top tax rates when he became president in 1981.

In the early 1980s, Reagan was joined by supply-side economists and congressional Republicans like Senator Bill Roth (R-DE) and Rep. Jack Kemp (R-NY) in a push for low tax rates, which they all argued would spur economic growth. Reagan also found common ground in loathing the tax system with a Democratic senator, Bill Bradley (D-NJ). While the former paid top rates as a Hollywood actor, the latter suffered the same fate as an all-star forward for the New York Knicks.

Democrats like Bradley and Rep. Dick Gephardt (D-MO) proposed to clean up the tax code by eliminating scores of tax credits, deductions, and other write-offs. These provisions not only made the code hard for average Americans to understand but they also made it fundamentally unfair because the benefits of such tax breaks accrued mostly to special interests.

The combined Republican quest to cut taxes and Democratic quest to simplify the code drove the Tax Reform Act of 1986, a landmark bipartisan achievement. It was the biggest reform of federal taxes in more than thirty years.

What none of these legislators anticipated was that the act would fundamentally transform America's economy—in particular, its corporate sector—by driving an explosion in the number and size of a once-arcane type of business entity known as the pass-through.

The explosion in pass-through businesses helped usher in the Age of Millionaires, and it also created a paper trail that made Main Street Millionaires visible for the first time.

* * *

Let's briefly step back in time.

From the founding of the Republic until the early twentieth century, the nation raised tax revenues largely through import tariffs and excise taxes on goods like whiskey. To finance the Civil War, President Lincoln and Congress established an income tax in 1861, but lawmakers repealed it in 1872. The Supreme Court ruled in 1895 that a federal income tax on property was unconstitutional.

The excesses of the Gilded Age spurred efforts to find a viable way to sustain a federal income tax. Ratified in 1913, the Sixteenth Amendment granted the federal government the necessary authority.

The income tax rate on the very rich, which was only 7 percent in 1914, rose dramatically to 77 percent by 1918, helping to finance America's involvement in World War I. In the decades to come, lawmakers raised or lowered tax rates to reflect the mood and needs of the times. After falling to 25 percent in 1925, the top tax rate rose to 63 percent during the Great Depression and to as high as 94 percent during World War II. To finance wars and, especially after World War II, pay for ever-growing federal domestic programs, the government also collected revenue from corporations but at a lower tax rate (which peaked at 53 percent in 1968).

The individual tax had more brackets than it does today, and the top rates applied to a narrow sliver of the population. In 1950, the highest tax rate applied only to those making more than $2.5 million a year (in 2025 dollars)—three times higher than the top threshold today—and only those above the top 0.01 percent in income were in that tax bracket. Nevertheless, through the 1970s, the top 1 percent of earners still faced marginal tax rates of at least 60 percent.

The tax code has long given business owners several tools to minimize their taxes. Historically, business owners preferred to pay corporate rather than individual income taxes because the top individual tax rate was always at least as high as, and often higher than, the corporate rate. By creating a traditional C corporation, business owners could pay the lower corporate tax rate on their earnings. They could also enjoy extra tax benefits like writing off company cars, family vacations, and country club memberships as business expenses.

When Reagan was elected president in 1980, the top individual tax rate was 70 percent, and the corporate rate was 46 percent. Tax reform in 1986 cut the top individual rate to *below* the corporate rate—triggering a multi-decade transformation in the structure of American business ownership.

That brings us to pass-throughs. The income that a pass-through generates is not subject to corporate or dividend taxes. Instead, its profits (and losses) flow through to the individual income taxes of its owners. From 1986 to 2017, with top individual income tax rates lower than corporate rates, and with lawmakers giving pass-throughs more tax breaks, business owners had big incentives to organize as pass-throughs. Millions of business owners converted their C corporations into pass-throughs or set up new businesses as pass-throughs.

In essence, tax reform changed the face of American business. Before the 1986 act, traditional C corporations produced almost all business income, and nearly all employers adopted this form. Now, 95 percent of all businesses are pass-throughs. They employ half of all workers and generate the majority of business income.

And this transformation served another purpose. Because pass-through tax obligations flow to each owner, pass-through tax returns marked a new trail for us to follow the money.

* * *

The Treasury building sits next to the White House on Pennsylvania Avenue, in the heart of downtown Washington.

In the plaza outside the Treasury's south wing, atop a nine-foot marble base, stands a ten-foot bronze sculpture of Alexander Hamilton, the nation's first Treasury secretary, in knee breeches and ruffled cuffs, a hat in his right hand and a coat draped across his left arm. His eyes are steady, his face is calm, and his stance projects the resolve of a man who built the nation's financial foundations. Anyone who wants to enter the building must pass through multiple security checkpoints. Inside, one traverses checkerboard marble floors, gazes at vaulted ceilings and towering pillars, and walks on circular staircases. It's a humbling place to work.

If you descend one of the staircases to the basement, you find a row of windowless offices, with bookshelves of tax code reference manuals and fifteen-year-old IT equipment. It was in one such space, in Treasury's Office of Tax Analysis (OTA), that we started our investigation. When a president wants to propose a change to the tax code, OTA estimates how much it will cost (if it's a tax cut) or raise (if it's an increase). OTA is a nerdy place; we fit right in.

In the summer of 2014, we finished graduate school—Zidar at the University of California at Berkeley, Zwick at Harvard—and moved to Washington with Danny Yagan, a friend who had finished his graduate work at Harvard two years earlier and who joined us on the project to help the Treasury Department figure out how much tax business owners were paying. As we would soon discover, that was no easy matter.

We rented a three-bedroom apartment in Shaw, a gentrifying Washington neighborhood not far from the Treasury Department. The owner was an artist who decorated the place with exhibits from

Peeps, the Easter candy. We commuted to work in shared Ubers, and we wrote, ate, coded, and brainstormed together.

Our office mates called us the "Three Amigos" but, privately, we adopted a sillier nickname: the Tax Ninjas.

* * *

The IRS collects voluminous, confidential information about businesses and their owners. But it's stored in a labyrinth of separate systems and databases, making it hard for anyone to use it to paint a clear overall picture of those businesses and owners. That is what we were trying to do.

One system stored information on the revenues, profits, and industries of millions of businesses, while a separate system stored information on hundreds of millions of individual taxpayers, including tens of millions of people who might or might not be business owners. Another included information on how we might connect the data in those two systems. Each system was designed to help tax auditors investigate cases of alleged wrongdoing by specific taxpayers, not to enable anyone to conduct an economy-wide analysis of all taxpayers.

Policymakers, pundits, economists, and others perennially propose different ways to tax rich individuals and profitable firms. That explains in large part why policymakers have changed the tax code so often over the years. Two years before we got to Washington, that issue once again took center stage when President Obama squared off against Republican nominee Mitt Romney in the 2012 presidential election. At issue was what to do about President George W. Bush's tax cuts of 2001 and 2003, which were set to expire soon after the election. (As it turned out, lawmakers extended the vast majority of them before their scheduled expiration.)

As White House and Treasury officials over the years sent tax proposals to OTA to evaluate, staffers identified a problem. Because of the siloed IRS databases that did not link to one another, they couldn't fully understand how the existing tax code influenced taxpayers and shaped federal revenues, much less predict the impact of any reform. This blind spot was especially large in the case of pass-throughs.

Over sandwiches at Woodward Table restaurant a block from the Treasury, we debated how to link everything together. Danny would order the merguez sandwich, which was so spicy it caused him to break out in sweat every time he ate one.

We had already dug through dusty IRS codebooks to understand the different names that various databases gave to the same information. For example, "profits" in one database meant "total income" in another. The names in the IRS books corresponded to boxes of tax forms that didn't always match the tax forms stored on the server. Names would change from one system to another. And all these items required translation to become useful as economic concepts.

We drew diagrams over lunch to map out a plan to build a new dataset. After finishing our sandwiches, we returned to the office and tacked our sweat-stained notes to a corkboard.

* * *

The data are massive. They cover every company and individual in America multiple times. Working with such data required numerous security trainings and background checks as well as the constant vigilance of researchers to prevent the unauthorized disclosure of protected information. Gaining access to each dataset required documentation, justification, and multiple approvals.

Meanwhile, the IRS computers storing all this information were outdated and, as a result, slow. Starting around 2010, Republican lawmakers began a successful decade-long effort to slash the IRS budget, forcing staff cuts and leaving the agency without the funds to serve the public well and modernize the IRS's computers.

Working for the federal government in an underfunded agency meant using legacy servers with limited file storage space, putting up with frequent service outages, and enduring automatic security upgrades that left our computers unable to function. When many users were on the server, the system would slow between keystrokes.

We waited hours for others to finish running their programs before we could run our own.

Poorly structured queries from us to the computers would take days to run, if they ran at all. Often, the first few times we tried something, we'd wait long hours for the computers to process code until we received an error message or the computers stopped pursuing our task because, for instance, we left out a semicolon somewhere. We'd then have to rerun the whole program. Zwick's experience as a software developer proved helpful when we needed to use arcane programming languages from the 1980s to circumvent system limitations.

We spent hours waiting on the IRS technical help desk to troubleshoot the random times when our passwords refreshed, our data access changed, or some other computer update prevented us from working. We eventually learned the best way to move our help desk ticket to the front of the line: scream the words "complete work stoppage."

* * *

Late afternoons, we'd leave to buy salads or tacos and return before the building's entrance closed.

When most Treasury staff had left for the day, the server's bandwidth expanded, enabling us to work far more efficiently. At around the same time of day, the Secret Service would shut down the building for the evening. Leaving after hours required navigating a set of underground tunnels to the one exit that was still open. Conveniently, an entrance to the tunnel stairs was located near our basement office.

Before leaving for the night, we set code running and decamped to a beer garden where we debated puzzles that emerged from the data during the day. Why didn't simple totals match across systems? How could we separate real companies from shell corporations that obscured a firm's true ownership?

Over a few months, we solved some of our linking problems, reconciled differences in the totals across systems, and distilled thousands of variables into a few dozen core economic measures, such as revenue, cost, wages, profits, and total owner pay. We were making steady progress toward figuring out who owned all the businesses in America and how much tax they paid.

The quest led us to unexpected places. Of the eighty thousand IRS employees, only a few understood the structure of some of these systems. On his way to lecture at Utah State University, Zwick stopped for a lunch appointment at a burger bar in the Salt Lake suburb of Ogden, a forty-minute drive north from the city. There, he met a man in his mid-forties whom we came to call "The Architect."

With cropped blond hair, a rounded beard, and a button-down flannel shirt, he looked more like a mountaineer than a database designer. But, from the IRS office in Ogden, he built many of the systems that we were trying to understand. He explained their construction and how each system was designed for data integrity rather than easy use by analysts.

We learned that esoteric details that had seemed unimportant to us unlocked mysteries with which we had struggled for months.

For instance, we learned that a data item coded as zero sometimes meant zero but other times meant that the item was missing. That could help explain the inconsistent totals we were finding in different databases. From the dusty codebooks, we learned how to connect variables in different systems, but only after reordering the digits of each variable to match one another.

So, where did all this take us?

* * *

After ten months working with OTA's economists, we built the first database that links the data on tax forms to individual businesses and their owners.

For the first time, researchers (in this case, us) had access to roughly everything of economic importance on tax forms. With all this information, we could identify every pass-through business and its owners and workers. We could then figure out how much money each owner made from the business. All this proved hugely important in our mission to answer the question that Treasury officials posed when they hired us: How much tax do businesses pay?

And, by enabling us to link individual business owners to their businesses and the businesses to their workers, we discovered something monumentally larger and altogether unexpected: the transformation in the landscape of American business that had begun decades earlier.

With our database completed, we decamped to our home universities but regularly returned to the Treasury over the years to continue our work, brainstorming about how to use the data to learn more about the economy. We took research walks around the basement corridor. With a full loop about the length of a quarter-mile track, we often would cover a few miles on one walk.

We began to write and talk about what we were learning.

* * *

We published our first scholarly paper based on our work in 2016. In it, we used data from 2011 on 3.6 million partnerships and found that pass-through income is especially concentrated at the top, even more than other kinds of income generated by businesses. Following pass-through income seemed to be a uniquely effective way to find the rich.

America's nine thousand C-suite public executives, which includes CEOs, CFOs, and other corporate leaders, earned a collective $38 billion in 2022. But pay for the top 1 percent of private business owners—comprising ten times as many people—was fifteen times more that year, a collective $570 billion. Moreover, the average private business owner in the top 1 percent made 1.5 times as much as the average public company CEO.

Since the 1980s, pass-through businesses have accounted for more than half of the rise in the share of income that accrues to the top 0.1 percent. Thus, understanding who is rich in America and understanding why inequality has widened means understanding pass-through owners.

We painstakingly unwound the very complex ownership structures of some pass-through firms. Some partnerships are owned by other partnerships, which are owned by still other partnerships, creating ownership pyramids and overlapping webs of more than thirty layers that we needed to strip away before we could link a pass-through to an owner. Pass-through owners often create this complexity in hopes of hiding information about their business from taxing authorities. In fact, we found that a third of partnership income could not be traced to an identifiable owner.

The average tax rate on pass-throughs was also quite low, both compared to salary earners and to other forms of business, reflecting the many tax breaks they have enjoyed over the last four decades. We came to understand how tax reform in 1986 unleashed the growth in pass-throughs.

For subsequent papers, we expanded the number of pass-throughs that we studied to eleven million and extended the data to cover all years since 2000. We also used income data such as wages, pension distributions, dividends and capital gains, and mortgage payments to estimate the wealth of Americans. We learned how people grow their wealth and where entrepreneurs come from.

In the top 0.1 percent of income, the number of people who earn most of their income from pass-through businesses exceeds those who earn most of theirs from wages and salaries. Our linked data showed that these wealthy people were running businesses across a wide range of industries and geographies. They came from all kinds of family backgrounds and jobs. And they were astonishingly rich.

* * *

Historically, researchers found it very hard to figure out who is rich and how they got there. Before our work, there were three main sources of information on the income and wealth of the rich: surveys, investigative reporting, and tax information in separate IRS databases that did not link to one another.

The Federal Reserve produces the highest-quality dataset on the rich, known as the Survey of Consumer Finances. While this survey of six thousand people is very informative, it includes information on only a few hundred ultrarich respondents. Tracking down even this small number of respondents requires an expert staff to conduct interviews and a budget of tens of millions of dollars.

Interviewers often struggle to convince rich people to respond. Only one in ten who are contacted cooperate with the survey, and they volunteer only the information they're willing to share. One interviewer told us that former Federal Reserve Chairman Alan Greenspan personally intervened and persuaded a wealthy interviewee to participate.

The small sample size creates other problems. The Federal Reserve cannot publish information on the location, industry, and other aspects of the businesses these rich people own without, in essence, revealing who they are—which is confidential. The survey also doesn't follow the same person's journey over time.

Other datasets, like the decennial Census and the annual Current Population Survey that the Census Bureau conducts with the Bureau of Labor Statistics, have larger sample sizes, but they generate even less information about the rich. That's because they don't ask anyone about their total wealth and they group all people above a certain threshold of annual income (e.g., $150,000) into the same upper-income category. Thus, they provide no real information about wealth or income at the top.

In *The Millionaire Next Door*, a best-selling book of 1996, Thomas Stanley and William Danko used marketing surveys to describe the consumption patterns of high-wealth individuals. Their findings mirror several of the stories in our book, though their data are limited and three decades old.

* * *

Perhaps the most popular gauge of wealth in America is the Forbes 400, which relies on public data and investigative reporting to identify the nation's richest people. While *Forbes* magazine works hard to compile the list, it is not a definitive source of information about America's richest people.

As *Forbes* journalist Chase Peterson-Withorn recounts in a 2017 retrospective, the project began in 1981 when *Forbes* publisher Malcolm Forbes directed his editors to produce an issue on the richest four hundred Americans; in choosing that number, he reportedly was inspired by the ballroom of New York socialite Caroline Astor's Fifth Avenue mansion, which could accommodate four hundred people. The editorial staff doubted they could find the four hundred, let alone measure their wealth. While large owners of public companies must disclose their stock holdings, wealthy private business owners need not—and many don't. They closely guard details about their businesses and avoid the limelight.

Nevertheless, *Forbes*'s staff went to work, touring major cities and conducting thousands of interviews. They hunted for old money on the Eastern Seaboard, oil money in Texas, and new money in Silicon Valley, gathering tips and leads from local bankers, fundraisers, and journalists.

They then hit the streets. "We got this directory that showed who owned every single building in New York," Jonathan Greenberg, a *Forbes* reporter, recalled in describing a brute-force approach to tracing the origins of New York real estate wealth. "We went down Fifth Avenue and Park Avenue and Madison Avenue and looked at every building and looked for the names that reoccurred."

When Greenberg and his editor, Harold Seneker, reached out to potential list members, most didn't want to talk. Some shared tales of their success but, more often, of their competitors' successes. When *Forbes* staffers did acquire information about someone's assets, they often found it hard to verify.

(Over the years, Donald Trump took a different approach to inquiries about his wealth. He tried to inflate his *Forbes* rating by calling the magazine many times, on some occasions pretending to be "John Barron" from the Trump Organization, and claiming that he owned far more real estate buildings than he did and was worth far more than he was. Greenberg later discovered that, wealth-wise, he shouldn't have been anywhere near some of the Forbes 400 lists on which he was included.)

Forbes published its initial list on September 13, 1982. The magazine cover listed the names of all four hundred, each with assets of at least $100 million. Some hated the attention. Media magnate Malcom Borg complained that, after the publication, he received phone calls from "every goddamn stockbroker in the United States." Others worried that in naming the non-adult kids of those on the list, *Forbes* was putting them at risk of kidnapping or terrorism.

Others, however, savored the publicity. Donald Reynolds, another media mogul, said that "being a vain old man, I was terrifically impressed. I read it all the way through and am looking forward to the next one."

As of this writing, *Forbes* publishes these lists under Kerry Dolan, who leads a team of at least ninety-two reporters. While their approach is more systematic, their strategy has its limits. Asked about the type of billionaire she'd never find, Dolan said, "Someone who quietly sold a stake in a business for, say, $250 million in the 1990s and then invested it well."

How many such private business owners are there across the United States? How rich are they, and how did they become rich? Before we began our own work, neither the federal government nor anyone else knew.

* * *

The final source of data on the rich that drives much conventional wisdom about inequality in America is tax data. Back in 2003, French economists Thomas Piketty and Emmanuel Saez published a paper that used such data to show the fall and rise of the top 1 percent in income over the twentieth century.

They showed that income inequality had been rising steadily since the 1980s and was approaching the levels of the 1920s. Unlike in the late nineteenth and early twentieth centuries, when the "leisure class" derived its huge income from land rents and coupon payments on financial securities, labor income in the latter part of the twentieth century drove the incomes of top earners. That is, the "working rich" had replaced the "coupon-clipping rentiers" as central players in the story of U.S. inequality.

Piketty and Saez's paper propelled the "we are the 99 percent" slogan of the Occupy movement of 2011, which began with encampments in Manhattan's Zuccotti Park near Wall Street. Protesters raged about rising income inequality and the uneven policy response to the 2008 financial crisis, which, they said, bailed out the rich and huge financial institutions and left everyone else behind. By directing its rage at financial institutions and big business, the Occupy movement presaged a more general revived attention on rentiers.

Soon after the Great Recession of 2007–9, however, economists, scholars (including Piketty), and other seasoned observers began to question whether focusing on labor income to explain inequality made sense for the economy of the twenty-first century (as opposed to the twentieth century).

But if labor income did not explain inequality in the new century, what did? Well, experts said, "capital" (i.e., assets such as stocks, pensions, real estate, and businesses) and the capitalists who owned it.

In his bestselling book of 2014, *Capital in the Twenty-First Century*, Piketty argued that capital was driving the surge in inequality since 2000. The returns to capital owners, he explained, were outpacing the returns to workers.

Some of Piketty's conclusions were based on his work with tax data in which he tried to disaggregate income into labor and capital income. He faced the same limitations, however, that previous scholars and government officials had faced when using IRS data: It was siloed in separate buckets, limiting what anyone could learn about the rich. One could see that lots of business profits were flowing to rich people but not learn anything about the businesses themselves.

Nevertheless, Piketty and his collaborators continued their influential work. In a 2014 paper titled "Capital Is Back," Piketty and Gabriel Zucman wrote that wealth-to-income ratios in the United States, United Kingdom, Germany, and France had risen in recent decades back to the high levels of eighteenth- and nineteenth-century Europe.

Then, in a 2018 paper, Piketty, Saez, and Zucman concluded that the road to riches in America no longer ran through working in a well-compensated position, like an executive of a publicly traded company. Instead, it increasingly ran through the accumulation of capital.

Their work was important but—however influential—the picture they painted was incomplete.

* * *

Scholars, pundits, and politicians who focus on inequality largely neglect Main Street Millionaires.

Scholars like Piketty and his collaborators don't write about auto dealers, travel center owners, beverage distributors, and innumerable other rich private business owners, and politicians like Senators Elizabeth Warren and Bernie Sanders don't talk about them. They focus their proposals to reduce inequality far more on higher-profile billionaires than on this broader group of very rich Americans who collectively hold a greater share of the nation's wealth.

All told, conventional wisdom about America's rich has been shaped by anecdotes and limited data—the *Forbes* lists, reports from public companies, siloed tax data, and media coverage of celebrities and coastal elites. In the absence of systemic data on the whole economy and whole country, we've missed the vast forest of American entrepreneurs for a few redwoods in Silicon Valley.

Until now.

2

Millionaires Everywhere

> *We service the seamless gutter industry. That's all we do. If it has to do with gutters, we're either doing it, thinking about doing it, or planning to do it. We're thinking about gutters all the time.*
>
> —A. B. Walters,
> Founder and Chairman of the Senox Corporation

In Dothan, a city of about 71,000 in the southeast corner of Alabama, a wealthy oral surgeon completed his 10,000-square-foot dream home in 2015.

Ten years earlier, Craig Schmidtke launched his oral and maxillofacial surgery center. As of this writing, he's also CEO of ORCA Oral Care Products, which makes an oral pain putty out of essential oils.

Schmidtke taught himself to use home-building software and drew up the blueprints for a $5 million neoclassical mansion for his family. It includes a movie theater and golf simulator, a splendid pool and terrace, and a fountain of Neptune, Roman god of the sea, inspired by the court in Bologna, Italy.

As of June 2024, over eight million homes in America (nearly one of every ten) are worth at least $1 million; two million are worth at least $2 million; and around 255,000 are worth more than $5 million. Many of these homes belong to Main Street Millionaires, and they live all over the country.

To go to some of these homes, learn a bit about their towns, and meet more Main Street Millionaires like Schmidtke, let's take a road trip from Dothan. We'll drive west and stop at a few places across the South, and head north through the Rocky Mountains before again turning west and arriving in the picturesque Northern California town of Petaluma.

Our goal is to replace faceless statistics about top wealth with the stories of real people, where they live, and what kinds of businesses they run.

* * *

The biscuit capital of the world is four hundred miles west of Dothan.

Nestled along the banks of the Mississippi River, the town of Natchez, Mississippi, hosts an annual biscuit festival on the 300 block of South Broadway Street. With a population of about 14,000, Natchez sits near the Louisiana border, ninety miles southwest of Jackson, Mississippi's state capital. Before the Civil War, Natchez was a key port along the river. During the era of Reconstruction, the city elected one of the first Black mayors in America, Robert H. Wood.

Aside from flaky biscuits, the town is perhaps best known for its one thousand antebellum buildings. One of them, the Gloucester mansion, dates to 1803. It was built for David Williams, a tobacco and timber plantation owner, who was one of the nation's wealthiest men in the late eighteenth century.

A. B. Walters and his wife, Elizabeth, acquired the mansion, located seven minutes from downtown Natchez, in 2022. Surrounded by more than five acres of woods and lawns, the property is worth around $2 million.

Walters left a career in computer science to pursue a more lucrative calling—manufacturing and installing seamless gutters. He started out installing rain gutters for Sears. After learning the business and growing frustrated with low product quality, he bought his first gutter machine in 1972 and founded Senox Corporation. It's now the largest supplier of seamless gutters in Texas, employs around 350 people, and, according to the National Establishment Time Series database, had around $50 million in sales in 2021.

We estimate that the company is worth more than $100 million.

* * *

If we drive another four hundred miles to the west, we hit the Texas town of Colleyville (where one of us—Zidar—once lived). It has a population of about 26,000 and is named for Dr. Lilburn Howard Colley, who practiced medicine there for forty years starting in 1880.

Over the years, Colleyville's fortunes fluctuated with changes in agriculture, transportation, and demography. Colleyville first benefited from the nearby railroad. When more and more families found the means to buy cars, making the railroad less indispensable, the city suffered. When the population of the Dallas–Fort Worth metroplex expanded into the suburbs and exurbs where Colleyville is located, the city recovered.

In 2017, Alfonso and Sharon Chan designed their 10,500-square-foot home in Colleyville, now a wealthy residential suburb. The classical limestone home echoes the design of historic estates from the Gilded Age and the English countryside, with columned porticoes, a four-car garage, a kitchen based on an English country house (Holkham Hall), a two-story mahogany-paneled staircase, and a bell board that rings to several rooms throughout the house.

"Long ago," Sharon Chan told *The Wall Street Journal*, "if you were upstairs you'd ring for tea or food or snacks. I thought it would be funny to flip it. So from my bell board, I can ring the kids downstairs." The Chans enjoy entertaining and, she said, they can easily host 150 people. After their kids moved out, the Chans listed their home for $6.75 million in September 2023.

Like his wife, Alfonso Chan is an engineer. He grew up in the Philippines and joined the U.S. Navy after high school on a ROTC scholarship. He majored in materials science and engineering at Rensselaer Polytechnic Institute in New York and applied his skills in the Navy's "Silent Service" on nuclear submarines. He earned a graduate certificate in nuclear engineering from the Bettis Reactor Engineering School near Pittsburgh in 1994, then attended Southern Methodist University's Dedman School of Law in Dallas, specializing in complex intellectual property cases and graduating in 1999 before becoming a prominent patent lawyer.

Chan is now a partner at King & Spalding, the nation's seventeenth-largest law firm in terms of profits per partner in 2021. The firm generated $2.1 billion in revenue in 2023, and its annual profits per partner amounted to $5.3 million—about enough to buy the 10,500-square-foot mansion with two years of pay, after taxes.

* * *

From Colleyville, a 215-mile drive north brings us to Oklahoma City, home to the Gaillardia Golf Club development, which features dozens of luxury homes ranging from 5,000 to 15,000 square feet.

One home on Wisteria Drive was recently owned by Johnny Morris and listed for $2 million. Born in Springfield, Missouri, Morris grew up "running around in a diaper with a fishing pole in [his] hand." His parents loved to fish and hunt and, in their family liquor store, they also sold fishing tackle.

From that humble beginning, Morris built a privately owned sporting goods juggernaut, now known as Bass Pro Shops, with 177 retail locations throughout the country. The largest store is the 321-foot-tall "Memphis Pyramid" in Tennessee, reportedly the world's tenth-tallest pyramid. *Forbes* estimates his net worth as $8.4 billion as of December 2025.

* * *

Some 670 miles northwest of Oklahoma City, the Great Plains meet the Rocky Mountains in Boulder, Colorado. In that city's northwest corner, an 8,700-square-foot house on Lee Hill Drive was listed for $10 million in October 2024. The home sits on five acres at the foothills of Colorado's Front Range, and features a ninety-foot lap pool, a heated driveway, and four limestone fireplaces.

A lifelong ski racer, David Jacobs attended St. Lawrence University in upstate New York, twenty miles from the Canadian border, for its ski program. He won a national championship in ski racing and became an instructor after school, but he didn't know what to do with his life.

Then it came to him in a conversation with his son. "One of my kids . . . was at a [ski-racing] training camp in Argentina and he met the Italian ski team," Jacobs recalled, "and came back with this padded race sweater. . . . He said, you know, kids'll kill for it, but you can't buy them . . . they're not in the stores. So a kind of light went off in my head and I said I'm going to get into the market and make a race sweater. And now it's the biggest in the world in the high-end skiwear market . . . in forty countries."

David sold his company Spyder for $100 million to private equity firm Apax Partners in 2004.

* * *

From Boulder, a five-hundred-mile drive northwest around the Rocky Mountains would bring you to Limekiln Gulch, at the base of the Wasatch Mountains in the northeastern corner of Salt Lake City, Utah.

If you saw a $12 million, 12,000-square-foot mansion, surrounded by thirty acres of trees, in Limekiln Gulch, you might think the owner was a tech executive who fled Silicon Valley. But this is the home of Kurt and Dawn Larsen, cofounders in 1992 of a human resources company aptly named Resource Management Inc.

The Larsens had worked for four years at a professional employer organization. Its owner, however, let his kids collect paychecks without doing anything. "The idea of giving people money for not working didn't sit well" with him, Kurt Larsen later told an audience at his alma mater, Utah State's Jon M. Huntsman School of Business. He and Dawn left and started their own firm, with him as president and CEO and her as CFO.

"Here in Utah we have a lot of entrepreneurial people," Kurt later said. "Just because you're adept at making a widget, it doesn't mean you're good at paying taxes, dealing with all the Department of Labor requirements, being able to shop for health insurance . . . and so that's been one of the big things [driving our growth]. People say, 'We want to focus on our core business' and to outsource everything else to us."

By 2020, Resource Management Inc. was generating $640 million in annual revenue and represented around eighteen thousand employees in 350 companies located in every state in America. They target clients with anywhere from five to one thousand employees in property management, doctors' offices, and trades like engineering, architecture, and construction.

Together with another cofounder, the Larsens sold their business in October 2023 to Vensure Employer Solutions, a privately held company based in Chandler, Arizona. The terms of the sale were not disclosed but, given the size of the company, it was likely in the hundreds of millions.

* * *

These Main Street Millionaires are hardly the only well-to-do private business owners in their local areas. In fact, they have many rich neighbors. (The IRS publishes local statistics by income group that reveal just how many, and you can find that number for your own zip code.)

In 2021, 310 owners of pass-through businesses in Schmidtke's zip code in Dothan were in the top income group (those making at least $200,000). They generated $74 million in pass-through income. Those business owners represented nearly half of all top-income taxpayers in that zip code, reminding us of how much pass-through income drives top wealth.

In the Larsens' zip code in Salt Lake City, 670 top-bracket pass-through owners collectively earned $243 million in 2021. And in Jacobs's zip code in Boulder, 940 top-bracket pass-through owners earned a collective $230 million in 2021. That's a lot of Main Street Millionaires living next to each other!

They say everything is bigger in Texas. When Zidar moved from suburban Chicago to Colleyville, Texas, he was struck by all the mansions in his town. Indeed, IRS data show, nearly two thousand top-income pass-through owners earn a collective $560 million a year in Chan's zip code in Colleyville. And that is far from the richest zip code even in that local area.

* * *

We don't hear about Main Street Millionaires as much as we hear about the rich in New York and San Francisco because many of them live in smaller cities like Atlanta or remote towns like Dothan. They're not near media centers, and they don't typically work in newsworthy businesses. Even within a given place, we aren't as likely to hear much about them.

When most people think about uber-rich business owners, they think about the tech moguls in Palo Alto, California, who "move fast and break things." The mythology of Silicon Valley dates back at least to Hewlett-Packard's founding in 1939 by two Stanford students in a garage. The surge in venture capital from institutional investors in the 1970s and 1980s led many VCs to locate near Stanford, including along Sand Hill Road in Menlo Park, where early firms like Kleiner Perkins and Sequoia Capital established headquarters. Sand Hill VCs funded many of the most successful technology companies of the twentieth and twenty-first centuries, including Apple, Google, and Facebook, whose headquarters are all within a twenty-minute drive of Palo Alto.

But, when it comes to understanding wealth in America these days, we should be thinking not about tech moguls but about people like Terry Collins. Drive 740 miles southwest from the Larsens' part of Salt Lake City and you will arrive at our penultimate stop, Petaluma, California, just north of San Francisco. There, you will find a $12.5 million, 11,741-square-foot Mediterranean-style estate called Villa Terra Rosa.

Olive trees adorn the grounds, which span thirty-five acres of wine country in Sonoma County. Near the fifth hole of the Petaluma Golf and Country Club golf course, the villa includes a home theater, billiards room, wine cellar, pool, spa, koi pond, and bocce court. Terry Collins and his wife, Rose, began custom building the estate in 2005, importing limestone floors and hand-painted frescoes from France.

Collins was born in 1941 in Escanaba, Michigan. He dabbled in several careers, which ranged from selling encyclopedias to owning a paint shop to selling insurance, before he found his footing in the food service industry.

Working at McDonald's, he rose from store manager to regional vice president, managing franchises in five states. He then bounced around leading chains from Burger Chef to Pizza Hut. In 1988, he teamed up with convenience store owner Robert Graham, who was working on a fledgling take-and-bake pizza company called Papa Murphy's. Collins bought 51 percent of it for $500,000, then bought another take-and-bake company, Papa Aldo's, for around $1 million, increasing his share of the company to 85 percent.

Two main features helped Papa Murphy's become the nation's fifth-largest pizza chain. The first is price. It sells a 16-inch pepperoni pie for $6. Since customers cook it at home, Papa's doesn't need large ovens, staff delivery drivers, or table service. Second, Collins created a franchising model in which franchisees paid Papa's a fee for initiating each store and 5 percent of revenues. Anyone who wanted to set up a small shop with a few workers assembling pies could start contributing to Papa's growth.

When Collins sold the company to Lee Equity Partners in 2010, it had hundreds of millions in yearly sales and more than a thousand outlets. Papa's did an IPO in 2014 with a value of around $350 million.

* * *

To close our journey, we arrive at the home of another Main Street Millionaire in the Bay Area. Nancy Mueller lives just on the other side of Stanford from Sand Hill Road. Her story exemplifies the many mundane paths to great wealth that come when, instead of moving fast and breaking things, founders move slow and make things.

When Mueller saw her first quiche in the early 1970s, she was raising two young children and working as a volunteer manager at a restaurant that benefited a local philanthropy. By the time she sold her frozen quiche company in 1999, Nancy's Specialty Foods had 350 employees and was generating nearly $60 million in revenue. Her 86,000-square-foot manufacturing plant in Newark, California, could make 1.5 million mini quiches a day.

Mueller, who turned eighty-one in 2025, hadn't set out to become a frozen mini-quiche mogul, but her triumphant path did not happen by mistake either. She followed her late first husband Glenn to California in 1964, where he was attending Stanford's Graduate School of Business. Typing up his papers, she got a bit of a business education herself. They married shortly after he graduated, and she eventually left her job as a pharmaceutical chemist to raise their children. Nancy didn't follow the traditional college-to-MBA track.

In 1972, the young couple threw their first Christmas party at their modest home in Palo Alto. Glenn had launched a fledgling venture capital fund. Their Christmas parties later became a legendary Silicon Valley tradition that would last more than two decades, but in those early years the Muellers couldn't afford a caterer.

In fact, Nancy admits in our interviews with her, they could hardly pay their insurance bills at the time. Nevertheless, their parties were grand affairs of about two hundred, with Glenn's work contacts mingling with Nancy's friends from the Junior League. Steve and Laurene Jobs, neighbors from across the street, came to one with their little son in their arms.

* * *

To prepare for each party, Nancy baked three thousand appetizers over the course of months and stored them in a freezer in her garage. She fantasized about the convenience of going to the supermarket to buy appetizers like hers. They didn't exist.

"I made the product myself with two little children on my lap," she recalls. She hired her children's teenage babysitters to pass the appetizers around on trays at the party. Everyone told her that they were delicious. But, she said, "nobody ever said, you should start a business."

A 1976 career development program at the Junior League changed that. She completed some two hundred questions on a questionnaire and emerged knowing that she wanted to be in the appetizer business, not as a caterer but as a manufacturer.

By then, the Muellers' son was eight and their daughter was five. Nancy had a few free hours a day when the kids were in school. Driving down the road to play tennis with friends one day, she stopped to think about where she wanted to be in ten years and realized that she didn't want to be a better tennis player. Instead, "I wanted to have something to show for the next ten years. I wanted to make it count."

She convened friends to taste her various appetizers. In the end, it didn't matter which ones they thought tasted the best. "The only one that I could really envision mass producing was the petite quiche. I had those little mini muffin tins. I could dip the batter in there and bake them and they were really, really good."

She placed an ad in the Junior League newsletter before the holidays, offering to deliver the appetizers for $3.00 per dozen. By Christmas 1976, she had sold $2,000 worth—666 dozen appetizers.

* * *

Nancy launched her business, the Hors d'Oeuvre Factory, leasing space from a dilapidated empanada factory that was vacant while the owner served time in jail.

She made necessary repairs to the kitchen and hired a few part-time workers, mostly her babysitters and their boyfriends, to come after school and help make the quiches. They would roll the dough very thin, cut it into circles, and put it in a mini muffin tin, adding the creamy quiche filling with a coffee scoop.

While her young workers assembled tiny appetizers, Nancy loaded a thick cardboard carton in the back of her Volvo station wagon with dry ice and made sales calls, delivering petite quiches to supermarkets across the San Francisco Bay Area. In 1978, she changed the name to Nancy's Specialty Foods and moved to a bigger space. Sales rose from $14,000 in the previous year to $80,000.

As sales increased, technical upgrades made the production process smoother. With a Maytag washing machine on spin cycle, she removed excess water from spinach. A switch from radiant heat ovens to convection created a more consistently crispy pastry shell. A package designer made custom packaging. A disgruntled aerospace engineer, who had left the industry in protest of the Vietnam War, popped in off the street one day and offered to help upgrade her equipment, eventually crafting a semiautomated quiche line. The business expanded into neighboring buildings, doubling its square footage, and later moved to a larger facility nearby.

Before long, Nancy could churn out 100,000 mini quiches a day. She was selling larger entrée-size quiches and ready-to-bake pie shells too. The business was growing and so was Glenn's venture capital firm. The couple talked business at dinner every night. But Nancy's Specialty Foods was in the red. No matter how many quiches they could sell to grocery stores, profit margins weren't high enough to offset the costs of securing shelf space in those stores.

"The problem," she recalled, "is that retail just takes all the profit out of the product. You're almost paying them to be there."

Personal bank loans funded the operation's growth. If the quiche business defaulted, the Muellers would be personally on the hook. Though Glenn later became a storied Silicon Valley venture capitalist, at this point the borrowing felt very risky. Nancy's father, a CPA, told her, "You're shipping dollar bills with every case of quiche," because she wasn't charging enough.

* * *

Nancy landed on the cover of *California Business Magazine* in 1980, prompting an invitation to meet with buyers from the supermarket Trader Joe's.

Soon, she was manufacturing Trader Joe's–branded quiches and some mushroom puffs, generating enough revenue to cover her payroll. Even then, she still needed to borrow money for inventory.

Every fall, the business went into overdrive, stockpiling products for the busy make-or-break holiday season. Half of Nancy's annual sales came in December. Yet no matter how many cases she could ship, the margins with twelve mini quiches to a package were not big enough to turn a profit. They generated brand recognition but not cash.

By the fall of 1983, seven years into the venture, Nancy was becoming frantic. She had a goal to hit $20,000 in sales through one of her distributors and realized they weren't going to reach it.

"I was getting ready to close the business down right after Christmas," she says. "I couldn't make my numbers, and I wasn't making any money. I wasn't shipping dollar bills, like my father warned. I was shipping $10 bills, $100 bills in those cases of quiche."

Desperate, she approached the warehouse store Price Club two weeks before Christmas. To her delight, she secured an order for twenty-five cases to be delivered to each of four Northern California stores the following week. Her crew worked all weekend to fill the orders. The day they debuted, the products sold out by 11:00 a.m.

Winning the Price Club account was an inflection point that catapulted Nancy's Specialty Foods to tremendous success. By year's end, it had reached $1 million in sales. "It didn't happen overnight," she said. "But within a couple of months, I was busier than I could ever be."

As the warehouse store industry grew, so did quiche sales. Finally, Nancy was baking and freezing her way to a profit.

* * *

The warehouse stores, which offer larger volumes of product per package, helped Nancy's margins.

"Retail was a great platform to introduce people to the product," she explained. "But the club [i.e., warehouse] stores sold it. And the economics were much better for me because I could price it right. I had 18 percent pretax profit at one point, and that's really good."

Nancy believes her background as a chemist gave her the methodical, operational abilities to scale production. "It's the thought process and the organization," she reflected. "I didn't use equations or anything. It's just that the logic was there." She hired engineers, expanded production space, and bought her first automated quiche assembly line in 1987, tripling her production to 300,000 quiches a day.

She hit $10 million in sales in 1988 and doubled that figure three years later. Ventures in Japan and Mexico were unreliable because the value of the dollar fluctuated too much. But Canadian business was robust. In the week before Christmas in 1992, Nancy's products were the second-biggest seller at Price Club's Canadian operations, behind only toilet paper.

Along with Price Club, which merged with Costco in 1993, warehouse stores Sam's Club and BJ's were placing orders as well. As these warehouse club stores surged in market share, so did Nancy's business. Holiday sales extended into Super Bowl sales, and soon her mini appetizers were on the club store freezers' shelves year-round.

Sales in 1993 hit $30 million, and the factory was operating at capacity. Nancy began building a new, state-of-the-art manufacturing facility.

Business was tremendous, but all was not well.

* * *

Glenn Mueller had become a pivotal figure in the booming Silicon Valley technology venture capital scene, accumulating $100 million in private wealth. But the competitive pressures he faced became unbearable and he died by suicide on his sailboat off the coast of Mexico in April 1994.

Nancy's children were young adults by then, her son living in Southern California and her daughter a month from graduating college. She huddled with them and considered what lay ahead.

"I knew I had to be the leader, so I just picked up and kept going," Nancy said.

Her 86,000-square-foot plant in Newark, California, just across the San Francisco Bay from Palo Alto, opened on time and on budget in May, about a month after Glenn's death. Giant tanks stored milk and eggs, and a silo held 60,000 pounds of flour. The hors d'oeuvre fillings, which were mixed in 40-gallon drums at the old facility, came together in a single 300-gallon computer-controlled mixer and blender that fed into four holding tanks. Three separate production lines hummed at a time, two for quiches and a third for petite mushroom turnovers, mini calzones, and something called cream cheese bouchées. Nancy added new products to the business, from crab cakes to party spirals—sandwich wraps that could be defrosted and served cold without any reheating required.

With $50 million in sales in 1998, Nancy's Specialty Foods was thriving. The business had never been stronger. But Nancy started to panic. She was waking in the middle of the night, worrying about what would happen if one of her giant club stores canceled its account.

"I had a $17 million mortgage on my company," she said. "I had all that inventory. I mean, I had probably $30 million sunk in that company, and I was not going to get paid out unless I could sell the product."

She knew that the warehouse stores that were paying her bills were known for abruptly changing tactics. They could call a good supplier out of the blue and say that they weren't going to sell the product anymore and ask whether the supplier wanted to come pick up the inventory or have them donate it.

"I became frantic," Nancy recalled. "That was my nightmare."

"I factored in that possibility, and said, that's the truth. It's reality that this could happen," she said. "That handwriting was probably on the wall, and I was seeing it even though it hadn't happened yet."

* * *

She and a friend took her 56-foot cabin cruiser yacht to Mexico over Thanksgiving, and Nancy spent four days thinking things through.

"I came back and I said to my team, 'I need to sell the business,'" she remembers. Soon thereafter, at the height of the dot-com boom, when Palo Alto was teeming with internet start-ups and the stock market was booming, Nancy cashed out of the quiche business.

After two decades, Nancy's Specialty Foods now belonged to a leveraged buyout firm, Kohlberg & Company, and Nancy was building the luxury yacht that would buoy her through the next decade. "No tears were shed," she said. "Only relief."

"You don't sell when you've lost Price Club. You sell when you're getting accolades," she explains. "I would have kept my company if I wasn't so scared about losing it."

In her den at home, behind a row of stately olive trees, she says she doesn't miss Nancy's Specialty Foods and has no regrets about selling while she was ahead. "If I had waited two or three years, I probably would have gotten more money for it, but I didn't. So I'm not going to cry over that spilled milk," she insists.

Six years later, Kohlberg & Company sold it to the Heinz Company. Her nightmare of losing the business never happened, but today her quiches have largely faded from warehouse store shelves. When they pop up at Safeway around Christmas, she buys as many as she can for the freezer.

Nancy's story shows that the path to wealth need not run through elite universities and technology start-ups. Sometimes, the key is spotting an unmet need and doggedly pursuing it, even when the early results are disappointing.

She always kept a careful eye on operating metrics and used that data to tweak the strategy and grow the business. And she knew herself well enough to recognize when it was a good time to exit, cash out, and sail off into the sunset (on her yacht, *The Andiamo*).

* * *

Whether in small towns or Silicon Valley suburbs, the Age of Millionaires has reshaped wealth across the map. Looking at the economy across industries gives another perspective that reveals their prevalence.

We categorized each pass-through business in America based on whether any of its owners were in the top 1 percent in income. Here are the leading industries that generated the most pass-through income for those owners in 2021:

1. *Legal services ($109 billion).* Most of this activity is in law partnerships.
2. *Financial investment activities ($104 billion).* These would include venture capitalists, private equity, and hedge fund managers.
3. *Auto dealers ($50 billion).* America is a nation of drivers.
4. *Professional and technical services and management consulting ($46 billion).* America is home to a lot of consultants.
5. *Oil and gas extraction ($34 billion).* Imagine fracking companies in North Dakota and Pennsylvania.
6. *Doctors' offices ($32 billion).* Think doctors who have stand-alone practices instead of working for hospitals.
7. *Residential and nonresidential builders ($31 billion).* Picture general contractors for building and renovation projects.
8. *Real estate activities ($24 billion).* In other words, managers of rental and other commercial real estate.
9. *Restaurants ($24 billion).* Most restaurateurs don't reach the top, but some do, especially when they have restaurants in several locations or multi-unit franchises.
10. *Accounting and bookkeeping ($20 billion).* Every firm in America must track its books.
11. *Specialty trade contractors ($20 billion).* These include contractors who focus on building project components, like drywall, cabinets, or foundation work.
12. *Nondepository credit intermediation ($18 billion).* Think mortgage companies, credit card issuers, and other non-bank lenders.
13. *Fabricated metal product and miscellaneous manufacturing ($18 billion).* Picture a company making plumbing fixtures, artificial Christmas trees, jewelry, flatware, cigarette lighters, umbrellas, wigs, and toys.
14. *Durable goods merchant wholesalers ($16 billion).* They, for instance, sell home appliances to retail stores or distribute garbage trucks.
15. *Building equipment contractors ($14 billion).* Picture contractors who install and maintain HVAC, plumbing, and electrical systems.
16. *Computer systems design ($13 billion).* Think software and internet technology companies.

17. *Securities and commodity brokers ($12 billion).* These include stockbrokers and other financial market middlemen.
18. *Insurance agencies and brokerages ($12 billion).* These include, for example, title insurance companies.
19. *Architectural and engineering services ($12 billion).* Every building in America has a designer.
20. *Realtors ($11 billion).* Nearly every home sold in America has both a buyer's agent and a seller's agent.
21. *Dentists' offices ($10 billion).* Everybody's got teeth. There are over 200,000 dentists—or, six dentists for every 10,000 people across the country.
22. *Nondurable goods merchant wholesalers ($10 billion).* Think distributors of paper products, groceries, and cleaning supplies to retailers.
23. *Building material and supplies dealers ($10 billion).* These include lumberyards, hardware stores, and home improvement suppliers.
24. *Non-auto motor vehicle dealers ($9 billion).* Think boat, RV, and motorcycle dealerships.
25. *Employment services ($9 billion).* These include staffing agencies and temp firms.

Each of these industries has propelled thousands of Main Street Millionaires to riches. The leading industries are not concentrated in a few firms but instead reflect a multitude of midsize companies and their owners.

For example, 12,100 professional and technical service firms, 16,400 construction and contracting firms, 1,300 fabricated metal production manufacturers, and 9,900 auto dealerships have at least one owner in the top 0.1 percent of income. Put another way: There are 25 ultrarich auto dealers for every member of the Forbes 400.

* * *

Doctors like Rakesh Ranjan represent one of the top industries for pass-through business income.

He founded the Charak Center for Health and Wellness in Cleveland, providing psychiatric care to patients. After he grew his private practice to five locations in northeast Ohio, his business generated around $20 million in sales in 2021 and his estimated wealth is now $40 million.

More than six thousand doctors' offices generate enough income to put at least one of their owners in the top 0.1 percent in income, which means they make more than $6.7 million per year.

Similarly, Peter Boulden of Atlanta owns eight local dental practices. The market for dental services, he told Sieva Kozinsky in an interview, is way bigger than Formula One, the NFL, the NBA, Major League Baseball, all NCAA sports, and the PGA—combined. Total revenue from dentistry is $165 billion a year, says the American Dental Association. The NFL generated around $23 billion in 2024, while the NBA generated $12 billion.

When David Alameel, an immigrant from Lebanon, was picking strawberries and pumping gas at age twenty, he could not have imagined how much money he'd make from dentistry. He enlisted in the Army, worked as a pharmacy specialist, and completed his dental training before founding a network of thirty clinics in the Dallas–Fort Worth area. He sold his company at age fifty-seven and listed his net worth at around $75 million.

Not surprisingly, many lawyers, financiers, and insurance providers occupy the top ranks of pass-through owners. There are ninety thousand law firm owners in the top 1 percent, and fourteen thousand in the top 0.1 percent.

In one corner of the pass-through world, mainly finance, business structures are so opaque that the IRS can't even find a way to audit the underlying firms. The world of Main Street Millionaires, however, is not dominated by a hyper-sophisticated white-collar technocracy of complex business pyramids, tax and regulatory loopholes, and paper-pushing. Indeed, the typical millionaire is more Main Street than Wall Street.

Less than 20 percent of millionaire-owned pass-through profits come from finance, insurance, and real estate.

* * *

Main Street Millionaires usually provide valuable goods and services. They meet customers' needs, employ many workers, and form connections with clients, suppliers, and the community.

While law partnerships, financial firms, and insurance companies can also provide valuable services, they mostly do their work digitally and at a distance. By contrast, the typical Main Street businesses are tactile, personal, and tangible.

These industry statistics suggest that there are more systematic ways of finding Main Street Millionaires. In the next chapter, we will explore several. For example, along our road trip, we surely would have stopped for gas, snacks, and clean bathrooms. Let's meet some of the folks who are making millions keeping fellow voyagers filled up and well fed.

3

Many Roads to Riches

[An auto parts maker is] not a sexy business by any means, but it's a very lucrative business that grows exponentially. It clicked for me in my brain. It's like, non-sexy is sexy for me.

—Russell Westbrook, NBA MVP who has owned Pizzana restaurants, auto dealerships, and other unsexy businesses, May 2023

Arch "Beaver" Aplin III didn't set out to be a convenience store owner. As he told a crowd at Texas A&M's Mosbacher Institute in 2022, "I ended up where I was because I didn't have a job."

When he opened a small convenience store in Lake Jackson, Texas, Aplin had no idea it would grow into a behemoth of fifty-four Buc-ee's gas and convenience mega-stores on highways across Texas, in growing swaths of the American South, and as far west as Colorado. After he brought in a partner in 1985, Aplin's share of the business is, as of this writing, worth several hundred million dollars.

* * *

In a sense, Main Street Millionaires are hiding in plain sight. The supermarket where you shop, the restaurant where you order a burger, and the convenience store where you buy gas, newspaper, and coffee may all be parts of huge chains that have made their founders very rich.

You may see these outlets on the Main Street of your local town that you drive down every day or, as with Buc-ee's, you may pass them on the outskirts of town when you head out on a long drive.

Behind the food and other businesses that you see, however, are many others that you don't; they, too, have turned their founders into Main Street Millionaires. They include food suppliers that deliver—to restaurants and other food establishments—meat for hamburgers, chicken for cutlets, bread for sandwiches, cheese for pizzas, and milk for ice cream.

Main Street Millionaires also have made their fortunes on the other end of the food chain. They, for instance, provide the toilet paper for the bathrooms of convenience stores like Buc-ee's or fast-food giants like Wendy's, or for the shelves of supermarket chains like Publix and Wegmans.

The same, of course, is true of industries far beyond food. When you pass by car dealers on Main Street or out in the suburbs, think about all the suppliers of all the parts that go into all those cars. Or the suppliers of materials to build buildings or rebuild highways and bridges.

So, let's take a closer look at how grocery store owners, paper product distributors, fast-food franchisers, plastic product manufacturers, and meat, poultry, and cheese distributors became Main Street Millionaires.

* * *

Beaver Aplin sports a neatly trimmed beard, metal-rimmed glasses, and wavy, shoulder-length hair under an off-white cowboy hat. When he spoke at Texas A&M, he had just pledged $50 million to create a program at the university in hospitality and entrepreneurship.

He accepted the school's McLane Leadership in Business Award wearing a navy jacket over a crisp white shirt and tie, and brown cowboy boots with the Buc-ee's logo—a cartoon of a bucktoothed beaver face—peeking out from under his khakis.

Decades earlier, when he was graduating from A&M's construction sciences program, Aplin wanted to build high-rise buildings. Weeks before graduation, he secured a job as an assistant project manager for a new building on the A&M campus.

"I thought, how could anything be better?" he recalled to his A&M

audience. "I'm going to have a job and a paycheck and still be living in College Station, so I was very, very excited and I put all the eggs in that basket." But A&M put the project out to bid, and Aplin lost the job because his would-be employer lost the bid.

After something like that, he explained, "you got to pick yourself up and dust it off and just do something. So I immediately went to work because I was graduating within a few days of that . . . and started working for my dad. My dad built houses and light commercial [real estate] and apartments and those kinds of things . . . but it wasn't my passion. It wasn't what I really wanted to do."

Growing up in Louisiana, he had spent time in his grandfather's little general store. He wasn't allowed to run the register, so he worked at the store's full-service gas pump.

"I decided," Aplin said, "I was going to build a convenience store. I designed the store myself."

An avid duck hunter, Aplin trained Labrador retrievers, one of whom was named Buck. "My nickname's Beaver and I had a dog named Buck so I called [the store] Buc-ee's and I made the logo a beaver and here we are.

"I knew absolutely nothing about the convenience store business and so that was a big challenge," he recalled. "You're always undercapitalized when you start out. I built the first store probably a quarter of a mile from where I grew up, so that made it pretty handy. My cost of living, my overhead was very low. I lived in one of my dad's apartments for free and my mom cooked meals three days a week."

The first Buc-ee's store was 3,000 square feet, just a bit bigger than the typical 7-Eleven of those days. It had two gas pumps. The second store was twice the size and had four pumps.

"I just kept tinkering with the design and changing things," Aplin told his audience at Texas A&M. "It was always difficult to get any traction because every time I would open a store then I would experience it and then change it, so I was always in changing mode."

In hindsight, he said that was probably the best approach for him to take. "Looking back, I needed to go slow then and kind of develop my business so the model has evolved through all the years."

In 2003, he settled on the concept of what he now calls a travel center, which built on the basic convenience store by adding substantial food offerings. "Of course we're in Texas, so I chose to do barbecue."

Aplin's strategy had four main prongs:

- *First, locate travel centers along highways mainly outside of major metropolitan areas.*

  That's largely because the land is cheap and the competition in terms of other travel centers is more spread out, leaving each Buc-ee's a wide geographical area in which to operate alone.

  So, you won't find a Buc-ee's in central Atlanta, Austin, Dallas, San Antonio, or Houston. Instead, you'll find one on the outskirts of those cities and in places like Robertsdale, Alabama; Fort Valley, Georgia; Crossville, Tennessee; Madisonville, Texas; and Temple, Texas.

- *Second, use gas as a loss leader—that is, as a product sold at a loss to attract customers into a Buc-ee's to buy higher-margin items like barbecue and merchandise.*

  For decades, slightly below-market gas prices have proved a powerful sales tool for Buc-ee's. "There's no product, arguably, that people are more price sensitive to than gasoline," Jeff Lenard, an industry expert and vice president of strategic industry initiatives for the National Association of Convenience Stores, explains to us. Even before the cost of credit card fees, labor, and all the other costs associated with selling gas, Lenard explains, the profit margin on gasoline alone is just 15 to 20 cents a gallon. "So let's say you're at the upper end. If the typical fill up is 10 gallons, you can make $2."

  Inside the store, however, the profit margin for a brisket sandwich is closer to that of a restaurant, which Lenard said can be around 100 percent. "Gas prices get you to the store," he said, so charging a shade less for gasoline than the competition is a low-margin way to drive traffic.

Their brisket sandwiches, branded beaver logo merchandise, homemade fudge, and private-label beef jerky have earned Buc-ee's a cultlike following. Its top-selling snack is crunchy, sweetened corn puffs called Beaver Nuggets. There's even a burgeoning online resale market for Buc-ee's merchandise, with one Texas operator claiming more than $250,000 in aftermarket Buc-ee's snack sales a month.

"People have Buc-ee's tattoos," Lenard told us.

- *Third, keep the toilets gleaming.*

The company claims its oversize restrooms are attended and cleaned 24-7. Billboards urge travelers to hold it in until they arrive at one of Aplin's landmark emporiums. And by all indications, millions do.

"It's a business built on porcelain," said Chris Aarons, a lecturer at the University of Texas McCombs School of Business. "Those bathrooms are really important. That's what we're all worried about because we've gone into sketchy roadside gas stations where the bathroom is broken."

Buc-ee's has won awards for the cleanest bathrooms in America, including a nationwide-award from Cintas in 2012 and top rankings from GasBuddy. Buc-ee's even installed a "Tooshlight" outside each door to let you know if the stall is occupied.

- *Fourth, provide entertainment.*

Buc-ee's locations create a shoppers' playground, making each travel center a destination in and of itself.

"Buc-ee's is not convenient if you look at the traditional definition of a convenience store," Lenard said. "The typical in and out at a convenience store on average is three minutes and thirty-three seconds. That's the length of a song," such as the Rolling Stones' "Start Me Up."

"But the experience at Buc-ee's, getting from your car, just even inside the store, is probably more than that," said Lenard. "You're taking a picture of the Beaver statue, you're walking through a massive parking lot. The pit stop is the destination and it's a total shift in mindset. And then by changing that mindset, you just introduce customers to a new mindset and how they might want to spend money with you."

"You can buy everything," Aarons said, "including an entire wardrobe, kitchenware, and a $1,000 smoker, which by the way, I hear from people who've bought it who say the Buc-ee's smoker is the best one."

* * *

Today, Aplin and business partner Don Wasek oversee a dominion of massive twenty-four-hour Buc-ee's stores.

Each man owns half the company, Buc-ee's Ltd. Wasek heads up operations, while Aplin focuses on expansion, construction, and marketing. Their holding company, CSMS Management, LLC, buys the land. Aplin's the president, Wasek's the vice president. The firm owns two jets—a 2020 Cessna Citation Longitude and a 2009 Global 5000—and, in 2015, the company generated $959 million in sales and was valued at more than $500 million. More recent estimates are hard to find but, based on per-store revenue estimates and revenues from comparable firms, these values could well have doubled in the decade since.

The Buc-ee's in Sevierville, Tennessee, outside Knoxville, was once the world's largest convenience store at 74,707 square feet—until it was outdone by a new Buc-ee's in Luling, Texas, in 2024. Meanwhile, a Buc-ee's in Katy, Texas, near Houston, has the world's longest car wash, and the store is as long as a football field.

Built to replace the original 2003 travel center in a building next door, the Luling location covers 75,000 square feet, has 120 gas pumps, and employs about 250 people. But it won't be the biggest Buc-ee's for long. A store in the works in Ocala, Florida, is planned for 80,000 square feet.

"What we do is so basic but it's hard," Aplin said at a recent megastore opening. "If it wasn't hard there would be a lot of other people doing it."

* * *

But others *are* doing it, though with less flair. The nation is home to more than 152,000 convenience stores, according to Lenard. "That's roughly equal to every drugstore, dollar store, grocery store, Starbucks, and McDonald's combined."

America's richest convenience store owners may be the Loves of Oklahoma. In 1964, Tom Love borrowed money from his in-laws to lease an abandoned gas station in rural Watonga, Oklahoma, for $5,000. It was a modest beginning, born of necessity. Tom, a Chickasaw Nation tribe member and former Marine, was looking for a way to support his wife, Judy, and their young children.

Their little business grew to forty stores in eight years. Judy managed the books until she returned to college in 1975. "When we got married," Tom told a reporter in 2018, "I couldn't even balance my own checkbook. She did all the books, all the payrolls, covered all the overdrafts."

In 1972, Tom and Judy were supposedly the first to combine a grocery–convenience store with a gas station when they opened the first Love's Country Store in Guymon, Oklahoma. They serve motorists and truckers. Love's giant yellow sign with a red heart now towers over highways across America.

By the time Tom died in 2023 at age eighty-five, his family's empire had grown to 640 locations in forty-two states. Love's Travel Stops & Country Stores had $26.5 billion in revenue in 2023, according to *Forbes*, ranking it the nation's eleventh-largest private company. The family's wealth amounts to around $13 billion.

Over the years, the role of a convenience store has changed. A few decades ago, it was a place to get directions when you're lost and maybe buy just a few things. "Let's get some film," Lenard said. "Let's get a magazine. Let's get a newspaper. Let's get a map because we're lost and let's buy some greeting cards. That's all changed. What you sell and how you sell it is constantly changing and the customer always wants more."

Shaping the convenience store of the future might fall to a third generation of Loves. Tom and Judy had nine grandchildren and several great-grandchildren. The family has resisted purchase offers, "but we've done a pretty good job on family succession," Tom told the same reporter in 2018.

"Several months ago," Tom said, "one of my grandsons was graduating from the University of Oklahoma with a degree in entrepreneurship and supply chain management. He wasn't sure what he wanted to do. I said, 'Why don't you learn how to drive a truck? Get your CDL [commercial driver's license]. If you think you're interested in coming to Love's, you'll get to know our most important customer from that side of the windshield.'

"And he has done that. And he loves it. He was able to begin hauling loads solo recently. The first night the air-conditioning [in the cab] went out on him. He's learning a lot." Another grandson worked with the company's sales group on the East Coast, working with truckers and fleets. "So the third generation is creeping into the business, which is great."

Though Buc-ee's and Love's have taken widely disparate approaches, each has grown in one generation from a single roadside gas station to a sprawling multistate network. And both have kept their businesses firmly—and very lucratively—in private hands.

* * *

Ask people to tell you about the richest person they know. You'll learn a lot about the many roads to riches.

For example, someone we know from St. Louis said the richest kid in the local high school was from the Tracy family, which owns Dot Foods—the nation's largest food redistributor. The nation's forty-second largest private company in 2025, according to *Forbes*, it has nearly seven thousand employees and around $10.6 billion in annual revenue.

Born in the summer of 1924, Robert Tracy grew up during the Great Depression working on his family's dairy farm in Jerseyville, Illinois. He served as a Marine in World War II and studied dairy technology at the University of Illinois after the war. He met his wife, Dorothy, in college. At thirty-six, after he worked a decade at Prairie Farms, he and Dorothy decided to found a powdered milk delivery company in the small farming town of Mount Sterling, Illinois. With little money, they launched the business from the back of the family station wagon, which usually helped transport their eight (and eventually twelve) children.

They had planned to deliver powdered milk to local ice cream and dairy manufacturers, but demand for more products and deliveries prompted them to expand. They added a warehouse and bought a few trucks. A key to Dot Foods' success was the redistribution model. Usually, food manufacturers only shipped full truckloads, which was too much product for small distributors. Dot Foods bought full truckloads, stored products in their warehouse, and resold items in smaller quantities to distributors.

Sales doubled every few years in the 1970s and '80s as the Tracys added more warehouses and transportation fleets. During this time, the couple handed over the reins to the second generation. The second son, Pat, was president for eleven years starting in 1985 and became CEO in 1996. Four brothers (Tom, John, Jim, and Dick) joined the family firm around this time.

An early adopter of electronic transportation and logistics technologies, Dot let customers track their shipments online. The Tracys steadily added warehouses and expanded product offerings, including nonfood items like over-the-counter drugs.

The second generation of Tracys has continued to run Dot Foods. Dick was named CEO in 2023 after serving as president for six years. Of the forty-six grandchildren of Robert and Dorothy, eleven work full-time at Dot as of October 2024.

* * *

If you are wondering where those food distributors are selling their wares, think about the grocery store chains we all drive by. Many are regional family businesses that continue to build lasting multigenerational wealth.

George Jenkins, the founder of supermarket giant Publix, which *Forbes* lists among the nation's largest private businesses, grew up in Harris City, Georgia. Like other Main Street Millionaires, he got an early exposure to business in his family's general store. After his freshman year at Georgia Tech, he hitchhiked to Ybor City, Florida, to chase opportunities in real estate. After realizing that dream wouldn't pan out, he thought about hitchhiking back to Georgia.

Before he could pack his bag, he met a local grocery store owner who convinced him to earn some money by working at his store, Piggly Wiggly. Jenkins learned the ropes, doing well as a clerk and then store manager. He was transferred to another Piggly Wiggly, in Winter Haven, a central Florida town dotted with several lakes. But when the absentee owner of that Piggly Wiggly wouldn't see Jenkins when he traveled to meet with the owner in Atlanta, Jenkins spitefully opened a new store next door.

Enter Publix in 1930. Jenkins focused on customer service, employee welfare, and innovation. With air-conditioning, wide aisles, and an in-store bakery, Publix did well and began expanding. Jenkins encouraged employees to buy shares of Publix and, in 1959, Publix began an employee ownership program. Today, it's the nation's largest employee-owned company, with employees and former employees owning around 80 percent.

Publix operates 1,360 stores in the Southeast, employs a quarter of a million people, and generated $55 billion in revenue in 2023. The Jenkins family, whose net worth is $11 billion, according to *Forbes*, retains about 20 percent of the company, which was led by Jenkins's grandson, Ed Crenshaw, from 2008 until 2016. It also has a few other family members on the board.

* * *

In Kansas City, brothers Jim and Jerry opened Cosentino's Food Stores in 1948. They expanded from one grocery store to other store formats and now operate thirty-one stores, employing more than four thousand people and, based on a revenue-per-worker industry average of $220,000, generate around $900 million in annual revenue.

Cosentino's remains family-owned and operated, as have many chains across the country. Heinen's in Cleveland is now run by the grandsons of Joe Heinen, who founded the company in 1929. It employs thirty-five hundred and generates $600 million in revenue a year from twenty-three stores, mostly in northeast Ohio.

Privately owned grocery stores earn billions in revenue, employ tens of thousands of people, and make their owners lots of money. We found nearly sixteen thousand pass-through owners of grocery and convenience stores who, collectively, own around ten thousand businesses and are in the top 1 percent in income.

Other prominent examples include Wegmans in New Jersey, owned by Danny Wegman and other family members, with $12 billion in revenue and fifty-three thousand employees; Meijer in Michigan, owned by the Meijer family, with $21 billion and seventy thousand; Brookshire Brothers in Texas, owned by the family until they sold it to employees in 1999, with $3 billion and seven thousand; Houchens Industries in Kentucky, owned by the family until they sold it to employees in 1988, with $4 billion and nineteen thousand; and K-VA-T in Tennessee, owned by the Smith family, with $3 billion and fifteen thousand.

One of the richest store owners is Charles Butt, who inherited H-E-B, the family-owned and San Antonio–based grocery store that does over $46 billion in revenue and employs one hundred and fifty-four thousand. He's worth around $10 billion.

* * *

Maybe instead of heading to the grocery store after work, you're thinking of picking up some takeout on the way home.

Born on the banks of the Ohio River as one of eight kids in a working-class family, Scott Schmidt started working as an assistant manager at a local Wendy's in 1975. After a decade and a half, during which he learned the ins and outs of each position in the restaurant, he had saved up enough money to buy two franchises. He gradually expanded his holdings into a small empire of Wendy's restaurants.

The Schmidts now own seventy-seven Wendy's franchises across Ohio, Kentucky, West Virginia, and North Carolina. In 2004, Schmidt bought a few Buffalo Wild Wings franchises as well. He appointed his son, "Juice," president of the family company in 2015. Scott and Juice have both won the Wendy Award, which each year honors the company's top general managers of Wendy's franchises, the former in 1997 and the latter in 2018.

As of the end of 2024, Wendy's had seventy-two hundred restaurants, and 95 percent of them were franchise-owned by around three hundred owners.

Ulysses "Junior" Bridgeman built a $1.4 billion fortune from owning 450 fast-food restaurants, primarily Wendy's and Chili's. The son of a steelworker, Bridgeman played in the NBA for the Milwaukee Bucks, but was not a superstar. He drew inspiration from one of the Bucks' owners, Jim Fitzgerald, and the general manager, Wayne Embry, who owned several McDonald's.

After retiring, Bridgeman pursued his franchising career. He bought a few Wendy's and enrolled in their franchisee training program. "He'd be working in the restaurant like he was an hourly worker," Sidney Moncrief, a former Bucks teammate, recalled to ESPN. "I was thinking, 'What the heck is he doing in there flipping burgers, washing dishes?' And he had those work pants on." Bridgeman passed away in 2025, leaving behind several business interests, including 240 Wendy's and a 10 percent stake in the Bucks.

Larry Fleming opened his first Wendy's franchise in Wichita in 1975. He grew his holdings to include forty-three Wendy's as well as several beverage distributorships in Kansas and Oklahoma. As of 2002, his businesses generated $100 million in revenue and employed more than 1,500 people. He sold his Wendy's franchises in 2017 for an undisclosed—but certainly sizable—amount.

A common type of Main Street Millionaire, franchise owners are harder to spot because we only see the franchise brand on the business.

* * *

The next time you're in a fast-food restaurant, ask yourself how many people got rich along the supply chain to your meal.

John Paterakis, a.k.a. "the bread man," was one of the largest suppliers of hamburger buns for McDonald's. When he passed away in 2016, he owned at least twenty-two bakeries that employed thirty-five hundred people, and was worth around $250 million.

Paterakis began his bread-baking business in the basement of his parents' row house in Baltimore. Although McDonald's did not promise that it would buy from him, he boldly invested $1.5 million in automating bun production. "You've got to keep spending money to keep updating to remain competitive," he said. "If you don't keep up, the big fish will eat you."

Paterakis didn't wear suits. He drove a Lincoln with more than 200,000 miles on it. He lived in the same house in the Baltimore suburbs for nearly fifty years. "You gotta remember," he said after he was inducted into *The Baltimore Sun*'s Business and Civic Hall of Fame, "I'm just a little Greek baker that got lucky."

He wasn't the only fortunate Greek baker in America. Louis Kuchuris founded East Balt Bakeries, the first supplier of buns to Ray Kroc in the original McDonald's location in Des Plaines, Illinois. His bakery business would go on to serve around nine thousand McDonald's outlets worldwide.

East Balt acquired the Wendy's company baking business in 2015. Two years later, the Kuchuris family sold East Balt for $650 million.

* * *

The meat supply business has also been a route to great wealth.

Chicago's Joe Grendys is one of two "Chicken Billionaires" we found in our search for Main Street Millionaires. When he started in the mid-1980s as a 50 percent owner of his company, Koch Foods (which is not affiliated with Koch Industries of Kansas), it had one room and thirteen employees who would remove chicken bones and cut up meat for processing. Joe bought the other half of the business from the founder, Fred Koch, in 1992. Over time, and partly through acquisitions, Grendys amassed a fortune of around $4.5 billion.

Tommy Bagwell of Cumming, Georgia, is a chicken centimillionaire. Among other products, his American Proteins business converts chicken guts into feed for pets and farm animals throughout the world. With four rendering plants in Georgia and Alabama and thirteen blending facilities in the Southeast and Midwest, the company employs around seven hundred people. He sold it to Tyson Foods in 2018 for $850 million.

For those who don't have the stomach for processing meat, processing cheese can be just as enriching.

James Leprino owns the world's largest mozzarella maker. Leprino Foods opened in 1958 with $615 as a family grocery store in Denver's Little Italy. In the late 1950s, when major pizza chains began operating and frozen pizzas started to become more popular, Leprino noticed the growing demand for pizza cheese. "Pizzerias in this part of the country," he later recalled, "were buying 5,000 pounds of cheese a week." Around that time, the first Pizza Hut opened in Wichita, Kansas.

About ten years after Leprino began selling cheese to Italian restaurants and pizza places, Pizza Hut started looking for a supplier that could standardize cheese portions. In response, Leprino Foods created presliced frozen blocks and deployed a "preservative mist" technique to extend the cheese's shelf life. He grew alongside Pizza Hut, which had one thousand stores in 1972.

Leprino then secured long-term contracts with California dairy farmers and co-ops, giving his company a stable supply of milk to process cheese. The company's "Quality Locked Cheese" (shredded and individually frozen portions) became an industry standard in 1986.

Now, Leprino Foods sells more than a billion pounds of cheese each year, supplying most of America's major pizza chains—including

Pizza Hut, Domino's, Papa John's, and Little Caesars—and controlling up to 85 percent of the market. The reclusive Leprino, who rarely gives interviews or lets others photograph him, is worth around $3 billion; *Forbes* dubbed him "one of America's all-time monopolists."

* * *

Many Main Street Millionaires have made their fortunes at the very end of the supply chain as well.

Steven Tabak's family business—a distributor of a wide range of paper products, including toilet paper—dates to the 1930s. His grandfather, Aaron Tabak, established Jersey Paper in 1935, and Steven's father and uncle assumed control of it in the 1950s. "I was the youngest grandchild," Steven recalled to us, and "the only one who wanted to be in the business out of four."

Steven remembers going to work on Saturdays with his dad, Joseph, working during school breaks or after sleepaway camp. "I'd go in a lot," he said. "I learned from my father because he was like me, or I was like him. He would come home, we would talk about it, and I just became like him."

When he was a twenty-year-old junior at Syracuse University in 1981, however, his father called to tell him that he (Joseph) and his brother had sold the company to Bunzl PLC.

"What am I going to do?" Steven asked his father.

"You'll figure it out," his dad replied.

He did. After working for Bunzl for five years, Steven left to buy a paper company in Carlstadt, New Jersey. He grew the company, bought another one, and eventually changed the name of his company back to Jersey Paper in 2000.

Fast-forward to 2017. His company raked in around $70 million in sales before it was acquired by Imperial Dade, a larger independently owned distributor of disposable food service and janitorial supplies.

Some forty years after taking over, and with his company now owned by Imperial Dade, Tabak still comes to work. He says he doesn't have much else to do. "I don't play tennis," he said. "That's why I'm still there."

The company serves customers throughout New Jersey, the greater New York City region, and eastern Pennsylvania. It's a consistent industry, with many clients receiving weekly deliveries; "these guys use it and then throw it out," he said. The customer base is broad too. It includes "anybody who uses toilet paper or towels, or soap or cleaning mops, brooms, hot cups, bags."

In a crowded disposable paper products market, Tabak said that customer relationships are key. Many of the products might be carried by a big box retailer, and pricing can be competitive. "We're selling a hot cup, a bakery box," he said. "Everybody sells it. In order to really have that [relationship], you've got to go talk to the customers."

That's why you might have found Tabak on the other end of the line if you called at 6:30 in the morning. As he told industry publication *Maintenance Sales News*, he made a habit of coming in early and heading out late. Even if offices didn't open officially until 8:00 a.m., he picked up the phone. And if a customer called to voice a complaint, no matter how belligerent the customer was, Tabak would start his answer with, "Thank you for calling. We appreciate that."

* * *

Carl Allen of Irving, Texas, made $300 million in 2016 when he sold his company, Heritage Bag, which produced trash bags and liners for restaurants and other customers.

Allen leveraged his trash-derived wealth into a literal treasure hunt. In 1656, a Spanish treasure ship sank in the Bermuda Triangle. Marine archaeologist Jim Sinclair believes that most of its treasure, which he told CBS was probably worth "well over $100 million," is still there. Allen decided to take a look.

He bought a 164-foot-long yacht, which he named for his wife, Gigi, along with a 183-foot-long research vessel that carries a Triton submersible and a seaplane. Exploring the North Atlantic Ocean floor, he has collected over ten thousand artifacts, including dozens of gold chains, silver bars, and pendants.

"If we don't do this, Mother Nature gets it, or pirates," Allen explained. "And that doesn't do anybody any good.

"I am a treasure hunter. I fully admit it."

* * *

Another way to find Main Street Millionaires is to think about Adam Smith and his description of a pin factory, which is how he begins his classic economic treatise, *The Wealth of Nations*.

In that story, each person working in the factory specializes in one aspect of making pins, whether it's shaping the heads, elongating the necks, or putting them in boxes. Today, many successful companies specialize in making niche inputs along a supply chain. Although they are largely invisible to the average consumer, such businesses play key roles in making the products we use every day.

When the Obama administration wanted to save the auto industry amid the financial collapse that began in late 2008, it calculated that making one Jeep Wrangler requires three thousand American workers scattered across dozens of firms. They work at places like ADAC, a massive family-owned supplier of door handles, with thousands of employees, in Saranac, Michigan. We suspect that very few people have heard of ADAC, even though it employs twice as many people as Twitter ever did.

Nor have most people heard of most of the smaller companies in America where, in fact, most people work. Firms with fewer than five hundred employees account for around half of employment in the United States. Small firms with fewer than one hundred workers account for about a third.

Many of these firms are owned by Main Street Millionaires. Each person we met in this chapter represents hundreds or thousands of other business owners who operate in small niches across the economy. And there are a lot of niches!

The Tabaks are among 1,300 pass-through owners in the top 1 percent in income who made their living in the paper and paper product merchant wholesaling business. Also in the top 1 percent are about 4,400 pass-through owners of plastic product manufacturing companies like Carl Allen.

Our cheese and chicken billionaires also have plenty of company. More than 500 pass-through owners of dairy product manufacturers are in the top 1 percent in income. The animal slaughtering and processing industry has propelled another 560 pass-through owners to the top 1 percent.

* * *

Following his tour of America, Alexis de Tocqueville wrote in 1835, "What strikes me most in the United States is not the extraordinary greatness of some industrial enterprises, it is the innumerable multitude of small enterprises." A lot has changed since then, but the statement still resonates nearly two hundred years later.

There are Main Street Millionaires everywhere. Look around. And now you know how.

4

The Typical Top Earner

You have to make a choice between having fun during the weekend or fun during the week.

—A. J. Wasserstein, founder of ArchivesOne, 2024

A. J. Wasserstein told us that he opted to have fun on the weekend. He made millions growing a company that just stored documents for medical and financial firms. He likened the experience to watching paint dry. People would ship him boxes of documents, and he would put them in a locked building and keep them dry.

Some seventeen years after founding ArchivesOne, he sold it to a publicly traded company, Iron Mountain. For more fun on the weekend, he then became president of the nation's third-largest bottle-less water service business before selling it in 2016. Now Wasserstein is imparting wisdom (such as this chapter's opening quote) to graduate students about the virtues of boring, steady businesses as a senior lecturer in the practice of management at the Yale School of Management.

Many of A.J.'s students aspire to get rich like him. But what does it take to be among the richest Americans?

In 2022, you would have needed $60 million to be among the top 0.1 percent in wealth. If you wanted to be in the top 0.1 percent in income, you would have needed to earn $2.3 million that year, making your wage effectively $1,140 an hour before taxes.

Imagine being that rich for a moment. How might you spend your money?

To start, you'd send lots of money to Uncle Sam. Taxpayers who earn more than $1 million a year have an average federal income tax rate of around 25 percent and an average state income tax rate of another 5 percent (although some millionaires, especially private business owners, pay much less by putting their money in tax shelters and taking lots of other tax breaks). At a combined 30 percent federal-state income tax rate, $3 million in income shrinks to $2.1 million.

Let's say your primary residence was worth $3.5 million. After a 20 percent down payment and with a 5 percent interest rate, you'd have a monthly mortgage payment of around $14,000. Property taxes would add another $3,000 to $6,000 each month, depending on where you live. After accounting for utilities, maintenance, and insurance, you'd probably have a total monthly bill of around $23,000. That means you'd be spending $276,000 a year on your primary house.

For the person with $2.1 million in after-tax income, that leaves around $1.8 million for the year, or $150,000 per month. So, each month, you'd have nearly twice as much to save or spend as the typical household earns in a year.

What would your life be like?

Among those who fly on their private jets, sail their yachts, enjoy their summer home in the mountains, and vacation in extravagant style are lots of Main Street Millionaires who came from far humbler beginnings.

Let's look over the shoulder of typical Main Street Millionaires as they go about their work. Who are they and what are their lives like? How do they spend their time and money? Are they really as bored as Wasserstein describes?

* * *

In Frisco, Texas, Ben Caballero wakes up every morning at 5:00 a.m. Looking in the bathroom mirror, he sees a thinly trimmed white beard that matches the white horseshoe of hair on his head.

After eating a breakfast of oats with milk and berries, he watches the news and checks email and his home-selling platform, HomesUSA.

At 7:00, he leaves for work in his GMC, arriving a half hour later at his real estate office in Addison, a suburb fifteen miles north of Dallas and seventy miles south of the Red River, on the border with Oklahoma.

With twenty-two employees, his firm specializes in selling new homes. On a typical morning, he catches up with his team, meets with clients, and gives a presentation to a client's salespeople about HomesUSA.

Caballero eats lunch—usually the vegetable plate—every day at Luby's, a cafeteria-style diner with several locations across Texas. A few times each week, and after some post-lunch meetings with employees, he meets his personal trainer at 4:30 at the local gym.

He then heads home, arriving around 6:15, when his fiancée greets him with dinner. After they eat together, Caballero may watch a football game on TV, but usually calls it a night before 10:00.

Don't let Caballero's modest lifestyle fool you, however. A real estate agent, a former homebuilder, and the founder of HomesUSA.com—an online platform for builders—he was worth an estimated $3.7 billion in 2022.

* * *

Caballero started learning his business early in life, just like Beaver Aplin and other Main Street Millionaires we've met.

He spent summers in Tampa, Florida, working with his parents, who were real estate agents. His father, a Cuban immigrant, assigned him to help manage some rental units and call customers.

His parents divorced, and he moved with his mother to Houston. He left home after high school to serve in the Air Force. From his base in Oklahoma City, Caballero took some classes at the University of Oklahoma and in his free time pursued a real estate license.

One weekend when he was traveling from Oklahoma City to his

mother's house, his car broke down in Dallas. He found the people there very friendly and decided to move to the "Big D" after the Air Force.

He passed his real estate exam at twenty-one and, at age eighty-three at the time of this writing, has been an agent for more than sixty years.

* * *

Caballero dabbled in a few real estate–related business ventures, starting in the apartment rental business in the early 1960s. After struggling to find a place to rent, and frustrated by the local rental service he was working with, he started a business to help prospective renters find apartments in Dallas. He made money by taking commissions.

"I was going around in an un-air-conditioned car, using the pay phone, calling owners of apartments, and telling them what I wanted to do," he explained on his podcast. "And hell, they were taking me to lunch and just being very gracious about it. That was not like I was used to in Florida because back then, it was like, 'Where did you go to school? Who is your daddy?'—they really didn't accept you the way that I was accepted here in Texas."

He then built custom homes for eighteen years. Through his work, he realized that many of his fellow homebuilders weren't listing their homes in any organized way. They had binders of new home listings that constantly needed updating. The problem offered Caballero an opportunity.

In 2007, he launched a platform for builders—HomesUSA.com—to track their listings. The service now provides listing and marketing assistance for more than seventy builders in four markets in Texas. The platform enables him to funnel new homes to his real estate agent services on an unrivaled scale.

Caballero is the first real estate agent to top $1 billion in home sales in a single year (and the nation's top-ranked real estate agent for ten years straight). Assuming a 2.5-to-3 percent commission per home, $1 billion in sales gives his business $25 million to $30 million in annual income. In 2023, he sold 7,012 homes, representing $3.6 billion in sales, which translates to around $100 million in income. Selling that many homes in a year means selling around 20 per day—almost twice what the typical agent sells in a year!

Like those of many Main Street Millionaires, Caballero's days are full, busy, and mundane. The turnkey operation he established over the years still requires a fair amount of oversight and involvement. And, at eighty-four in 2024, he was still the one making presentations to clients.

* * *

In its structure, Caballero's firm is fairly typical.

We looked at every pass-through firm in America, and we found that the median firm with at least one owner in the top 0.1 percent in income generates around $25 million in revenue every year. It has around thirty employees and only two or three owners. A firm is generally worth about one to two times its revenue, so a firm with $25 million in revenue generally is worth between $25 million and $50 million. (Why? Because a firm's owners effectively own the right to receive its current and future profits, and practitioners use formulas to convert those profits into a single valuation—expressed as a multiple of current assets, profits, or revenues.)

Each of these firms is not only "closely held"—i.e., only a small number of people own most of it—but the owners also tend to be singularly focused on it rather than on a host of business ventures. To put it another way, most top business owners own only one firm. And more than nine out of ten pass-through owners say they actively participate in their firms.

Some business owners grow very wealthy by closely holding their one company and reinvesting the profits into it over the long term. Owning a big share of a small company is the typical path to pass-through wealth. Around three-quarters of all profits accruing to the top owners of pass-throughs come from firms with less than $75 million in profits.

The superstar public companies with galactic executive pay packages that we often hear about, such as Apple, Nvidia, and J.P. Morgan, are quite different from pass-through firms. Four-fifths of pass-through profits come from firms with less than $750 million in annual revenue. By contrast, essentially all the profits from traditional C corporations, including publicly traded companies, come from firms that are larger.

We often hear stories about the cozy relationships between managers and corporate boards that set excessive pay packages. In a famous example, the Mattel CEO resigned in 2000 amid poor performance at the company, and the board rewarded her by forgiving a $4.2 million loan and allowing unvested stock options to vest. These payments came on top of a $26.4 million termination payment and retirement benefits of more than $700,000 per year.

When such favoritism occurs, a firm's owners lose out because there are so many of them, which limits the control that any one of them can impose over executive decisions. These stories, however, don't apply to the vast multitude of Main Street Millionaires because pass-through owners are often both the managers and the majority owners of their own firms.

* * *

Who is the typical business owner?

Let's start with the typical decamillionaire business owner. He—and it's usually a "he"—is a white, sixty-two-year-old, working college graduate.

Nine out of ten decamillionaire business owners are married (compared to 60 percent of the overall population of those aged forty to seventy).

Jon Zimmerman fits the profile to a T. He and his wife bought a car wash in Milwaukee in 2010, expanded their business to four locations over the next thirteen years, and sold it in 2022 to a private equity firm for $19 million.

That sale put them in the top 1 percent in wealth, which in 2022 included everyone with at least $13.6 million.

* * *

Most decamillionaire business owners are in their fifties, sixties, or seventies. Less than 10 percent of them are younger than forty simply because accumulating wealth and growing a business take time.

You might think that, since they're predominantly well advanced in years, these business owners are all self-made men. However, some of them were lucky enough to inherit a business but didn't assume full ownership of it until the older generation (normally, about thirty years older) passed from the scene.

Because the wealthy tend to be older, younger readers of this book might be wondering if they themselves are on track to reach the top 1 percent of income or wealth at some point. To help answer that question, they can calculate where they are among their age group at the moment. As of 2022, if you're in your twenties, you need to be making at least $300,000 in income and have $2.1 million in wealth to be in the top 1 percent among twentysomethings. In your peak earning years of your forties, you need around four times as much income and wealth to be in the top 1 percent—$1.2 million in income and $8.5 million in wealth. In your sixties, you need $1.8 million in income, and $19.4 million in wealth. In your seventies, when many stop working, you need $1 million in income and $18 million in wealth.

The thresholds for the top 0.1 percent follow similar patterns, although peak incomes come earlier—when those in this elite group reach their forties. The threshold for income grows from $4 million in your thirties to $8.4 million in your forties, and it then declines to $5.9 million in your fifties and $4.7 million in your sixties.

For the top 0.1 percent in wealth, the thresholds climb rapidly with age through the sixties and then fall a bit—$9.6 million in your twenties, $19.5 million in your thirties, $41.8 million in your forties, $62.8 million in your fifties, $112.4 million in your sixties, and $94.0 million in your seventies. In other words, a person in their sixties must be almost six times richer than a person in their thirties to make it to the top 0.1 percent of wealth in their age group.

All told, baby boomers (born between 1946 and 1964) hold 50

percent of private business wealth, Gen Xers (born between 1965 and 1980) hold a quarter, and millennials (born after 1980) and the silent generation (born between 1925 and 1945) each hold around 12 percent.

* * *

Some 80 percent of decamillionaire business owners have a college degree, and 40 percent have a postgraduate degree (e.g., MBA, MD, DDS, JD, PhD).

These decamillionaire business owners are twice as likely to attend college and postgraduate school as the general population. But, interestingly enough, they're *less* likely to go to college and graduate school than decamillionaires who don't own businesses.

Main Street Millionaires who attend college are likelier to start businesses that provide legal, medical, dental, and veterinary services, which require specialized degrees. Those who don't attend college are likelier to start businesses in the trades, retail, wholesale, and multi-establishment restaurants.

As for decamillionaires who don't own a business, nearly all of them went to college and three out of four of them earned postgraduate degrees. Thus, a college degree appears essential to growing rich if you don't start a business but far less so if you do.

* * *

Many Main Street Millionaires tend to work at and manage a single location (unlike the owners of massive chain stores like Walmart). Their customer bases are often geographically concentrated as well.

As these businesses grow, however, their owners' day-to-day management scope expands beyond one location. Firms with 20 to 99 workers have 1.3 establishments on average, and firms with 100 to 499 workers have around four.

Managing more than one location requires additional organization, formal accounting systems, travel, and a greater delegation of responsibilities. But the businesses of Main Street Millionaires usually don't grow so large that they sprawl across multiple states and employ thousands of workers. In that sense, businesses like Buc-ee's and Dot Foods are exceptions.

The number of a business's locations tends to differ across industries, reflecting differences in the nature of those businesses. Beer wholesalers with 100 to 499 employees have 1.6 establishments on average, whereas nursing and residential care facilities of that size have an average of 3.3.

The competitive landscape varies across industries as well. Some industries, like oil, telecommunications, and air travel, are dominated by the largest firms, with more than five hundred employees, while others like beer wholesalers are predominantly comprised of smaller firms. In fact, only 17 percent of beer wholesalers have more than five hundred employees. Nursing and residential care firms fall in between, with 63 percent having fewer than five hundred employees.

* * *

Main Street Millionaires like Caballero don't tend to have much interest in hobbies or anything else unrelated to their businesses.

Remember Nancy Mueller, who decided to start Nancy's Specialty Foods after realizing that she'd rather spend ten years building a business than improving her backhand? She's hardly unique among Main Street Millionaires.

"I'm still doing the same thing I did thirty, twenty, ten years ago," Terry Taylor, a secretive billionaire auto dealer who now lives in Palm Beach, Florida, told *Forbes* in 2024. "I'm still at our headquarters most days."

Remember John Paterakis, the "bread man" we met in the last chapter? He remained dedicated to the business into his seventies.

Over the years, according to *The Baltimore Sun*, Paterakis put in twenty-hour days and even came to work on Thanksgiving and Christmas. On Saturdays, you would find him in Broadway Market, where he would meet with local officials. In his later years, he would set up shop in the Harbor East Deli, where his usual lunch order was the JP Special—sausage, egg, and cheese on a toasted English muffin, his favorite bread.

Jamie Shah, of Wood Dale, Illinois, recounts a revealing story about her father, who founded a specialty chemical distributor, Chem-Impex: "My dad came to work late on Tuesday and he said, 'Oh, my God, I'm so sorry I'm late to work on Tuesday,' and I replied, 'Oh, don't worry about it. You're the owner of the company.'"

When she asked why he was late, his answer was illuminating: "I was just doing my chai and I was doing work from home and I just thought it was Saturday."

Rather than seeing this as confusion, Jamie Shah recognized something profound: "That's amazing that he's confusing a Tuesday with a Saturday. To him, there's no difference between weekend, weekday. He's working. He's loving it. There's not this concept of work-life balance."

This integration runs deep in many family businesses. Shah recalls vacations to "different peptides symposiums" as a child. "We would go to these conference halls as kids and then we would go visit different sites or we'd stay at customers' or vendors' houses . . . it just felt like these are my dad's friends." Summer breaks meant "packing orders and stuffing envelopes" in the warehouse.

The result is a fundamentally different relationship with work than most employees experience. "I don't really feel like I work when I come to work," Shah explains. "It's like I just do the thing. It's like you're honing on your craft." This doesn't mean Main Street Millionaires work less—quite the opposite. Shah's father regularly confused weekdays with weekends because he worked equally on both.

But, of all the Main Street Millionaires we found, no one had a more profound distaste for leisure than John Osher.

* * *

Osher can't sit still.

As he's telling his story to a gathering of entrepreneurship students and professors at the Technion – Israel Institute of Technology, he's wearing an untucked, short-sleeve Panama shirt and sporting reading glasses that hang loosely from his neck. He has a compact build, paunchy but athletic for a sixty-eight-year-old, a five o'clock shadow, and short brown hair.

Born in 1947 in Cincinnati, Ohio, he jokes that his entrepreneurial career started at the age of five. His parents took an art class, which included nude paintings, and stashed the paintings in the attic. Young John charged his friends a nickel each to view them. "I've never had better profit margins," he quips. "This early success taught me what it means to have a business."

Osher spent seven years completing college, bouncing around a few universities. During that period, he started two businesses: the first an antique clothing store and the second a specialty earring store called the Ear Hole, the latter of which had an 85 percent profit margin. He sold them both and finally received his BA in psychology from Boston University in 1971.

After college, Osher worked for about five years as a licensed carpenter, plumber, and taxi driver while living on a commune in Amity, a small town in upstate New York. He then returned to Cincinnati and started an eclectic entrepreneurial venture in 1978 that sold a range of energy-conservation products, including hot-water heater insulation, toilets, and fans.

But he also produced and sold baby gyms, and Gerber bought that business in 1985 for mid–seven figures. Osher agreed to stay on as a product designer but stayed only eighteen months.

* * *

Many entrepreneurs don't like working for other people, and Osher is no exception.

"I realized I was vice president in charge of nothing," he explained to *Knowledge at Wharton* magazine. "I went on vacation for two weeks and came back, and my inbox was empty." Every time he sold a business, he spun up his next venture within two years.

He founded a new company, CAP (Children at Play) Toys, in 1988. After some initial stumbles (e.g., debuting a blooming flower puppet that turned into a doll, which flopped in the market), the company was going broke while Osher was getting divorced. He told his Technion audience, "Toys-R-Us didn't want anything to do with us, the bank didn't want anything to do with us, and our investors didn't. It was a very difficult moment, and honestly, I wanted to cry and get into bed. And I probably did."

He met with a vice president at Toys-R-Us and described the dire circumstances facing his business. "You know, we can afford it," the vice president replied. "We need new toy companies. I'll take your goods." Toys-R-Us bought all the inventory at a discount. Osher found a new bank to inject some financing, restructured agreements with his investors, and put more of his own money into the company. "I got a second chance," he recalled, and "it changed my whole life."

Reflecting on the experience, Osher noted that successful entrepreneurs find a way. "It's not about how smart they are or how creative. It's what do they do when they have to get over, under, or around something. Every one of them will have a story of the moment when they had to stand up and figure out how to do it."

* * *

He developed a home version of the "Pop-a-Shot" basketball game that's popular at arcades, one that could hang from bedroom doors and track how many baskets you made. The toy was massively popular.

CAP's biggest toy, however, was the Stretch Armstrong doll. And the company's biggest category was the SpinPop, a battery-powered rotator of lollipops.

Neither product was original. Stretch Armstrong, an action figure doll made of corn syrup, was developed in the late 1970s and was in production for a few years. The SpinPop was designed by four postal workers.

Osher acquired the rights to both. He started selling Stretch in the early 1990s, and he sold fifteen million SpinPops in 1994, eventually selling one hundred million of the latter. Each lollipop sold for $4 but cost only 80 cents to make in China. Three years later, when CAP's candy division was generating $70 million in sales, Hasbro bought CAP for $120 million.

After selling CAP, the fifty-year-old Osher tried to retire. He took up golf and moved to Florida. But he quickly came to terms with his mediocre golf game and decided he'd rather create new products than refine his swing.

He gathered a few colleagues and started generating ideas for the next venture. They thought of a hundred and pursued the top three.

* * *

The best idea built on the team's experience and relationships.

With SpinPop, they already knew how to build a battery-powered rotating device that could safely go in a kid's mouth. What if, instead of a lollipop, they put a toothbrush on the end of it? As he joked with his colleagues, after rotting kids' teeth with lollipops, he was ready to sell them the solution. Dr. John's Spinbrush was born.

With SpinBrush, he would replicate the manufacturing and distribution success of the SpinPop. Osher and his team used their contract manufacturing relationship in China to produce an electric toothbrush that cost less than $1.50 to make and sell it for $5 at Walmart.

Within a year of starting Dr. John's, Osher placed SpinBrush prototypes on the shelves of big store chains. His preexisting connections with account managers at Heinen, Meijers, and Albertsons and with others he met at trade shows enabled him to reach customers quickly. His team tested the SpinBrush's quality and appeal, and they continued to improve the product.

SpinBrush was an epic success. Its initial sales rate of seven per day per store was fifty times greater than those of other toothbrush brands.

By early 2000, less than two years after launching the product, Osher was selling six thousand a day.

To sell to Walmart at the time, a company needed a sales representative who lived in Bentonville, Arkansas, home of Walmart's headquarters. So Osher hired a top sales executive who was based there and had recently left Clorox. That helped boost sales to twenty-four thousand per day. Dr. John's booked $20 million in profits in 2000.

Osher approached Procter & Gamble (P&G) to propose an agreement to license the SpinBrush for its Crest brand. At the time, P&G was struggling to develop an electric toothbrush and, when Osher was uncomfortable with what P&G proposed for the licensing agreement, P&G offered to buy Osher's company instead. P&G paid $165 million in cash and provided an incentive program for Osher and two other employees based on net revenues from the product as long as they agreed to stay on with the company for three years.

By 2002, SpinBrush had a 50 percent market share in the electric toothbrush market. Rather than continue to pay so much to Osher under the incentive program, P&G bought out the rest of the contract for an additional $310 million.

In the shadow of the dot-com boom and bust of the late 1990s and early 2000s, when internet founders and venture capitalists graced the covers of business magazines, Osher and his team made half a billion dollars selling $5 electric toothbrushes.

Of course, they didn't stop there. Within a few years, Osher filed a patent for a vibrating hand razor and developed and distributed lighted dog leashes, among other projects. He has dozens of patents and many lessons to pass on: Start with a big market (e.g., for the SpinBrush, "everyone's got teeth"), use your network, leverage what you know, prepare to make mistakes, and learn from them.

And don't worry if golf isn't your thing.

* * *

When it comes to new businesses, how typical is the extraordinary success of Dr. John's SpinBrush?

As it turns out, most new firms are small and remain that way. Of all new businesses in America each year, only about 10 percent reach $2 million in sales within two years. By then, they have about twenty workers, including active owners. Even after ten years, the top 10 percent of firms based on their size are only slightly larger, at $2.5 million in sales and around thirty workers.

For the top 1 percent of new businesses, sales reach an average of $30 million in the second year and $50 million in a decade. They each have more than one hundred workers after a few years and about three hundred workers after a decade.

Osher grew his business so much faster than the typical high-growth firm by using his experience and the relationships he developed while working on similar projects over the prior twenty years. Unlike many Main Street Millionaires, he is more of a creator than an operator, choosing to exit each venture relatively early in its growth cycle.

Looking at Osher's overall career, however, you can see more of the slow and steady upward journey that better resembles the typical Main Street Millionaire's story. He also shares their distaste for hobbies, their resilience and ability to pivot, and a remarkable tolerance for working on seemingly boring projects.

* * *

Ben Caballero and John Osher come straight out of central casting from *The Millionaire Next Door*, which emphasized the relentless work ethic and surprisingly frugal consumption habits of America's millionaires.

Our data paints a more nuanced picture of the lifestyles of the many rich Main Street Millionaires we have encountered. As they reach their golden years, some live far more extravagantly after becoming prolific consumers.

The sales records of luxury homes in resort destinations like Aspen are replete with examples.

Joel Tauber ran a manufacturing firm in the stainless steel and alloy scrap industry in Detroit. He grew his father-in-law's business to a billion-dollar conglomerate, with thirty factories and two thousand employees. He bought his "ski-in, ski-out" Aspen mansion—that is, one close enough to the slopes to enable someone to ski directly to the lifts and back from the trails at the end of the day—from department-store heir Ted Field for $9 million in 1996 and sold it for $65 million in 2023.

In Aspen's most expensive home transaction to date, Terry Taylor, the stealthy car dealer we mentioned earlier, bought another ski-in, ski-out mansion, this one for $76 million. "He's like Batman," a source told *Forbes*. "You hear about him and you admire his work, but nobody has really ever seen him in real life." He only attends conferences on the condition that no one introduces him to others. He doesn't list his name on his dealerships that, instead, often keep the name of their previous owner, although the limited liability company that officially owns them often has a name like "TT of Palm Bay, Inc." Taylor also lists his initials on other prized assets, including his $45 million private jet.

To find other wealthy private business owners who live extravagant lives, we bought owner registries of twenty-two thousand private jets and fifteen hundred superyachts. These lists come from public registrations for private planes and boats. Unlike the tax data, the names are not confidential.

These registries are full of Main Street Millionaires. Paul Andrews of Fort Worth founded TTI, an electronic components distributor, and owned a $40 million superyacht, *Abbracci*, as well as a private jet. Ralph de la Torre, a doctor who runs the nation's largest physician-owned hospital system, with 12.5 million patients per year, has a $40 million superyacht, *Amaral*.

Dozens of auto dealers own superyachts, including Alan Jay Wildstein of Sebring, Florida; John Eagle of Dallas; Bob Giles of Lafayette, Indiana; Chris Dagesse of Gilford, New Hampshire; Mike Maroone of Colorado Springs; David Wilson of Laguna Beach; Joe Buzzetta of New York; Larry Van Tuyl of Kansas City; Mark Bretlinger of

Dublin, Ohio; Bradley Hubler of Franklin, Indiana; and John Rosatti of Brooklyn.

Some superyacht-owning car dealers also recently owned professional sports teams. Norman Braman owned the NFL's Philadelphia Eagles; Gail Miller owned the NBA's Utah Jazz; and, before his death in 2018, Tom Benson owned the NFL's New Orleans Saints and the NBA's New Orleans Pelicans.

Not surprisingly, plenty of Main Street Millionaires who did *not* make their money from cars also own both yachts and professional sports teams. Rocky Wirtz, a Chicago beverage distributor, owned a yacht called the *Blackhawk* as well as the NHL's Chicago Blackhawks. Tilman Fertitta, a restaurateur, owns multiple yachts as well as the NBA's Houston Rockets.

* * *

All these cases of conspicuous consumption, along with the Brockways and their wedding of the century, show that Main Street Millionaires are central characters in the saga of rising inequality. They're earning huge incomes and amassing great wealth, and they're driving consumption inequality over time and across the country.

Up to this point, we have shown how the Age of Millionaires began with the pass-through revolution, which spurred the rise of Main Street Millionaires and made them visible for the first time. We have seen that they live all over the country and dominate most industries. We learned how to find them and what they're like: modest in some ways and ostentatious in others.

But where did they come from? How were they raised? What advantages did they enjoy? And what factors set them apart from the many business owners who didn't make it to the top?

It is to these questions that we turn next.

PART II

How to Get Rich

5

Where Do Entrepreneurs Come From?

The American Dream is that dream of a land in which life should be better and richer and fuller for everyone, with opportunity for each according to ability or achievement.

—James Truslow Adams, 1931

In 1963, Dick Portillo opened a hot dog stand in Villa Park, Illinois, though he'd never cooked a hot dog in his life.

By 2014, that single stand had grown into the Midwest's largest privately owned restaurant company, with four thousand employees and forty-nine businesses in four states, including shopping centers and a catering and shipping division. He had no franchises and no outside investors.

What he did have at the time was a Chicago-area mansion, a private jet, and a 12,000-square-foot penthouse in Naples, Florida, with its own dock to moor his 130-foot Westport yacht, *Top Dog*.

Twenty-five years after Portillo opened The Dog House, Karen Bentlage of Shelton, Connecticut, was suffering through the first semester of her junior year at Central Connecticut State University.

She wasn't getting anything out of college, so she dropped out—without a plan. Over the next several decades, she built the nation's second-largest distributor of tanning beds. She reinvested millions from that business to develop a regional franchise model for waxing salons. That business then expanded into multiple states, employing several hundred people.

Bentlage's success gave her the means to enjoy a lifestyle beyond her wildest childhood imagination.

From different generations, Portillo and Bentlage achieved the American Dream, starting with almost nothing and becoming two of the many Main Street Millionaires the vast majority of Americans have never heard of.

In the details, of course, Portillo's and Bentlage's particular stories are each unique. But, in their general path from limited means to fabulous wealth, their stories are not that uncommon at all.

* * *

We built a novel dataset on the founders of every new firm started in the United States since 2000. That gave us eight million entrepreneurs to study. We tracked them from early childhood through the decades that followed, tracing the full arcs of their careers. Our dataset contained comprehensive information on the childhood backgrounds of entrepreneurs—including information on their parents, neighborhoods, demographics, and test scores.

Just as tax data enabled us to trace the rich to the sources of their wealth, it also created a paper trail back to the childhoods for millions of entrepreneurs. We could ask questions that were previously impossible to answer for the entire U.S. population. Where did founders come from? Where did they grow up? What were they like? How rich did they grow on average? How often did they fail?

We wanted to learn what backgrounds, traits, and circumstances make someone likelier to be a successful entrepreneur—indeed, a Main Street Millionaire—and what we, as a society, can do to help make more of them. The lives of successful entrepreneurs like Portillo and Bentlage help illustrate some of the general lessons that emerge from our broader research.

* * *

In his memoir, *Out of the Dog House: Turning a $1,100 Investment into a Billion-Dollar Profit*, Portillo tells the story of his hardscrabble rise from daunting poverty to spectacular wealth.

The youngest of three children, Richard "Dick" Portillo was born in Chicago to immigrants from Mexico and Greece. "I came from a poor family and at one time thought I didn't have anything to offer the world," he wrote. Neither of his parents graduated from grammar school, "but they were good people and raised on hard work. That's all they had known their entire lives."

When he was young, the family lived in the city's infamous Mother Frances Cabrini Housing Project, which became known as "one of the scariest places in urban America," until his father could afford to move them to a better neighborhood and ultimately buy a home in the suburbs. (After decades of rising crime and decay, the city began to demolish the project in 2000.)

"The walls were so thin," Portillo said, "that you could hear the conversation in the next room, even hear the person going to the bathroom. You could hear the echo of gunshots outside. People looked down on you when they found out you lived in the projects."

To keep her children clothed, his mother once stole shoes for him or his brother from the nearby Montgomery Ward store. At one point, his parents were so short of cash that they had to sell his tricycle.

Portillo was snubbed or underestimated throughout his early years: dismissed, for instance, by a popular girl in high school because her parents didn't want her to date him; humiliated by two Irish brothers who jumped him in front of his girlfriend; rejected by a loan officer at a bank.

When we talked to him six decades later, he remembered every insult and said the fear of losing it all and returning to poverty is what motivates him to this day.

* * *

"I loved to fight," Portillo said, recalling that for his first date with his eventual wife, Sharon, he took her to a lake but told her that he also had to participate in a rumble there.

Successful entrepreneurs often exhibit certain personality traits as youths. On average, they have a stronger sense than others that they—and not luck—control their future. As a result, they are prone to act quickly when challenges arise. They're also likelier than others to engage in illicit activity—likelier as youths to use force to get what they want, damage property, fight at school, shoplift, gamble, take drugs, and be stopped by police for non-traffic offenses.

Among the general population, surveys show, only 4 percent of people used force to get things as kids, and 19 percent were stopped by police at some point. By contrast, 8 percent of founders used force, and 26 percent were stopped by police. Portillo is far from the only troublemaker among successful entrepreneurs.

The excitement of fighting, he thinks in retrospect, helped him to mask some of his shame and sense of inferiority from being a slower learner than his peers. "I always thought I was dumb," he recalled. That fear would prove a powerful fuel to propel him forward. "It was always, always in the back of my mind," he said recently. "Fear will give you a lot of energy and ideas."

"Everything came hard for me in high school," he wrote, "and I was unsure of myself. I thought I was destined to a career of odd jobs and unskilled labor."

* * *

But if, in his troubled youth, Portillo was like other successful entrepreneurs in some ways, he was unlike them in others.

On average, teenagers who go on to found companies score well on aptitude tests, exude self-esteem, show creativity, and have strong problem-solving skills. Having said that, standardized test scores do not predict entrepreneurial success nearly as well as they predict other financial outcomes.

Test scores strongly predict future income: For individuals born between 1978 and 1982 who scored at the median level for the SAT or ACT, average earnings in 2019 were about $90,000 (in 2025 dollars). For those who scored at the 80th percentile, average earnings were about $113,000; for those in the top 10 percent, they were about

$132,000; and for those in the top 1 percent, they exceeded $200,000. (Test scores are also correlated with parents' social class.)

Test scores, however, correlate less strongly with the entrepreneurial spirit. The top 10 percent of test scorers become founders of businesses only 1.3 times as often as those at the median. Such factors as children's exposure to a family business (for example, Beaver Aplin running around his grandfather's general store in Louisiana as a youngster) and their labor market experience early in their careers are more important determinants of their entrepreneurial success.

Owning a business is a promising pathway for success, especially for those who can't otherwise find a good job. Of all kids born between 1980 and 1982, 3.7 percent became business owners. But, of all kids born between 1980 and 1982 *who rose from the bottom fifth in income to the top fifth*, 9 percent became business owners (nearly three times as high of a share).

By contrast, elite colleges don't play nearly as large a role in taking someone from rags to riches. Of all kids born between 1980 and 1982, only 0.9 percent went to an "Ivy-Plus" college (an Ivy or MIT, Stanford, Duke, or the University of Chicago). And, of all kids born between 1980 and 1982 *who rose from the bottom fifth in income to the top fifth*, only 1.3 percent attended an Ivy-Plus school (just a little higher of a share than the 0.9 percent above).

One reason is basic math: There are fewer available slots at elite schools than there are paths to entrepreneurship. But a deeper reason centers around the difference between academic prowess and the skills that make a great entrepreneur.

* * *

Dick Portillo didn't go to college.

Instead, he enlisted in the Marine Corps seven days after graduating high school in 1957, and he considers his two years at Camp Pendleton, California, in the 1st Marine Division among the most important years of his life. They taught him teamwork, organizational planning, and a deep appreciation for proper training, all of which he later put to good use in building his business.

When Portillo returned from the service and married Sharon, he didn't have a plan. "We had literally nothing," he said. He worked on his wedding day, and the couple didn't go on a honeymoon for seven years. "I always worked to make ends meet, and most weeks it felt like 24/7."

After his Marine service, Portillo worked at a forging plant for eighteen months, leaving him with burns all over his shoulders, arms, and back. "I knew I couldn't do manual labor forever," he wrote. "There had to be more to life than working dead-end jobs. I had to figure something out. I had to create a future for us."

"At age twenty-three with two small children," he went on, "I knew I had to act. And it was our shared love for hot dogs that gave me a crazy idea in 1963. Our neighborhood needed a hot dog stand, I believed. I wanted to be the one to meet that need."

Portillo had discovered his opportunity.

"There's nothing more symbolic in Chicago than its hot dog," he said. "It seemed as if you could find great hot dogs in every corner in the city."

But not in the suburbs.

* * *

The couple had $1,100 in savings (worth about $11,000 today), and Sharon had a thought about what to do with the money.

She wanted a house with a nice yard in the suburbs. Who could blame her? She worked nights as a waitress and, Portillo recalled, "we literally saw each other in passing; when she arrived home from her shift, I left for mine."

When he told her that he wanted to use the money to build a hot dog stand, she insisted that they keep it for a down payment on a home.

Sharon's mother thought otherwise. "Josephine told Sharon she should back me up because I was working hard, job after job," Portillo said, "and, unlike some other men my age, at least I 'had ambition.' She credited me with having a dream and encouraged her daughter to support me."

Though Sharon relented, Portillo soon realized that he needed more than $1,100. Like many entrepreneurs struggling to fund an initial venture, he turned to his family for what investors like to call the "Thanksgiving round" because it's good to wait until after Thanksgiving dinner, when the family is full, satisfied, and a little tipsy, to ask them for money. Frank Portillo, Dick's older brother, agreed to match his $1,100 and become his partner.

They called his stand The Dog House, and Portillo modeled it after a California building he had seen in a magazine. He built a six-by-twelve-foot utility trailer with a hitch to look like a doghouse, with a steep pointed red roof.

And he set it up in the parking lot of a discount store, near a busy stoplight, in a blue-collar neighborhood.

* * *

Portillo offered four hot dogs with fries for $1 and a drink for 10 cents. With a coupon that he left on windshields in nearby parking lots, a customer could feed a family of four for $1.50.

But when he opened for business, the food was terrible and the buns were rock hard. "I didn't know a thing about steaming a hot dog," he recalled. "I didn't know how to steam a bun."

Leaving Sharon to mind the trailer, he took his two young sons to Gene & Jude's, one of Chicago's better hot dog stands, for a reconnaissance mission. There, he left two-and-a-half-year-old Michael to watch six-month-old Joe in his stroller and walked into an "employees only" door to survey the storeroom. He noted the brand of relish before an employee kicked him out.

After walking around to the front and placing an order, he leaned over the counter to get a peek at how they steamed the buns. "They had a little screen," he wrote, "but it wasn't placed on the hot metal. They also had a piece of cardboard on it, the steam came over it and they laid a box of buns on it. And boom! I found out how to steam a hot dog bun and I found the product to put on it."

His coupons proved a good marketing tool, and it wasn't unusual for fifty or sixty people with coupons to line up at his stand. But he wasn't making much money, especially not on sodas. Lacking access to running water, he relied on premixed sodas, which had a very low profit margin. A friend who worked as a pipe fitter helped him hook up a 40-gallon water tank, which he filled with a 250-foot garden hose from a spigot across the parking lot. Now, he could mix his own sodas. "I had Coca-Cola, I had root beer. I had a profit," he recalled.

Portillo opened every day for business from 11:00 a.m. to 10:00 p.m. At lunch, Sharon would back her Ford Falcon station wagon against the back door of the trailer and lift the hatchback. With the little boys and their toys in the back, she watched them through the screen door while helping with the lunch crowd.

Portillo brought the dishes home every night and he and Sharon washed them in the bathtub, leaving a ring of mustard around the tub.

Along with his focus and gumption, Portillo in his early years leveraged his personal traits to drive his rise: a huge tolerance for risk, a capacity for mischief, and a willingness to enlist help from a small circle of family and friends. Like Main Street Millionaires we've already met, he also worked extremely hard.

* * *

After dropping out of college, Karen Bentlage found a job in the weight-loss industry and then worked for two years at a medical device company, where she sold a light therapy device that dermatologists used for treating psoriasis.

The company wasn't prospering, however, and she felt it was time to move on. Then, a Michigan distributor with whom she had worked told her about something he believed would prove very popular. If you changed the wavelength of the medical treatment lamps she sold, they made people look tan. He told her she was a natural salesperson, and he wanted her to join his indoor tanning business.

"Tanning?" replied the blond, light-complexioned, and very bemused Bentlage. "I'm Irish. I literally had sunstroke on spring break in Florida, where I was in the hospital with an IV because I dehydrated. I'm not a tanner at all."

"No, girl," he persisted, "I'm telling you, this is a big business opportunity. You fly out here to see me. I'll teach you everything I know, and I'll give you Connecticut and New York as a territory."

The job paid commission, but no salary.

* * *

Bentlage had saved $3,000, which she planned to spend on a car. Instead, she spent it on a tanning bed to demo at a beauty trade show in Manhattan.

"We sold a few units [beds]," she told us, "and I thought, this is really something that can maybe make some money."

A friend of hers owned a hair salon. With her earnings from the sales, Bentlage offered to buy a tanning machine, put it in the salon, and split whatever revenue it generated with her friend. The machine would have cost her friend $6,000 to buy but, through her job, Bentlage bought it at the wholesale price of $3,000.

"I put it in, and she was charging $10 for ten minutes," Bentlage said. "And within two weeks, she was handing me almost $1,000 a week. I came from a job making $26,000 a year. This is back in the '80s. So I was like, wow, $1,000 a week."

"I sat on the floor in my parents' living room when she handed me that bag of cash," she recalled. "And I showed my parents. And I said, 'I think I'm gonna be rich.' It was this weird epiphany because I wasn't setting out to be rich. I said, 'I think I know how to make a lot of money.'"

* * *

Bentlage's parents were children of the Great Depression—her father, Joseph, a postal worker; her mother, Marion, a medical secretary.

Money-wise, Marion was very conservative. Her father had died of a heart attack when she was nine, leaving her mother working two jobs in a bakery and a factory just to survive. Now, Marion hoped that her daughter, Karen, would return to school and become a dental hygienist so she could make a steady income.

"I went to my parents, and I said, 'I think I've got something here,'" Bentlage recalled. "I don't want to sell these. I want to do vending, like a Coca-Cola machine. Because why would I make the $2,000 or $2,500 I can make selling one of these units when, if it's a good location, I can make, you know, $50,000 a year on it? It's a no-brainer. Why would I take the short cash?"

She had no money to start a business, and neither did her parents, "but they owned their house . . . And I convinced them to take down a second mortgage on [it]. It was huge for them, because they were very risk averse."

Bentlage took out a life insurance policy on herself so that if something happened to her, she wouldn't leave her parents in debt. Joseph and Marion borrowed $10,000 against their home so that Karen could buy two more tanning machines to place in two local gyms.

"Those places were on track to pay me $30,000 to $40,000 a year a piece," she said. "So I was making my money back very quickly and buying more machines. Nobody knew about this. Tanning was new at the time."

She repaid her parents within a year and invested the profits back into her business as quickly as she could, buying more tanning units and placing them in salons and gyms. (Not until she reached her thirties, however, did she tell her mother that she didn't finish her junior year of college.)

* * *

Recently retired, Marion had time to help her daughter.

She fielded Karen's phone calls and collected payments from her various partners. When Joseph finished work at 3:00 at the post office, he accompanied Karen to tanning locations to install equipment.

Karen named the company MJK Corporation for her parents and herself, and she never told anyone at work who they were.

Two years in, someone from Massachusetts who was in the tanning equipment business called to say he had a sales rep out in the field trying to sell his equipment. But every time the rep went into a place, he discovered that someone named Karen had already secured a deal.

Bentlage told him that she wasn't looking for a job. "I was making maybe $90,000 to $100,000 a year at that point, which was big money for some twenty-four-year-old back in those days, unheard of," she recalled. "And I was playing softball at night, really having a very balanced, fun life."

But the caller didn't want to hire her. He offered her a chance to buy into his business, and she bought 10 percent of it for about $30,000. "I became an owner, and we started really accelerating the company, moving into Connecticut and upstate New York. I was making good money."

Enough money, in fact, that she could share her good fortune with her parents. She flew them first-class with her to a trade show in Las Vegas. And when she was twenty-five, she bought her father a new red Ford Explorer for Christmas. It was the first new car he had ever owned.

To surprise him, she parked it at a neighbor's house across the street and put the keys in a Rolex watch box. He already had three watches and, as she recalled, "he's trying to pretend he's excited, but I can see like he's completely confused and bummed out, and then he opens it up, and there's keys in there."

"I bring him outside, and he was confused," she said. "And I go, 'Here you go, Dad, this is yours.' It's the first time I can remember seeing my father cry. It makes me cry now, even thinking about it.

"It was one of the best moments of my life."

* * *

The American Dream is about starting low and ending high, but what does it mean to end high? To earn more than your parents? To rise from the bottom of the income scale to the top?

With the available data, we can now analyze the trajectories of all kids born in 1980. Of those who grew up with parents in the bottom 20 percent in income (those making less than $37,000 a year in 2024 dollars), 70 percent wound up earning more than their parents (in inflation-adjusted dollars).

For those born in 1940, however, the picture was rosier. More than 90 percent of kids from the bottom 20 percent wound up earning more than their parents (also in inflation-adjusted dollars). Based in part on the declines in mobility in recent decades, people worry that the American Dream is dying.

* * *

Children of immigrants, like Portillo, who start at the bottom have had higher rates of upward mobility than children of U.S.-born parents who start at the bottom.

That's true for immigrants from nearly every country of their origin, historically and today. Why? For one thing, immigrants tend to settle in metropolitan areas that offer better prospects of upward mobility for their children. They have more flexibility to choose their location because they don't tend to have ties to any one place in America.

In fact, their decisions to settle in places with better schools, lower unemployment, faster wage growth, and other positive features explain about half of the mobility gap between immigrant and U.S.-born children.

Why else do immigrant children enjoy higher mobility? Parents of immigrant children often earn less in the United States than their skills suggest they should. Think, for instance, of immigrant parents with professional degrees (e.g., doctors, engineers) in their old country who wind up driving taxis here due to their inadequate English or limited contacts or discrimination against them.

The artificially low earnings of immigrant parents make it easier for their children to surpass them when they grow up.

* * *

Entrepreneurs come from every socioeconomic class. Based on our data for every founder, 70 percent come from families outside the top 10 percent in income and a third come from families outside the top half.

Having said that, they're likelier to come from families with two well-educated parents and higher incomes. People from families in the top 1 percent in income are 2.4 times as likely to have founded a firm as those from families at the 90th percentile, and 4.1 times as likely as those at median income. Meanwhile, men are twice as likely to start a firm as women.

Entrepreneurs are also likelier to come from certain racial and gender groups. According to Census data, Asians are about seven times as likely, and non-Hispanic whites nearly five times as likely, to own an employer business as Black individuals.

The differences in founding rates across groups are several times larger for firms that drive employment and growth. Of all firms started in the same year, we classify firms in the top 10 percent and top 1 percent (in revenues or number of employees) as stars and superstars, respectively. Among our findings:

- Individuals from families in the top 1 percent in income are four times likelier to found a star firm, and seven times likelier to found a superstar firm, than those at the 90th percentile.
- Racial gaps in business ownership are even larger for bigger firms. Non-Hispanic whites are ten times likelier than Black individuals to own a firm with more than five hundred employees.
- Men are more than three times likelier to found a star firm and more than four times likelier to found a superstar firm as women.

All told, most entrepreneurs are from middle-class families, but rich kids are much likelier to start a business. That may sound contradictory, but the answer lies in the relative size of these groups.

There are ninety-nine times as many people in the bottom 99 percent in income as in the top 1 percent. That helps explain why there are more than four times as many founders from families in the bottom third as from the top 1 percent. Even among star founders, there are 2.5 times as many from poor families as from the top 1 percent.

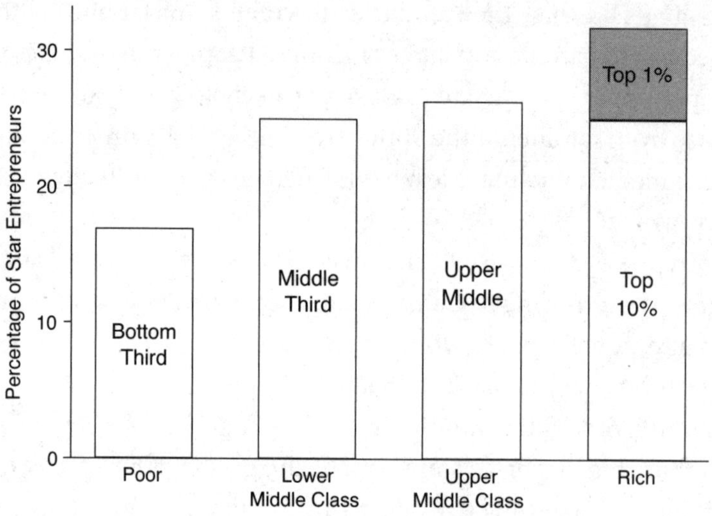

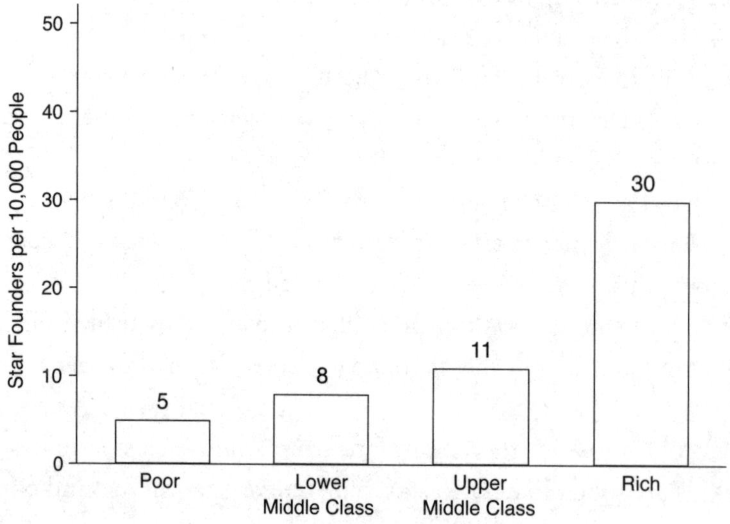

* * *

Successful entrepreneurs come not just from all backgrounds but also from every region (i.e., metropolitan area) of America.

Among the hundred most populated commuting zones, the most entrepreneurial cities (based on number of star entrepreneurs per ten thousand people) are Austin; Cape Coral, Florida; Port St. Lucie, Florida; Dallas; Denver; Nashville; Salt Lake City; Toms River, New Jersey; Las Vegas; Miami; and Atlanta.

Places with lots of entrepreneurship tend to have high job growth, small shares of single parents, and high shares of foreign-born and Hispanic people and of people living within a fifteen-minute drive from work. High rates of regional entrepreneurship are not strongly associated with high third-grade test scores, high median household income, or high shares of people who attended college.

The odds of rising from the bottom fifth to the top fifth are twice as high among kids who grew up in Salt Lake City than in Columbus, Ohio—10.8 percent versus 4.9 percent. Salt Lake City has been dubbed "Silicon Slopes" for its high number of start-ups, including unicorns (i.e., unusually successful start-ups) like Qualtrics, Vivint, and Ancestry.com and older tech firms like Novell and Omniture—the latter of which is now part of Adobe.

When we visited Silicon Slopes, several local boosters offered the following hypothesis. Mormonism, which is far more concentrated in Utah than in any other state, is "the world's most capitalist religion"—and this capitalist ethos draws from Mormons' "self-discipline, stemming from missionary work" (when recent high school graduates go door-to-door to proselytize). That experience develops sales skills, such as learning to pitch ideas and to take no for an answer and keep going.

* * *

As for upward mobility, when colleagues of ours examined the characteristics of places that most foster it, they found that five factors matter: (1) lower residential segregation, (2) lower income inequality,

(3) better primary schooling, (4) higher social capital, and (5) higher family stability.

In Chicago, where Portillo grew up, the chance of rising from the bottom fifth to the top fifth is 6.5 percent (6.5 for every 100 individuals), lower than the national average of 7.5 percent. Chicago has more residential segregation, more income inequality, and lower social capital (voter turnout and participation in community organizations) than average. It's around average in primary schooling (with a public school student-to-teacher ratio of 18:1) and in the share of single-mother households (21 percent of households with children).

In Shelton, Connecticut, where Bentlage grew up, the rags-to-riches odds are 7.9 percent. The region is slightly more racially segregated and unequal than average, but it also has substantially higher social capital, better student-to-teacher ratios (15:1), and about an average share of single-mother households.

In both cases, the places where they were born are neither exceptional generators of upward mobility, nor are they places where low-income kids are doomed to poverty.

Turning to entrepreneurship, regions also differ in the rate of founders among children who grew up there. The West Coast generates more entrepreneurs per child than the South and parts of the Rust Belt.

Surprisingly, the San Jose region—in the heart of Silicon Valley—does not score particularly high in its rate of founders among kids who grow up there. That region scores slightly better than average when it comes to producing founders of tech companies, though it still lags considerably behind places such as Salt Lake City and Minneapolis even within tech.

Among the hundred most populous regions in the 2000 Census, the top origins of star entrepreneurs per thousand kids are Reading, Pennsylvania (3.1); Salt Lake City (3.0); Toms River, New Jersey (2.9); New York City (2.5); and Spokane, Washington (2.4). The bottom places include Fayetteville, North Carolina (0.9); Brownsville, Texas (1.0); Virginia Beach, Virginia (1.1); Columbia, South Carolina (1.1); and South Bend, Indiana (1.2).

Intriguingly, the places with the higher rates of entrepreneurship for kids are not those with the highest rates of adult entrepreneurship. New York, Chicago, Fayetteville, and Detroit have higher rates of entrepreneurship for kids who grew up there than for adults who live there. By contrast, Salt Lake City, Seattle, Denver, and Austin have higher rates for adults living there than for kids who grew up there.

We looked at whether kids who move earlier in their childhood to areas with higher adult entrepreneurship rates are likelier to become entrepreneurs. We compared, for instance, a kid who moves to Salt Lake with her family at age fifteen to a kid who moves there at age five. If place matters, then ten years of extra exposure to the community in Salt Lake should translate into a higher founding rate for the younger mover. And it does.

Using a sample of 4.4 million movers across counties, we found that a child who spends twenty years in a one-percentage-point more entrepreneurial county is 40 percent likelier to found a business, and 24 percent likelier to found a star business, than the national rate for founding businesses. So, childhood exposure to entrepreneurial places matters a great deal in shaping future founding rates.

* * *

Based on all the data we've studied, the American Dream remains attainable for those of all backgrounds. Demographics are not destiny. But success is far from guaranteed, and it seems less likely today than decades ago.

When it comes to driving success—beyond what a child might learn while growing up in an entrepreneurial place—there is no substitute for hunger, ambition, perseverance, and hard work, as the life stories of Portillo and Bentlage illustrate so vividly.

Working grueling hours at The Dog House, Dick Portillo recalled, "I didn't have any balance in my life.

"Many nights I slept on the work table where we sliced the beef in the back room of the Bolingbrook restaurant," and used a makeshift shower in the basement before starting again the next day. "It had reached a point where I couldn't squeeze in another hour in a 24-hour day, no matter how hard I tried to make that happen. I realized I had to build an organization and hire people who truly understood the culture I wanted to implement at Portillo's."

He credits his time in the Marines for inspiring him to create a management structure as the business expanded.

By the time Karen Bentlage was thirty, she knew everyone in the indoor tanning industry. A friend was selling his small distribution company out of New Jersey. She sold her shares in the other company that she partly owned and bought the new firm for $75,000, opening her own office in Connecticut.

She went to meetings in Jonesboro, Arkansas, where the equipment was manufactured. When she arrived the first time, her business was second to last in volume out of fifteen distributors around the country, and she was the only female distributor.

"I remember thinking to myself, Okay, I'm going to get up into the top five really fast," she said, "because they're not going to know what's coming. They're not paying attention to me. And I ended up number three. I feel like you've got some advantage, because they underestimate you" as a woman.

What else explains the rise of Main Street Millionaires, from a start with little to a finish with lavish wealth?

6

What Do Entrepreneurs Need?

The component of entrepreneurship that really matters is domain expertise.

—Paul Graham, venture capitalist and cofounder of Y Combinator

Does it take money to make money?

Marceau Michel is a Black entrepreneur who had an idea for an on-demand staffing company that won him start-up pitch competitions and admission to a start-up incubator in Portland, Oregon. But he couldn't secure funding to get his idea off the ground because he faced what he called the "glass ceiling of being a Black entrepreneur," with potential investors constantly "moving the goalposts" in setting the conditions under which they would invest in him.

He was advised to raise money from family and friends but, as the son of Haitian immigrants in a stable but non-rich family, and with non-rich friends, his family and friends couldn't provide the needed capital.

His story is hardly unique. After surveying five hundred entrepreneurs, the Kauffman Foundation found that outside lenders and investors contributed about two-thirds of the capital for the businesses of white founders, while Black founders had to provide most of the capital themselves. Meanwhile, female and minority owners are much likelier to borrow on credit cards and against the value of their homes when they launch their own companies than white male founders are, other surveys show.

Nevertheless, having money matters far less to budding entrepreneurs than you might imagine. Paul Graham's lesson from Silicon Valley, cited above, is just as applicable for all entrepreneurs. Instead of financial capital, what really matters is human capital.

Early in their careers, successful entrepreneurs often acquire domain knowledge, make essential network connections, and learn firsthand how to start, run, grow, and eventually exit their businesses.

* * *

To learn how important liquid wealth is for entrepreneurial success, we examined whether people who suddenly come into great wealth tend to use it to start a new business.

When companies go public through an initial public offering (IPO), employees who joined the company soon after it opened its doors often receive substantial stock options that can turn into millions of dollars. We studied the behavior of half a million workers across more than two thousand companies that went public between 2000 and 2022.

For every $1 million increase in someone's wealth, the data showed, the probability that they would start a business rose by 0.4 percentage points (thus, for a $5 million increase, the probability rose by 2 percentage points). The probability that a person who suddenly comes into $1 million would start a star company rose by 0.1 percentage points.

So, wealth matters to someone's decision to start a business, but it doesn't matter much. Other researchers have found similar results when someone wins a lottery. Most of us aren't on the cusp of starting a business and just waiting for the right infusion of wealth to nudge us into action.

We also found that wealth differences explain less than 5 percent of the gaps in business creation across gender, income, geography, and demographic group. Policymakers, businesses, and nonprofits often provide capital to help would-be entrepreneurs, but other approaches would likely prove more effective in nourishing entrepreneurship. Closing gaps requires something beyond financial support.

If not wealth, what are the crucial factors behind entrepreneurial success?

* * *

Early labor market experience has proven very important in raising the odds that someone will become an entrepreneur and, beyond that, a Main Street Millionaire.

When Karen Bentlage found a job in the weight-loss industry, she worked for a graduate of the University of Pennsylvania's Wharton School of Business. He was only thirty-one, but he taught her quite a bit over the course of two years as she shadowed him everywhere he went. "I picked his brain and just learned," she told us, "and I thought, 'Wow, I can do this myself. Anybody can rent a storefront.'"

That relationship changed her life. "If I hadn't gotten that job that summer and met him, would I be a dental hygienist somewhere?" she wonders. What she witnessed, and what she heard from her young boss, taught her lessons in how to run a business that she couldn't have learned in school.

Similarly, Beaver Aplin started learning everything he needed to know about running a general store from an especially young age. Ben Caballero learned about real estate as a construction worker before he became America's top Realtor.

Early labor market experience also proved crucial for a sixteen-year-old boy from Lahore, Pakistan. In January 1967, he came to Urbana-Champaign, Illinois, in the middle of a blizzard, with $500 in his pocket, to attend the University of Illinois.

* * *

Through his years as a "Fighting Illini," Shahid Khan washed dishes at night to make ends meet before earning a degree in industrial engineering.

After graduation, he found a job as an engineering manager at Flex-N-Gate, a local auto parts company, where he stayed for seven years and developed a car bumper that was much leaner than bumpers on the market.

Drawing on that experience, Khan founded Bumper Works in 1978 in Danville, Illinois. He combined the $16,000 he had saved with a $50,000 U.S. Small Business Administration loan. He quickly found his first client, who wanted a lighter bumper for one of his imported vehicles.

Early on, Khan met adversity when Flex-N-Gate sued him for stealing trade secrets. With limited resources, he defended himself in court, spending nights in the university's law library to prepare his case after working all day. The lawsuit dragged on for two years, but he eventually prevailed—and then bought Flex-N-Gate, which at the time was losing $50,000 a month.

Later, General Motors threatened Khan's business by planning to use larger suppliers. But he cultivated relationships with Japanese automakers entering the U.S. market and, with strategic partnerships—particularly with Toyota making his company its sole supplier of bumpers by 1989—he transformed Flex-N-Gate into an automotive manufacturing powerhouse.

By 2012, his company's parts were featured in more than two-thirds of all vehicles sold in America, and his operations spanned fifty-two factories and employed thirteen thousand workers around the world.

With annual sales of $3.4 billion and a personal net worth of $2.5 billion, Khan had more than enough money to buy the NFL's Jacksonville Jaguars for $770 million in 2012.

* * *

Beyond Bentlage, Aplin, Caballero, and Khan, we explored more broadly the role of early labor market experience in nurturing entrepreneurship.

We focused on how the ebbs and flows of the economy affect career paths and how those career paths shape business creation. Imagine, for instance, two people graduating from Santa Clara University, in the heart of Silicon Valley—one in 2000 at the peak of the dot-com boom, the other in 2001 after the bubble burst. The 2000 graduate was much likelier to land his first job in the tech industry, which historically produces many more entrepreneurs than other sectors. Presuming he landed that job, the question is whether his early exposure to a more entrepreneurial industry made him likelier to start a business later in life.

We analyzed data from twenty-one million workers across the country who were born between 1978 and 1986 and followed them through their twenties and into their mid-thirties. We looked at which industries tended to produce more entrepreneurs and tracked how hiring patterns in these industries varied across different locations and times.

What did we find?

For one thing, the chance that someone will start a business substantially rises if that person gets his first job in an industry that produces more entrepreneurs. For another, experience in an entrepreneurial first job (such as computer systems design, accounting, and building equipment contracting) is critically important to the founder's chance of success.

As we can see, people gain specific skills and knowledge from these industries that make entrepreneurship more likely, and they develop valuable professional networks. We know that because people often started businesses in industries in which they first worked.

This early career experience explains 20 to 50 percent of the gaps in business creation by income, race, or gender. Individuals from low-income families, Black and Hispanic individuals, and women have significantly less labor market experience in entrepreneurial sectors than others and, not surprisingly, they start businesses at lower rates.

In essence, a first job matters as much for entrepreneurship as pre-career factors (like education and test scores) matter for future earnings. From a first job, someone could learn how an industry works, what customers want, with whom to partner, when to expand, and when to exit.

All of that suggests that we, as a society, could increase the rates of entrepreneurship significantly by providing more labor market experience in entrepreneurial sectors for more people, especially for those who are part of groups that are currently less likely to start new firms.

Female founders, for instance, are not just underrepresented as entrepreneurs, but they're also likelier to hire women in their company's early years—and that's true no matter what kind of businesses they start. As a result, helping more women become founders could position more women to gain the relevant labor market experience to create their own businesses.

* * *

Let's say that we, as a society, could persuade more people to pursue the path of entrepreneurship. Would their businesses likely succeed? Would these founders and their workers flourish?

In our data, around 5 percent of all business founders have firms worth more than $5 million after ten years, qualifying them as Main Street Millionaires. But, beyond this distinct set of very successful founders, how does the broader population of founders do?

We first looked at how entrepreneurs performed compared to similarly situated people who didn't start businesses. We matched entrepreneurs with non-entrepreneurs of similar backgrounds, incomes, industries, and locations before the entrepreneurs started their businesses.

Not surprisingly, the income of the entrepreneurs plateaued during the year they started their businesses. But, later, their income grew much faster than their counterparts who did not start businesses. Eight years after starting their businesses, entrepreneurs earned on average about 10 percent more each year than the non-entrepreneurs—and that accounts for cases in which start-ups failed altogether. Moreover, 10 percent is a very conservative estimate because it doesn't include a business's value based on what an entrepreneur could get by selling it.

What about the founders who don't succeed? Not only do many

firms fail to grow substantially, but many fail altogether. Five years out, around half of firms had stopped operating as stand-alone entities.

But failure does not mean that founders are starving. They might return to the workforce or even start another firm. When compared to their similarly situated, non-founder counterparts, more than half of founders do just as well. And of course, some exits aren't failures at all but lucrative sales (like Osher's sale of SpinBrush).

Starting a business is definitely risky, but the payoffs can be extraordinary for those who find good luck and manage that risk. Even failures can provide invaluable experience that drives future entrepreneurial success. Nearly 20 percent of founders in our data are serial founders, meaning we see them start more than one company over time.

How did Dick Portillo, the hot dog king, and Karen Bentlage capitalize on their own early experience to grow their businesses?

* * *

With one cash register, one steam table, and a customer line that moved slower than he wanted, Portillo was eager to expand.

He knew he was wasting time and leaving money on the table, and he desperately wanted a bigger trailer with running water and greater capacity. "I could serve twice as many people, twice as fast," he wrote. "Nothing else mattered in my life, that's how goofy I was."

Though he and his wife, Sharon, saved what they could, they needed another $2,500 to build a larger trailer. When Portillo's landlord at the shopping center stopped by and inquired about the expansion plans, Portillo told him the bank had rejected his loan request. The landlord asked him to stop by his office the next day and, when Portillo did, loaned him the money himself, writing him a personal $2,500 check on the spot. It was a lucky break that he never forgot.

With a second trailer that, at nine-by-seventeen feet, was twice the size of the original Dog House, Portillo hired a second cashier, who became one of his longest-tenured employees. "Business was doubling, doubling, doubling," he recalled. By 1971, eight years after he set up his first hot dog stand, he built a restaurant ("Portillo's") and moved the trailer to another shopping center parking lot. With a bigger trailer, he added more items to the menu.

"You're limited to how much you can make out of a hot dog," he explained. "The margins just aren't there. So what I thought was, if I could add some burgers and beef sandwiches and some other items," the margins would be better. "I focused on getting the best beef sandwich I could, the best burger I could, but keeping it at a decent price. And then things just skyrocketed."

Three years later, he had five Portillo's restaurants in the suburbs of Chicago.

* * *

"I wanted to be in the field, at the restaurants with my employees and customers. I wanted my supervisors in the field," Portillo wrote, explaining why he never gave desks to his supervisors.

He believed that every detail of the dining experience was important to attracting and retaining customers—the sights, sounds, energy, and decor of the restaurants; the service they offered; and their unique menu. (Even in the earliest days of The Dog House, he roasted peppers and left them out near the counter so the smell would reach customers as they ordered.)

"We sell a lot of hot dogs, 60,000 to 70,000 pounds a week," Portillo noted in his memoir, but they were now only 12 percent of his business. "We sell over 200,000 pounds of Italian beef a week. We have two kinds of chicken sandwiches, two kinds of fish, two kinds of sausage, salads. You can go into Portillo's and eat something different every day."

As the company expanded, he focused more on his employees. Many of his restaurants employed 150 people, any one of whom could make the dining experience more or less enjoyable for his customers. "So that's why operations, teamwork, and training is the backbone of the restaurant business," he explained.

Portillo developed his own processes and systems so he could outsource as little as possible. His office staff grew to seventy-four. "We had two attorneys. We had our own IT people and my own construction people. We built our own restaurants. I didn't source that. I had my own accounting group."

* * *

Portillo likes to boast about the lengthy list of fast-food restaurants that went belly-up when Portillo's opened nearby—or when those restaurants were dumb enough to open an outlet near him. The list, he is proud to note, includes Pro Football Hall of Fame tight end and coach Mike Ditka, a Chicago icon.

In 1990, Ditka announced he was opening a new restaurant, Ditka Dogs, near one of Portillo's most successful locations in Naperville, a Chicago suburb about thirty miles west of the Windy City. "They were coming straight at me," he recalled. "But I didn't know how to retreat."

Ditka's team began poaching his employees. "They were in my restaurants with $100 bills in envelopes trying to pick off my staff," Portillo recalled. "They copied our equipment layout plan from one of my managers they hired." Portillo and his son went to meet with Ditka's representatives but, despite their promise to back off, they hired away another manager at a higher salary.

A few days before the Ditka Dogs opening, Portillo asked the manager who had just left to meet him at his home. "I stopped at the bank and withdrew a boatload of money in cash," he recounted. Portillo and his attorney were waiting when the manager arrived. "I told him he did what every man, every leader of the house, every bread-winner would do" before he reached into his pocket and spread fistfuls of cash across the table. "There was probably a couple thousand dollars on the table."

He asked the manager to return to his job at Portillo's for a higher salary, plus the cash. He also asked him to persuade the employees who had been hired away to return, for $1 more an hour than Ditka had offered. All the while, he was emptying even more cash onto the table by the fistful. "There was about $12,000 on the table now. I told him it was all his if he did one more thing."

Ditka's was scheduled to open that Saturday and, in doing that "one more thing," the manager quit on Friday. Portillo attended the grand opening and sat with a cup of coffee to watch the mess unfold. It was "utter chaos," he wrote in *Out of the Dog House*. "They didn't have enough workers. Customers screamed and yelled that the food was cold; they didn't have anyone to make the sandwiches. The young financial backers—their jackets and tie off, their sleeves rolled up—attempted to help, but they didn't have any idea what they were doing."

Portillo also hired a plane to fly over Soldier Field during a Bears game with a banner: PORTILLO'S HOT DOGS, #1 IN CHICAGO.

Ditka Dogs didn't last.

* * *

Portillo grew his restaurant business the most during the '80s and '90s, during which he added seventeen restaurants.

By the end of 1999, he had twenty-two restaurants generating millions of dollars in revenue a year and, a year later, he added a catering and delivery business. Scouting new locations, he usually tried to buy the land outright and, since he always worried about assuming debt, he self-financed his expansions as much as possible.

"I didn't build a building till I had enough money for the building," he explained. "I always tried not to be over leveraged like that, because, God forbid, if something happens you lose everything. And I sure as heck did not want to go back to being broke." As a result, he continued to earn money on his real estate long after he sold his business.

Portillo received hundreds, maybe thousands, of franchise inquiries over the years. But he never considered it an option. Once you gave up control of your ownership and your vision, he believed, people would try to change things and, in doing so, they could dilute or ruin the brand.

He wasn't looking to sell his business, either. Portillo's was booming and he was happy. His average restaurant boasted higher sales than the average McDonald's—and without serving breakfast.

Even with the sizable organization he was building, Portillo remained deep in the weeds of his business, clearing any financial decision over $500. He prided himself on knowing where every penny went. "My bottom line was unbelievable because I was on top of everything," he said.

* * *

Future Industries, the company that Karen Bentlage created in 1990, eventually grew from about $1 million in annual revenue to $40 million, making it the nation's second-largest tanning distributor.

Amusingly enough, her mom still wasn't convinced that her daughter was financially secure. "She kept saying, 'Go back to school and become a nurse,'" Bentlage said. "And I'm like, 'Mom, I just bought the building. I have thirty people working for me. I'm not going to be a dental hygienist.'"

At that point, Bentlage could have relaxed, but she realized that the tanning craze would not last forever. Detractors were raising safety concerns; federal lawmakers had slapped a 10 percent tax on indoor tanning services; people were starting to buy their consumables (such as tanning lotions and moisturizers) over the internet instead of through salons; and, most important, being tan wasn't as stylish as it had been.

She came to recognize the latter of these challenges while watching a University of Connecticut basketball game in 2005. "I looked at those cheerleaders," she recalled, "and they were as pale as they come. Every one of them is pale, not even a spray tan on them. I said, 'This is going down.'"

But she also knew that she wasn't done making money.

* * *

Bentlage opened two Massage Envy franchise stores in Massachusetts in 2010, with an old friend from the tanning business, Pam Zerber, running the stores in exchange for equity.

While awaiting approval for their franchise applications, Bentlage and Zerber discovered a new, relatively unknown hair removal company out of Florida, European Wax Center (EWC). Bentlage loved the business model, which would give them regional distribution rights to the franchise. The two of them jumped on it, buying the rights for all of New England and most of New York, including Manhattan, for about $780,000.

Under the model, an area developer—in this case, Bentlage—received $20,000 in commission for each franchise it sold, plus 2.25 percent of gross revenues for their region. Bentlage realized they would have to open and operate some of the stores themselves. "I can't be selling a franchise concept if I'm not doing it," she explained. "And if we're going to do it, we better be good at it."

They opened their first EWC location in Massachusetts in 2010 and a second one soon after, and signed leases for the first two Manhattan locations as well. The Massage Envy in Massachusetts was making a profit within three months, as was the adjacent EWC within four months.

The two Manhattan EWC stores opened the same week in the spring of 2011, "and that in retrospect was a mistake," Bentlage said. "We had no idea the avalanche of business that would be unleashed in Manhattan. There were so many phone calls coming in, the girls couldn't even answer the calls. They had them on hold, and people were calling corporate, saying, 'We can't get through.'"

They were fielding seven hundred calls a day about those two stores. "It was a monster, and I thought, 'Oh, my gosh! We are ruining it,'" Bentlage worried. "You don't get a chance to make a second first impression."

The two brothers who had founded the EWC franchise, however, reassured her. "Don't worry about it," one of them said. "They're going to come back. I know this business. It is really pretty bulletproof."

They were right. After all, hair tends to grow back.

* * *

Bentlage rushed to establish a call center upstairs at her tanning business office in Connecticut and to hire more people.

"We didn't even have enough waxers. We trained six waxers, and we needed twenty by week one. And you're training them in the store. So how can you train them if now you're open for business?"

Somehow, they managed to build the ship even while steering it on the high seas. A few months later, however, a supplier tipped her off that something was awry with her Manhattan stores; as it turned out, the operating partner they had hired to open and run the two stores walked away from the business suddenly and without warning. Bentlage was at her New Hampshire house, and her husband and business partner, Twan, was in the Netherlands with his ailing father.

The couple needed to move quickly. They had invested about $1 million to open the Manhattan locations and had expensive leases on both. All told, they had poured about $7 million of their own money into the new businesses.

Zerber, who was running the location in Saugus, Massachusetts, parachuted into the Manhattan stores with another key employee and her lead waxer. They would return to Manhattan for three days every other week for about six months until the stores were running smoothly.

* * *

Eventually, Karen and Twan had 25 women working for them in the corporate office. They also had thirteen stores, with 20 to 30 employees in each, so their business was employing about 250 people in all.

Their success was thrilling, but Bentlage was tempting fate. She was so involved in the business that she was not making time to sleep and, in 2012, her peers from a business networking group staged an intervention to set her straight. She had a heart-to-heart with her doctor, who told her she would gain weight and age very quickly if she didn't start sleeping more.

She began to prioritize her wellness, leaning more on the managers she had cultivated. By paying more than other operators, she attracted top workers and kept turnover very low. "We became the employer of choice," she said. "A lot of these were women from other countries, in a lot of cases from pretty poor demographics. They had the ability to make good money, and I think we provided a nice working environment."

One of her Manhattan locations was EWC's number one grossing store for ten years. Karen and Twan only accepted franchisees with the resources to develop several stores at once, minimizing the number of relationships they had to manage.

Eventually, her territory boasted eighty-five EWC stores, fifteen of which belonged to Bentlage, and her region generated about $85 million a year in revenue.

* * *

Bentlage sold the tanning distribution company in 2018, and she planned to run the waxing business for another six or seven years but wound up staying for almost ten.

"Private equity was coming after us to buy our New York stores," she recalled. She and Twan held out longer than most other franchise owners because they found it fun to own the top-performing locations; their store on First Avenue was consistently number one in revenue among the franchises.

"We were always up onstage winning awards every year," Bentlage said. But it was also a hassle. "There was always air-conditioning breaking, or, you know, two girls fighting. These are some tough girls down there."

She realized the business may have peaked. In 2020, she and Twan sold most of their stores to two different private equity groups. And they sold the area development rights in January 2020 for $10 million.

"Our cash flow from that business was like a million and a half a year. So that was a really good return to give us $10 million, because that's maybe what we would have made over the next ten years anyway, but I would have had overhead."

* * *

In March 2020, Karen and Twan closed on the sale of their Manhattan stores. The check arrived on a Wednesday night and the following Sunday, New York governor Andrew Cuomo proclaimed a COVID-19 emergency and shut down most businesses in New York. It was a "complete blessing" that she exited just in time to avoid the business challenges of the pandemic.

At sixty-six, Bentlage recalled this time in her life from a sunny waterfront terrace at her expansive home in Guilford, Connecticut, with a glass-enclosed lap pool, shuffleboard court, and pool table, and with the Long Island Sound so close that you can hear the water lapping the shore from inside the house.

She and Twan had just returned from several weeks at their New Hampshire home, where they love to mountain bike and play pickleball, and he was heading out to shop at Costco and then stop at Karen's favorite Italian restaurant on the way home to pick up dinner.

The couple still own three EWC stores in Massachusetts that continue to perform very well. But without a business to run, Bentlage began investing in real estate, and she now operates some of her properties as vacation rentals.

"I knew I couldn't stay at home and be retired 100 percent," she said. "For me that would be very, very depressing, because it's just not who I am."

Today, Karen Bentlage is a business coach for several other entrepreneurs. She also supports a nonprofit in Uganda that, with her help, has built three schools and a bakery. "Over in Uganda, you can change three kids' lives for $1,000 a year," she marveled. She's raised tens of thousands of dollars for that nonprofit from others in her networking groups, and she's also the board chair of the Boys and Girls Club in her hometown of Shelton, Connecticut.

* * *

As Portillo's restaurant empire expanded, he noticed a certain investment banker appearing at all his new store openings.

He was Damon Chandik, at the time from Piper Jaffray Companies. Chandik wrangled a meeting with Portillo in 2012 and, two years later, brokered the sale of thirty-eight Portillo's to a Boston private equity firm, Berkshire Partners (which is not related to Berkshire Hathaway).

Portillo insisted numerous times that he didn't want to sell. "I was having too much fun," he recalled. He wanted to get back to the counter and wait on customers. "That's where I felt at home, in a Portillo's on the front lines."

But the more Chandik talked, the higher the potential sales price grew. And Portillo began admitting to himself that "the timing seemed better and better."

"Why would I sell?" he wrote wistfully in his memoir. "I had all the money I wanted and was making $60 million annually. I didn't have any debt—other than Sharon's Neiman Marcus credit card! My employees were happy, too. But I also realized the next step—to plow forward and take on national expansion—would take a great deal of time, effort and outside finances.

"And here was another piece of the puzzle that I thought more of each day. I wanted to enjoy the fruits of this incredible success, and at seventy-four years old at the time, turn to other endeavors and adventures with my wife, children, and grandchildren. There was no balance in my life."

As word spread that Portillo's was for sale, twenty-four private equity groups were looking at his business. "They were flying to Chicago on private jets and many times I had two meetings a day," he wrote.

The choice of Berkshire as a buyer checked two boxes for him. He believed they truly understood how special the Portillo's brand and its culture were. And they didn't have any restaurants in their portfolio, which was important because he wanted Berkshire to embrace Portillo's training methods and culture. With other restaurants, he worried that their practices "would bleed into ours."

Over the course of the negotiations, Portillo opened four new restaurants, including two in Arizona, and a commissary, within thirteen months. He financed them all himself without borrowing any money.

The closing presented one final challenge for Chandik. There was nowhere to safely wire the proceeds. Portillo had a generic business checking account that was in no way equipped to receive a transfer of that size. "It was so funny, because we're trying to get the wire and they had no way of fucking receiving it. I mean, there was nowhere to send the cash."

On the day the sale closed, Portillo said, he was worth $1 billion. Though his involvement in the company quickly dwindled after the sale, he continued to stop in every restaurant he drove by. "I still feel an incredible sense of pride when I visit a Portillo's," he wrote.

* * *

Seven years after the sale, Berkshire took Portillo's public under the symbol PTLO. The market value after the IPO was $1.3 billion.

As of this writing, Portillo still owns a substantial amount of Portillo's real estate, with about a third of Portillo's locations still paying him rent. His commissaries were still making all the Italian beef for the restaurants. He has expanded his real estate holdings to include shopping malls, apartment buildings, and high-volume restaurants, and—he wants you to know—he's still making good money.

But at eighty-four, Portillo has complicated feelings about the company he created and nurtured for most of his adult life. He doesn't own a single share of the company that bears his name, he said.

"I have absolutely no control over it," he said of today's Portillo's—the one with a ticker symbol, seventy locations, a plant-based hot dog on the menu, and a brightly colored website with a photo of his original Dog House. "That's a different feeling."

* * *

Dick and Sharon have traveled the world in their Gulfstream jet, motivated by his fascination with history and especially World War II.

They've cruised their yacht through the Bahamas, Mexico, and Alaska. With three granddaughters and six great-grandchildren, they split their time between their 10,000-square-foot estate in Oak Brook, Illinois, and their homes in Florida.

They support philanthropies that include diabetes and breast cancer research and rehabilitation programs for people with substance abuse disorders. At the high school where Portillo struggled to keep up, a gleaming performing arts center bears his and Sharon's names.

In his office hallway, Portillo keeps two photos side by side: one showing the housing project where he lived as a child, the other an aerial shot of his palatial home outside of Chicago. It's a reminder of the distance he traveled and the humiliations he suffered. But he's not without regrets.

"I wish I had never sold," he confided. "I'm bored." What would he have done if he had kept the business? "I would have just kept on opening up a couple of restaurants a year with no financing," he mused.

"My mind was going, you know, very, very active. And it was just exciting. It was like a drug. I loved it. I loved every minute of it. I was a lot happier than now, and I was making a lot of money. I mean, I had a nice boat, I had a nice condo on the beach in Florida. I had a nice home. I had no payments, completely debt free.

"I didn't owe 10 cents on anything, and I was making more money than I ever thought imaginable."

* * *

Neither Portillo nor Bentlage relied heavily on external finance. They didn't need to raise capital or start out with large nest eggs because they shrewdly reinvested the proceeds from their growing businesses into their expansions.

At each stage, they drew on what they learned from their hands-on operation to grow product offerings and invest in the most profitable parts of their firms. They kept very close watch on looming threats from competitors and stayed ahead of market trends. And, of course, they were lucky to find markets that grew dramatically.

Once their businesses are established, how do Main Street Millionaires like Portillo and Bentlage grow their value, and how do they decide who shares in the rewards? It is to those questions that we turn next.

7

Growing and Slicing the Pie

I think now more than ever, like especially with AI and the ability to outsource and this whole freelance economy, it's very possible to just keep your team as lean as possible.

—Jamie Shah, president of Chem-Impex, a laboratory chemical supplier

Jamie Shah runs Chem-Impex, a laboratory chemical supplier in Wood Dale, Illinois, that has become one of the world's leading suppliers of amino acids and their derivatives. The name nicely captures what the firm does: import and export chemicals. These specialty chemicals are building blocks for a wide range of products, from pharmaceuticals to cosmetics to food ingredients.

Chemistry and entrepreneurship run in the family: Her grandfather on her mom's side has a chemical manufacturing business in India; her grandfather on her dad's side owned a chemical distribution business in India. Entrepreneurship also runs in her family's culture: In the Gujarat region on India's west coast, where they lived, her last name means "businessman."

Her parents came to the United States on a visa in 1974 as her father was studying for his PhD in chemistry. He worked as a chemist for a large chemical distributor in Milwaukee, but he grew frustrated with the punishing hours and limited family time. He quit a year later to start his own venture, Chem-Impex.

He immediately got down to work, opening the white pages and cold-calling potential customers. As Shah explained to us, "He would just call people and be like, 'Hey, do you need a chemical?'" He "would sit on friends' couches in different states so he could call from a local line," and he called during off-peak hours to raise his chances of attracting attention. His first client was Pabst Brewing Company.

Shah, who earned a bachelor's in business administration from the University of Wisconsin in 2007 and an MBA from the University of Chicago in 2013, now runs the company, serving as its president. Today, it generates up to $20 million in annual revenue, enjoys a 75 percent gross profit margin, and employs thirty-five people—seventeen in India and eighteen in America. "When people [started] outsourcing in the nineties," Jamie explained to us, "my dad was very quick to jump on that."

The Indian team—mainly chemists and technical experts—works overnight to be on central time, reviewing quality data and handling technical matters. The U.S. team handles low-skill warehousing and fulfillment as well as high-skill customer relationships and management.

"I can hire the same level of employee for 20 percent of the cost in India," Shah said. Her reliance on foreign workers, who fall between blue-collar workers doing fulfillment and white-collar workers doing account management, reflects a broader trend of offshoring that's helping to hollow out the U.S. middle class.

Like many Main Street Millionaires, Shah keeps her operation lean and focused. "I want to hire as few people as possible," she said, "because a smaller team, a nimbler team, is able to accomplish more." At the same time, the company nurtures long-term relationships with its employees. "Most . . . have been with us for ten years or longer, which is great," she added. What keeps people loyal is "a sense of belongingness . . . feeling like you're part of this family."

As second-generation leaders, Jamie and her sister are bringing new perspectives to the business. "My sister and I are much more willing to think about things like profit sharing because we feel like this business wouldn't be here if it weren't for our employees," she explained.

Nevertheless, she sees opportunities to streamline her workforce even more while maintaining quality. "I think now more than ever," she said, "like especially with AI and the ability to outsource and this whole freelance economy, it's very possible to just keep your team as lean as possible."

As Chem-Impex's development illustrates, Main Street Millionaires are growing the nation's economic pie by launching new businesses that deliver new goods and services, but they're also grabbing bigger slices of that bigger pie for themselves—in part by limiting the size of their staff.

* * *

From 1980 to 2021, the business sector (as measured by businesses' profits and their payments for wages, salaries, and benefits) grew from \$4.2 trillion to \$11.4 trillion (in inflation-adjusted dollars). Of that \$7.2 trillion increase, pass-throughs generated \$4.2 trillion. In other words, 60 percent of the growth in the overall economic pie came from the pass-through sector.

Main Street Millionaires can boost their incomes in three basic ways: (1) capture more of the value of their businesses by limiting worker pay and keeping profits to themselves, (2) make their businesses more productive, or (3) expand, such as by growing the scope of their businesses, opening more locations, or acquiring other businesses.

Shah's family did all three:

- They captured a larger share of the value they created, employing workers in India at 20 percent of U.S. costs while maintaining American pricing for their supplies.
- They made their business more productive; her father adopted computer systems to track complex chemical specifications, while she leveraged AI and outsourced some tasks to keep operations lean.
- And they expanded their business greatly, transforming it from their father's cold calls from a couch into a global operation.

To better understand what Main Street Millionaires in general are doing, we brought together all our data for pass-through businesses with an owner in the top 1 percent of the income scale, and we analyzed what happened when they doubled their profits between 2001 and 2014.

What did we find?

* * *

Not surprisingly, these owners are using all three of the aforementioned strategies to boost their incomes.

For starters, they're keeping more profits for themselves. Among pass-through firms with owners in the top 1 percent, the share of value added—i.e., the sum of profits and worker pay—going to owners rose from 37 to 52 percent from 2001 to 2021, while the share going to nonowner workers fell from 63 to 48 percent. Owners also paid themselves more through tax-favored profits than wages, so the increase in their after-tax share was even larger.

Main Street Millionaires are also making their businesses more productive and capturing most of the resulting gains. At top-owned firms, labor productivity—i.e., value added per worker—rose from $34,000 to $52,000 a year. Of this $18,000 increase, owners took $15,000 and gave workers $3,000.

And, while profits soared, the owners did not hire many more workers. To be sure, employment at top-owned pass-through firms (including part-time workers) rose from twenty-six million to thirty-two million. Much of this growth, however, occurred because pass-throughs became a larger share of all businesses. That is, workers moved to the pass-through sector, but total employment across the economy did not rise significantly.

Of that $15,000 growth in owner income, half came from owners capturing a bigger slice and the other half came from rising productivity at their businesses. The fact that Main Street Millionaires kept more profits for themselves rather than share them with their employees helps explain why income inequality has widened in recent years.

Now, let's take a closer look at those three ways that Main Street Millionaires can increase their incomes.

* * *

Main Street Millionaires only have so many hours in the day to work, and what they bring to their firms can be unique and hard to replace.

Look what happens when an owner dies prematurely or retires. Peter Schorr was CEO of Retreat Behavioral Health, a privately owned drug and alcohol rehabilitation service provider with several hundred employees and facilities in Ephrata, Pennsylvania; New Haven, Connecticut; and Palm Beach, Florida. When he died suddenly in 2024 at age sixty-five, the company unraveled. Soon, its 160 employees in New Haven did not receive paychecks. Rather than continue under new leadership, Retreat closed multiple treatment centers in the weeks that followed.

Retreat's unraveling reflects a broader pattern. We studied 765 firms in which a top-earning owner (making over $1 million a year) died unexpectedly at no later than age sixty-five between 2005 and 2010. We focused on owners who were central to their businesses' operations (i.e., those who owned at least 20 percent of their businesses).

We matched each owner-death firm to similar businesses that didn't experience an owner death. We found firms that were identical in industry, size, age of owners, and recent financial performance. That enabled us to see what likely would have happened to profits if the owner had lived.

In the four years after an owner's death, firm profits per worker fell by an average of 82 percent compared to similar firms in which the owner was alive. About a third of that came from firms going out of business and the other two-thirds from firms shrinking.

We also analyzed 5,312 firms in which owners appeared to retire in an orderly fashion. The results were nearly identical: an 83 percent decline in profits per worker.

So, whether the owner's departure was unexpected or planned, losing the owner devastated the firm's profits. These postmortem declines tell us that owners often bring inalienable—in the sense of being embodied in the person—human capital or effort that can be hard to replace.

* * *

In some firms, technological changes make the contributions of their owners even more consequential.

Consider top doctors who attract lots of business due to their reputations. Their income is the profits left over after they pay rent, other bills, and their workers. If the demand to see these doctors grows fast enough, the rise in their profits will outpace the increase in their costs.

Or take the case of economic consultants who work for businesses and analyze the effects that a merger would have on them. If they can raise the odds that the federal government will approve a merger, their service can prove enormously valuable. The consultants' value has likely grown over time as the economy has grown and potential mergers have become bigger.

Rising profits for economic consultants and other Main Street Millionaires reflect the rising value of expertise in business circles rather than anything nefarious on the part of those business owners.

* * *

Along with capturing more profits for themselves, firm owners also increase their profits by boosting productivity. Understanding how productivity drives income growth requires understanding how firms make profits.

Firm owners use a formula (akin to a recipe) that combines their efforts, the efforts of their workers, and the use of machines, buildings, and equipment to produce goods and services to sell.

Take dentists. Their formula would involve the time and expertise of the dentist, the assistant who tracks appointments and manages payments, and the hygienist who sees patients before the dentist does, as well as the office, chairs, cabinets, dental tools, and X-ray machine that are all needed to clean teeth, fill cavities, and make and install braces.

Productivity growth occurs when a formula can produce greater output (clean teeth, braces, etc.) with the same amount of time and effort from workers. A better way to install braces would enable more patients to get braces each year. Improvements in X-ray technology could help the team identify more cavities to fill.

Other technological changes might enhance the skills of dentists and in turn their income; if, for instance, AI makes it easier for dentists to review dental scans quickly, then a larger share of the pie will go to them rather than their underlings. All these technology improvements will not only better fill the pockets of dentists but also grow the total economic pie.

Dentists also can capture more of the pie when the demand for their services goes up. Maybe more people move into the local area. Or people spend more on their teeth because a big local employer gives more generous dental plan coverage. Faced with higher demand and scarce hours, the dentist could decide to raise prices and might generate more profits per worker as a result.

Dentists' market power will be even greater if they lobby successfully for legal restrictions on the entry of new dentists into the profession or on the tasks that hygienists can perform.

* * *

Jamie Shah's experience at Chem-Impex highlights the power of productivity growth.

When her father launched the company in 1975, chemical distributors relied on paper catalogs, phone orders, and manual inventory tracking. As the business grew, her father invested in computer systems to track the complex specifications of thousands of specialty chemicals. That enabled Chem-Impex to offer something larger competitors couldn't: instant access to detailed product information, real-time inventory status, and rapid order fulfillment.

"We can tell you exactly which batch of amino acid derivative we have in stock, its purity level, and when it expires," Shah explained. "That level of precision and speed would be impossible without our systems."

Or, consider Nancy Mueller, the frozen quiche entrepreneur. Her evolution from home-based food production to industrial-scale quiche manufacturing shows how capital investments and operational tweaks can improve productivity.

Transitioning from making 3,000 appetizers in her garage to producing 1.5 million mini quiches daily requires a deliberate focus on productivity. Mueller systematically identified and eliminated bottlenecks. She switched from radiant heat ovens to convection ovens for consistent results, used a Maytag washing machine to remove excess water from spinach, and worked with an engineer to automate production.

Each improvement built on the previous one. Moving from individual packages to bulk warehouse club packaging reduced packaging costs and made the entire production process more efficient.

"Instead of selling two little boxes to move twenty-four quiches, I had them all in one box," Mueller explained. "But making these big boxes doesn't cost double what those small boxes cost, and the extra volume makes the labor much more efficient."

* * *

While most Main Street Millionaires focus on capturing larger shares of their existing markets, some seek to expand their successful models across multiple locations or through acquisition.

When Dick Portillo expanded his business beyond the original hot dog stand that he set up in 1963, he had to figure out how to maintain quality and speed across multiple locations that he was directly overseeing.

Portillo decided to systematize everything, drawing on his training in the Marines. He approached the challenge like a military campaign, developing detailed procedures for food preparation, customer service, and restaurant operations. He insisted that supervisors stay "in the field," working behind the counter with staff and interacting with customers, rather than sit in back offices. By not providing them with desks, he ensured the managers were on-site and on their toes—literally—at their assigned locations. His hands-on approach became the backbone of his expanding empire.

It delivered remarkable productivity. He averaged more than $8 million a year in sales per restaurant, and his most successful outlet generated more than $17 million in annual sales. And Portillo did this with roughly the same staffing levels as his competitors who were generating $3 million. The key was eliminating waste and inefficiency through standardized processes that gave each location a recipe for profit.

* * *

Ron Ross founded SRS Distribution, a roofing distributorship, in McKinney, Texas, in 2008. Turning immediately to growth through acquisition, he has acquired more than a hundred companies in the building supply industry.

Ross is a mergers-and-acquisition expert who enjoys "college sports, raising exotic deer, and making wine" at his vineyards, Triple "R" Ranch and Winery and Lone Star Wine Cellars. He led the company with then-COO Dan Tinker, who became CEO in 2017, in their ambitious growth-by-acquisition strategy.

They built a delivery fleet of four thousand trucks and helped newly acquired companies boost growth by using their fleet and technology, like the "Roof Hub" platform that helped contractors order, manage, and track deliveries. In many cases, SRS retained the local brand identities after acquisitions, which preserved goodwill with customers.

After a decade, their revenues had grown to $2.5 billion. In 2021, SRS shared a payout of more than $250 million with two-thirds of its sixty-five hundred employees. Three years later, Home Depot acquired SRS for $18 billion.

The $250 million payout may sound like a generous SRS gesture toward its employees, but that figure represented less than 1.4 percent of the company's $18 billion valuation. Most of the profits that SRS created over the years went to its owners and investors, not its rank-and-file workers.

* * *

To assess how often Main Street Millionaires capture the fruits of productivity growth for themselves rather than share them with their workers, we built a dataset on all firms that filed their first patent application between 2001 and 2011.

A patent represents both a new technology and a way to maintain higher prices because it grants the owner the exclusive right to use that technology. We studied how much patents boost profits and worker pay at newly innovative firms. We looked at the more than three million patent applications that were filed from 2001 to 2011 to estimate which workers benefit when a firm generates substantial productivity as a result of its first patent.

We focused on the most valuable patents—e.g., those that the government provides for such categories as business methods in finance, e-commerce, databases and file management, plastics, and computer architecture—with the predicted patent value ranging from $30 million to $60 million.

We found that total value added—profits combined with worker pay—rose by around $10,000 per worker after firms received a valuable patent. Profits accounted for $7,000 of that per-worker increase while worker pay accounted for $3,000 of it.

But, strikingly, almost all the wage increases went to high-pay workers—i.e., executives (who are often firm owners). Low-wage workers like janitors and those in the middle of firm pay scales received little pay increases.

* * *

Having said all that, Main Street Millionaires do sometimes boost productivity by paying efficiency wages, a strategy rooted in the belief that paying workers more than the market rate can be good for employers.

Higher wages lead to better productivity through higher morale, higher effort, and lower turnover. Buc-ee's tends to pay its workers above-market wages. When Texas governor Greg Abbott introduced Beaver Aplin at a public event in June 2024, he joked that a job at Buc-ee's would mean more money for him: "Beaver, I heard that a manager at one of these places can make up to $225,000 a year . . . The governor of Texas gets paid $150,000. So if this governor thing doesn't work out, Beaver, I may be coming to you applying for a job to be a manager and get a pay raise."

The company is known for paying above-market wages for the communities in which it has outlets. A sign outside a Buc-ee's between Houston and Austin touted starting wages at $18 per hour for cashiers, maintenance workers, and warehouse and grocery stockers, while the minimum wage in Texas is $7.25. A department manager could earn as much as $33 an hour, and the top salary for a general manager was listed as $225,000. The sign also touted a 100 percent matching policy for 401(k) retirement plan contributions of up to 6 percent of earnings, three weeks of paid vacation, and health care benefits.

With high salaries and good benefits providing the carrot, however, Aplin also uses the stick to control his employees. Kelly Rieves was hired as an at-will assistant manager in Cypress, Texas, at an annual salary of $55,000, but she had to sign an unusual "retention agreement" that let the company claw back a third of her total compensation if she left before forty-eight months. Buc-ee's could fire her at any time, but Rieves had to give six months' notice and repay that third—her "retention pay"—if she left early.

After trying unsuccessfully to negotiate her exit after three years, she quit—and Buc-ee's sued her for the full amount of retention pay that she'd earned during her tenure, over $67,000. A trial court awarded Buc-ee's $100,000 in damages and legal fees, but an appellate court reversed the verdict and ordered Buc-ee's to pay Rieves's legal fees.

Buc-ee's' retention policy illustrates a broader imbalance of power between Main Street Millionaires and their workers, which is part of an even larger story for workers.

* * *

From 1980 to 2024, the share of U.S. national income accruing to labor fell from 65 percent to 56 percent. That means that nine cents of every dollar that a firm creates that used to go to workers now goes to firm owners.

The reasons are manifold:

- Globalization has exerted downward pressure on wages, especially for low- and middle-skill workers, by exposing them to competition from lower-wage countries;
- Technological change and automation have increased productivity but also reduced the need for many low-skilled jobs, shifting income toward capital owners and high-skill workers;
- The fissuring of the workplace, with companies outsourcing functions to contractors or gig workers, has weakened labor protections and reduced compensation;
- Labor market concentration—with a few firms dominating hiring—has increased in many regions, giving workers fewer options of where to work and, in turn, increasing the power of employers;
- The rise of "superstar" firms like Apple, Amazon, and Walmart, which dominate markets with technologies that they use to expand their businesses and with relatively low labor needs, has further concentrated profits in capital as opposed to labor;
- Union membership since the 1980s has shrunk in half as a share of the workforce, from 20 percent to below 10 percent, reducing the power of unions;
- The federal minimum wage has lagged behind inflation, reducing its purchasing power—the last time Congress raised the minimum wage was in 2009; and
- Changes in corporate governance prioritize shareholder value over employee compensation.

These factors help explain why Main Street Millionaires have been able to capture so much of recent economic growth in the form of higher profits, and why those profits have surged even in the absence of meaningful job growth.

But what does this imbalance of power between Main Street Millionaires and their workers look like on the ground?

* * *

Business owners are increasingly using noncompete agreements to prevent their workers from leaving one job for a similar one nearby.

These clauses—which prohibit employees from working for competitors for some time period after leaving a job—have traditionally been reserved for executives or specialized positions with access to trade secrets. In recent years, however, noncompetes have increasingly appeared in low-wage and entry-level positions for which such justifications hardly apply.

In a notorious case that brought this issue to national attention, Jimmy John's required even its minimum-wage sandwich makers to sign agreements that barred them from working at any competing sandwich shop within three miles of a Jimmy John's outlet anywhere in America for two years after leaving the company. In practical terms, that meant that a sandwich maker in a major city could be legally barred from making sandwiches anywhere nearby for years. After the practice drew widespread criticism, Jimmy John's dropped these noncompetes in 2016 as part of a settlement with New York's attorney general.

Jimmy John's isn't the only sandwich shop to use tactics of this kind. Jersey Mike's, which Peter Cancro grew from humble beginnings to an $8 billion company, has a "no-poaching" clause in its franchise contracts (thus preventing other companies from hiring their workers).

Such tactics, however, extend far beyond sandwich shops. Jiffy Lube, a car maintenance franchise, imposed similar restrictions on low-paid oil-change technicians from taking jobs at rival shops. Companies ranging from Amazon (for warehouse workers) to Camp Bow Wow (for dog walkers) have used noncompetes.

In one striking story, the real estate firm Cushman & Wakefield sued a former janitor for taking a cleaning job with another company in the same building, claiming she violated a noncompete. After a public outcry, the company backed down, apologized, and admitted that applying a noncompete to a janitorial worker was "inconsistent with our policies and contrary to our values."

Firms' arguments about protecting intellectual property make no sense when applied to many of these jobs, since those who flip burgers, walk dogs, or clean buildings know few trade secrets.

* * *

And yet, noncompetes have spread across the U.S. labor market, benefiting large corporations and Main Street Millionaires alike. Some 18 percent of workers—about thirty million people—are now bound by a noncompete clause. Even among employees without a college degree—who are often lower-wage, blue-collar, and service workers—17 percent are subject to noncompetes.

By preventing an employee from taking a better job at a competitor or starting a competing business, noncompetes weaken workers' bargaining power; if you can't credibly threaten to take an outside offer, you have less leverage to negotiate a raise or leave for a higher-paying job. Workers bound by noncompetes tend to experience lower wage growth over time compared to similar workers without such restrictions.

In many cases, noncompetes have a "chilling effect on workers": They often won't even try to pursue new opportunities because they fear being sued, even if the noncompete clause might not hold up in court. Most people can't easily figure out whether their contract is enforceable to begin with. Nor can workers making just $8 to $15 an hour afford to hire lawyers to challenge their contracts. All told, noncompetes effectively lock many employees into their jobs, making them stay longer and accept smaller raises than they otherwise would.

Removing noncompetes, on the other hand, boosts worker pay and mobility. When Oregon banned noncompetes for hourly paid workers in 2008, workers in affected jobs enjoyed a 2 to 3 percent increase in their hourly wages. That ban also improved job-to-job mobility and career opportunities: Former hourly employees were likelier to move into higher-level positions, raising their occupational status while not diminishing the number of hours they worked.

Reviewing the evidence, the Federal Trade Commission (FTC)

reported that noncompetes have "resulted in reduced wages for workers across the labor force" by dampening overall competition for labor. In total, the FTC found, American workers would earn nearly $300 billion more per year if noncompetes were banned nationwide.

In July 2021, President Biden signed an executive order to encourage the FTC to clamp down on unfair noncompetes. In January 2023, the FTC in turn proposed a rule that would ban nearly all noncompetes nationwide. (As of September 2025, the FTC formally abandoned this Biden-era rule.)

Meanwhile, several states—including California, North Dakota, and Oklahoma—have banned noncompetes outright for nearly all employees. Others, such as Maryland, Illinois, and Oregon, have prohibited noncompetes for workers below a certain income threshold.

* * *

Main Street Millionaires benefit from additional structural advantages that enable them to capture a larger slice of the economic pie at the expense of workers. They are, for instance, exempt from key labor protections. Many important worker protection laws come with thresholds related to the size of their workforce, creating a significant regulatory gap for employees at smaller firms (even if those thresholds help small businesses reduce compliance costs):

- The Family and Medical Leave Act (FMLA) only applies to firms with fifty or more employees, leaving workers at smaller businesses with no federally guaranteed unpaid leave for family or medical emergencies.
- Title VII of the Civil Rights Act and the Americans with Disabilities Act—our primary federal antidiscrimination laws—only fully apply to businesses with at least fifteen employees.
- The Worker Adjustment and Retraining Notification (WARN) Act, which requires advance notice of mass layoffs, only covers companies with at least one hundred employees.

Thus, millions of workers at small businesses lack basic protections that their counterparts at larger firms take for granted.

Small businesses also present unique challenges for unionization. The workers at a particular business with few employees find it harder to build effective collective bargaining power or sustain a strike. The close personal relationships between workers and owners in small businesses often create social pressure against organizing. The resources of national unions are limited, making it far more efficient to organize one thousand workers at one large company than ten workers each at one hundred different small businesses. As a result, workers at small firms have significantly less leverage to improve their working conditions through collective organization.

The challenge of organizing workers in small businesses is further compounded in right-to-work states—i.e., states with laws prohibiting unions from requiring all workers who benefit from a collective bargaining agreement to pay dues. That creates a significant financial hurdle for unions, since they still must represent all employees in a bargaining unit—even those who don't pay dues. For workers at small businesses, the economics of organizing in right-to-work states often make unionization practically impossible.

Meanwhile, the benefits gap extends to critical areas like health care. While nearly all large employers offer health insurance, only about 20 percent of small businesses with fewer than ten employees do so, partly for financial reasons. Small businesses pay more per employee for health insurance because they lack the negotiating power and risk-pooling advantages of larger firms. The Affordable Care Act's requirement that businesses provide health insurance only applies to those with at least fifty full-time employees, further incentivizing businesses to keep their payrolls slim, hire part-time workers, or rely on independent contractors.

Similarly, small businesses often are exempt from pollution control rules that larger companies must follow. The Environmental Protection Agency designs many of its programs to reduce burdens on small businesses, which means allowing many Main Street

Millionaire–owned firms to avoid costly environmental controls that would otherwise protect local communities and those who work or live there.

While individual Main Street Millionaires may genuinely care about their employees and communities, their incentives and the regulations they face often favor owners at the expense of workers.

* * *

And yet, despite the prevailing trends, some Main Street Millionaires do, in fact, share their gains generously with their workers.

In Fort Collins, Colorado, in late 2012, Kim Jordan gathered her 450 employees of New Belgium Brewing for a major announcement. She had sold the company. As the room fell silent, Jordan asked all the employees to open the envelope placed in front of them to discover the identity of the new owners. Inside, they each found a mirror.

The workers would own 100 percent of America's third-largest craft brewery that produces around 800,000 barrels a year, distributed across twenty-eight states. The company's Employee Stock Ownership Plan (ESOP), which already had owned 42 percent of New Belgium since 2000, was now taking full possession.

Her gesture culminated the vision she had pursued since cofounding the company. In 1991, Jordan and her then-husband Jeff Lebesch founded the company after a bike trip through Belgium. She was thirty-two and recently married. The couple took out a second mortgage to start the company in their basement. At the time, craft breweries were relatively rare in America; they numbered only 322 and, together, they produced 220,000 barrels of beer a year (thirty years later, craft breweries produced 20 million barrels a year).

Jordan had worked as a social worker and never expected to be a businessperson. She built New Belgium on principles that balanced commercial success with employee well-being and environmental stewardship. "It was important to me that we acknowledged to our workers that their contribution meant something."

Her commitment to sharing prosperity began early.

* * *

After hiring New Belgium's second employee, Jordan started transferring ownership slowly to workers. In 2000, around the time that Lebesch semiretired from the business, New Belgium established its ESOP.

An ESOP is an employee benefit plan that enables workers to become owners of a company for which they work. Instead of buying shares directly, employees receive ownership stakes over time, typically as part of their compensation package. The shares are held in a trust and, as the company grows in value, so does each employee's equity. When employees leave the company or retire, they can cash out their shares, often giving them a significant financial windfall. ESOPs are designed to align workers' interests with the long-term success of the company, fostering a culture of shared responsibility and investment.

ESOPs emerged in the 1970s as part of a broader movement to expand capital ownership among working Americans. The federal government formally recognized them in 1974 through the Employee Retirement Income Security Act (ERISA), which established rules to ensure that retirement plans, including ESOPs, were fair and financially sound. Companies can deduct contributions of stock and cash to the ESOP and, in certain cases, owners who sell to an ESOP can defer capital gains taxes entirely. These advantages helped transform ESOPs from a niche idea into a widely used tool for business succession, employee motivation, and tax-efficient corporate finance.

As of this writing, America is home to roughly sixty-five hundred ESOPs, covering nearly 10 percent of the private workforce. ESOPs hold $2 trillion in assets, equal to about a quarter of the balances in 401(k) retirement plans. The median ESOP company is a Main Street Millionaire firm, with fifty-seven active employee participants, in industries such as professional, scientific, and technical services (20 percent of ESOP companies), manufacturing (19 percent), and construction (17 percent).

Jordan sought to create a "high involvement culture" in which employees knew the company's finances, participated in strategy development, and felt invested in outcomes. Along with ownership stakes, the company offered benefits like a free bike after one year of employment, a trip to Belgium after five years, free health care, and paid sabbaticals at ten- and twenty-year anniversaries.

When the ESOP sold the company to Lion Little World Beverages in 2019, employees received more than $200 million in total, with more than 300 ESOP participants each receiving at least $100,000 from the deal and another 450 receiving five-figure payouts.

* * *

In 1981, Willis Miller started making steel garage doors from his home in Arthur, Illinois.

A town of 2,000, Arthur sits in the middle of the heartland, 70 miles east of Springfield and 130 miles west of Indianapolis. As the company, C.H.I. Overhead Doors, expanded over the following decade, it began to use its own trucking fleet to sell to a broader set of distributors in the Midwest and to make commercial steel doors. In the 2000s, Miller filed for several patents on overhead doors, overhead door sections, and ratcheting winding cones.

By 2015, C.H.I. employed eight hundred people and was acquired for $700 million by a private equity firm. The deal set aside a pool of ownership for the employees that was unusually large for a private equity acquisition. Productivity continued to grow. Revenue more than doubled and profit margins nearly doubled over the next seven years.

In 2022, Nucor, a steel company based in Charlotte, North Carolina, bought C.H.I. for $3 billion. Most of the employees, from hourly workers to truck drivers, cashed in from that sale. The newest employees received $20,000 and the payouts increased with worker tenure all the way up to $800,000. Some employees received 6.5 times their annual pay.

Brad and Crystal Edwards told CBS's *60 Minutes* that they planned to use their mid-six-figure payout to start a college fund for their children, pay off debt, and finance Brad's education as he studied for a bachelor's degree at night. Previously, Crystal had taken a second job working the midnight shift at a local gas station and would often skip sleeping to make ends meet.

When the payouts to employees were announced, "The whole crowd went crazy," said Rhonda Jamison, an office manager who had been with the company for seventeen years. "Grown men were crying. I just about fainted."

* * *

Where do all these stories leave us?

Clearly, the economic pie is growing, Main Street Millionaires are central figures driving that growth, and they're capturing a big and expanding share of it.

Why are Main Street Millionaires capturing more of it? Partly because they're providing valuable services that people want to buy, and those services are hard to replace. And partly because Main Street Millionaires have capitalized on broader trends that have simultaneously boosted the demand for their goods and services and weakened worker power.

Not all Main Street Millionaires are sinister but, when given the choice of how to split an extra dollar of profit, most keep all but a few dimes. That's an important part of the story of how Main Street Millionaires are getting so rich.

But some individuals don't become Main Street Millionaires by starting and growing businesses. They take a shortcut.

8

The Shortcut: Inheritance

> *I can tell you the only reason I was on the payroll is because I was the son of the boss. . . . Any other corporation, I would have been thrown to the wolves.*
>
> —John Tyson, eventual CEO of Tyson Foods, testifying in court in 1998

In 2001, Ken Karns founded a company in Worcester, Massachusetts, to design trade show exhibits. Previously, he had worked for fifteen years at another firm in Worcester. When it collapsed during the dot-com boom, he ventured out on his own.

As he launched his new business, his son Adam watched and helped. A high schooler at the time, he worked for Ken after his class day ended, making cold calls and trying to set up appointments for his father.

In 2006, Ken merged his company with another firm to become Elevation Exhibits (which would later become Elevation3D), headquartered in Shrewsbury, Massachusetts. Adam graduated from Stonehill College in Easton (another Boston suburb) two years later and joined his father.

Over the next sixteen years, through the financial perils of COVID, a dramatic restructuring, and some clever estate planning, Adam would take the helm under a carefully crafted succession plan.

Today, with facilities in Boston and Las Vegas, Elevation3D is a thriving $37 million business that designs and builds trade show exhibits, produces corporate events, and builds out commercial interior spaces for high-impact business locations such as retail reception areas.

When COVID temporarily shut down the events business, the firm wisely pivoted to launch a digital engagement platform, providing video production and content creation for virtual events.

Like his father, Adam would become a Main Street Millionaire. And like a sizable share of other Main Street Millionaires, but unlike his father, he would come to his wealth via the shortcut: inheritance.

Most Main Street Millionaires whom we've met so far earned their fortunes the hard way: by taking risks, working relentlessly, and growing their businesses from scratch. So, how common is inheritance as a path to becoming a Main Street Millionaire? How does it shape businesses? Why do heirs often stumble? And why is this path poised to become even more important in the coming years?

* * *

America is on the cusp of the largest generational transfer in history—what many are calling the Great Wealth Transfer.

By the end of 2024, baby boomers and older generations of Americans had collectively accumulated over $10 trillion in closely held business wealth, $33 trillion in corporate shareholder equity, $21 trillion in real estate, $7 trillion in defined-contribution retirement accounts, and $18 trillion in other assets. Together, these assets total about half the nation's household wealth.

Several forces have combined to drive this impending tsunami of transferred wealth:

- First, the aging of the baby boomers—the seventy-six million Americans born between 1946 and 1964 amid the postwar economic boom—has concentrated great wealth among those older than sixty.
- Second, the postwar economy generated great wealth across society, especially since the "Great Moderation" (the period of low inflation starting in the 1980s and lasting until the financial crisis in 2008).

Low interest rates boosted stock prices, house prices, and business values. Rising globalization expanded markets for sales and lowered input costs around the world.

- Third, rising incomes at the top boosted savings rates and gave more well-to-do individuals the financial wherewithal to risk putting more of their assets in stocks rather than safer investments, further nourishing the fortunes of baby boomers as stocks continued their long-term climb. Shareholder equity, including in private business, accounted for a larger share of the portfolios of the wealthy.
- Fourth and finally, the economy shifted away from capital-intensive businesses, enabling more entrepreneurs to start businesses and grow them substantially without the need for outside investors who would have diluted their ownership stake and limited their rising wealth.

Whether the Great Wealth Transfer goes well depends on two questions: Is the next generation ready to seize the reins of running businesses, and are their parents ready to relinquish control and pave the way for a smooth transition?

* * *

During college, Adam Karns worked for a company in Boston that helped assemble trade shows at that city's Convention and Exhibition Center. The hands-on union job enabled him to learn about the industry on the ground.

He joined his father at Elevation3D in 2008 as a marketing manager, traveling around the country and supervising installations. At the time, the firm had twenty-three employees and was generating $6 million in revenue a year.

Father and son had an understanding about working together that dated back to when Ken coached Adam's sports teams. "You have to be twice as good if you're going to be the coach's son or the boss's son coming up in the industry," Adam told us. "That was really important to the two of us."

Two years later, Adam moved to Seattle and launched a satellite sales operation, adding what are still some of the firm's larger accounts. He moved back to Massachusetts in 2014 and, two years later, Ken bought out his partner's share of the business.

By now, the firm had grown to about forty people, and business had nearly doubled, to $12 million a year. Adam started earning equity in Elevation3D, and he and Ken began mapping out the next ten years of succession planning.

* * *

In 2018, looking to expand their business through acquisition, father and son identified a similarly sized company in their industry—EFI, which was based in Las Vegas. It had thirty employees, and was generating $10 million a year in revenue when Elevation3D bought it.

"All of a sudden we turned into a $22 million-a-year, eighty-employee company," Adam observed. "We had locations on both coasts, which was a big play for us." Now, the firm had two 80,000-to-90,000-square-foot facilities. Las Vegas was the world's trade show event capital. "It was a big advantage for us there."

The succession plan called for Ken to work another three to four years, but he was already starting to phase out gradually. The company finished 2019 with about ninety-five employees and $24 million in revenue.

But when COVID arrived the next year, the trade show industry came to a full and immediate stop.

* * *

The pandemic brought a great many family businesses to their knees, but Ken and Adam used that perilous moment to reset the business to function more efficiently.

Business dropped 95 percent in the first few weeks after COVID struck, and Elevation3D laid off seventy-five people. Almost immediately, the firm hired the consulting firm Cunningham and Associates to run scenario planning and help them leverage available government benefits, such as Paycheck Protection Program (PPP) loans and Employee Retention Tax Credits.

The consultants also helped them negotiate with their bank lenders over the lease on the building in Las Vegas. And most critically, Adam believes, they recognized the opportunity that the company's sudden drop in value presented for Adam and his father's succession planning.

Ken capitalized on the firm's greatly diminished value to transfer majority ownership of the business to Adam. The new valuation put the company's worth at about $600,000, which meant Adam could buy about 97 percent of it from his father through a promissory note for about $560,000. Ken retained his power to decide how to allocate the company's profits with his son.

Adam's purchase of the company's nonvoting shares enabled the family to escape the estate taxes that it would have owed if the company had changed hands at a higher valuation. In 2022, estates worth more than $12 million were subject to the estate tax.

* * *

Adam became the company's president in 2021.

He and Ken also worked out a deferment plan for rent payments with their Las Vegas landlord. Ken's former business partner still owned half the building, and the deferment plan enabled Adam to buy out that share of the building in 2021.

In 2022, as the nation emerged from recession, the company's revenue grew from $24 million to $30 million. By 2024, revenue was nearly $37 million for the year and Elevation3D had 105 employees, a bigger head count than before the pandemic.

"We were very intentional about our hire back," Adam said. "And I think that positioned us in a really advantageous way within the industry. We are about 5 percent higher in head count. We're 50 percent higher in revenue. And most [key performance indicators] in general are stronger than they were pre-COVID."

Ken officially retired in 2023, and he and his son completed the transition in a way that would shield them from taxes they would have owed if Adam had bought him out in a single lump sum.

With help from the same consultants, father and son agreed on a company valuation of $12 million—double the $6 million valuation of when they became partners. By splitting that growth in half, Adam would pay his father roughly $9 million in profits over a number of years by reallocating the profits between them.

"I'll give my dad all the credit in the world," said Adam. "It's not easy to transition a business you built and relinquish power. I think he was super gracious through the process and allowed me to step into the role earlier than many would have."

* * *

Needless to say, inheriting a thriving business is a lot easier than building one from scratch. But how common is inheritance among Main Street Millionaires? And, with it, what does succession look like?

Does succession commonly mirror Adam's story, with an heir inheriting a solid family firm but first learning the ropes right out of school and working his way up within the company so that he or she is ready to take over when the time comes?

Or is it more like the King-Lear-meets-Rupert-Murdoch-inspired drama *Succession*, with conniving but incompetent children competing for their father's approval and keys to the castle?

Let's look at all the Main Street Millionaires and ask how many started their companies themselves.

The Census conducts a large survey of business owners and their firms, asking the owners how they came to own their business. We used this information to determine how common inheritance is among business owners and whether these entrepreneurs look and operate differently from their self-made counterparts.

We focused on firms that reported at least $5 million in annual revenues, putting their valuation roughly between $7.5 million and $10 million and making them large enough for their owners to qualify as Main Street Millionaires.

In 2007, the most recent year for which the Census collected such information, 46 percent of all Main Street Millionaire firms were owned by the original founder, 32 percent by someone who bought it, 14 percent by someone who received it as a gift or transfer, and 7 percent by someone who inherited it. We combine the last two categories, which are similar in nature, and refer to them as inheritance.

But this measure of inheritance, which would include about a fifth of firms owned by Main Street Millionaires, may be too low. Consider Adam Karns. He received shares of Elevation3D in lieu of compensation, and he bought almost all the remaining shares during COVID.

Acquiring shares incrementally—often to stay below the annual federal limit above which gifts are subject to taxes—is a common way that family businesses transfer ownership. That, however, would likely be categorized as an acquisition even though it has all the trappings of an inheritance.

Under a more commonsense definition of inheritance, we estimate that the share of Main Street Millionaires who inherited their firms—i.e., including those that are inherited *or* bought within the family—is around 25 percent. Thus, while founding or acquiring a business is the typical path to becoming a Main Street Millionaire, the shortcut of becoming one by birth is not uncommon.

* * *

Other data points also suggest that 20 percent or so of Main Street Millionaires inherited their businesses.

We computed the share of rich private business owners born between 1980 and 1982 (a group that, as we've noted, we could link to their parents in Treasury Department files) who were self-made millionaires.

Among entrepreneurs who earn at least $1 million per year, only 17 percent were born to parents who were in the top 1 percent in annual income. These numbers alone don't tell us how many Main Street Millionaires inherited their firms. But, most successful business-owning parents would end up in the top 1 percent in income. So, the 83 percent of millionaire kids without parents in the top 1 percent likely didn't become millionaires by inheriting a company.

At the same time, using the Federal Reserve's Survey of Consumer Finances, we split up Main Street Millionaire business owners between those who received inheritances and those who did not. Among the 2.7 million private business owners who were worth at least $5 million in 2022, 19 percent inherited between $100,000 and $1 million, 13 percent inherited between $1 million and $10 million, and 0.7 percent inherited more than $10 million.

So, once again, we see that Main Street Millionaires mostly did not get rich through inheritance.

* * *

Inherited firms on average have been around longer than non-inherited firms, which isn't surprising since they've been passed down from one generation to at least one other.

Some 70 percent of inherited firms are at least three decades old, another 15 percent are at least two decades old, and around another 10 percent are at least a decade old. By contrast, less than a third of self-made Main Street Millionaire firms are at least three decades old. Main Street Millionaires who inherit their firms are a bit older (typically in their fifties and sixties) than those who don't (typically in their forties and fifties).

The ownership of inherited firms diffuses, mimicking the branches of a family tree. Accordingly, such firms have more owners (typically three) than non-inherited firms (typically two). Moreover, 18 percent of inherited firms have five to nine owners, compared to only 8 percent of non-inherited firms. More dispersed ownership structures within a family can complicate the firm's decision-making and governance.

Among Main Street Millionaires, heirs are a bit likelier to go to college than non-heirs, but non-heirs who pursue higher education are likelier to get postgraduate degrees than heirs. Both groups typically work at least thirty hours a week at their businesses. Inherited firms average ninety-nine employees; self-made firms average eighty-seven.

On average in 2022, a Main Street Millionaire heir who inherited at least $1 million was sixty-three years old, lived in a $2 million home, earned an annual income of $1.2 million, and was worth $20 million.

As we can see, Adam Karns's story seems typical along several key dimensions, including his educational background, his path to inheriting, and the features of his family's company.

His path is also not unlike those of several other Main Street Millionaires whom we've already met:

- Forty-six members of the Tracy family of St. Louis, Missouri, work for their family firm, Dot Foods (as of October 2024).
- H-E-B, based in San Antonio; Meijer, based in Walker, Michigan; and Cosentino's Food Stores, based in Overland Park, Kansas, are thriving grocery store chains with multigenerational owners.
- Chicken centimillionaire Tommy Bagwell of Cumming, Georgia, inherited his business.
- Tom Love of Oklahoma City proactively involved younger generations of his family in his multibillion-dollar convenience store chain, such as by having his grandson drive trucks after school.

* * *

In the 1994 movie *Richie Rich*, Macaulay Culkin plays a thirteen-year-old boy whose billionaire parents have presumably died in a plane crash. That's how he becomes a business owner. But, of course, he doesn't know anything about what the business does or how to run it. Hijinks ensue.

In real life, the children of wealthy business owners usually inherit their parents' assets much later in life. But, the Federal Reserve's survey and other data show, when Main Street Millionaires inherit a business, the ownership transfer typically occurs before the previous generation passes.

How do we know that? Well, most inheritances in general seem to come when heirs are in their fifties, sixties, or seventies. Most Main Street Millionaires, however, are younger—in their forties, fifties, and sixties, including those who own family firms—so their parents are younger and thus probably still alive.

If your parents are business owners, the chance that you will start a business (9 percent) is almost as high as the chance that you will inherit one (12 percent), based on our data on all eight million founders in America since 2000.

Even among those for whom inheritance would be the easiest path to successful business ownership, it's almost as common to start a new business. Why? Because, as discussed previously, the children of business owners often get the bug for entrepreneurship because of what they see, what they do, and where they grow up.

They see their parents live as business owners, they acquire early labor market experience by apprenticing, they develop entrepreneurial skills, and they decide to start their own businesses. They're also likelier to grow up in entrepreneurial places than other children.

All told, the children of business owners often would rather start their own business than wait for their parents to die so they can inherit one.

* * *

If the next generation has the right entrepreneurial exposure and temperament, they can build on the prior generation's success while evolving to meet the demands of a changing economy.

Mary and Vincent Grittani opened a tavern in 1923 in the Little Village neighborhood of Chicago. Nick Perrino, their son-in-law, worked with Mary to turn the business into a pizzeria in 1947, built around thin-crust pies cut into squares that they attribute to a family recipe from Bari, Italy. The company name, now Home Run Inn Pizza, dates to a (perhaps apocryphal) story about a batter in a neighborhood baseball game sending a home run through the store's window.

Joe Perrino, Nick's son, joined the family business in 1970, assumed operations in the 1980s, and became CEO in 1990. He grew Home Run Inn through regional expansion and innovation so that, by 2017, it was an $80 million business with nine restaurants and a frozen pizza factory that sold in over thirty-five states. Perrino was proud of Chicago, calling it the "pizza capital of the world," and acquired ingredients from the Midwest, including city water for the pizza's crust.

Perrino brought his son and daughters into the business early on. His nephew, Dan Costello, took over after Perrino died of a heart attack in 2018 at sixty-four. Costello has now worked in the business for more than thirty years—as a busboy at thirteen and then a sausage grinder before climbing the corporate ladder.

At the time of Perrino's passing, the frozen pizza business he introduced to the company accounted for 70 percent of revenues. Since then, the company has continued to invest in that side of the business and scaled down the restaurant side from nine locations to six. COVID and its protocols that discouraged people from eating out prompted them to grow the frozen pizza business even more.

* * *

Thus far, we've focused on successful inheritances of family businesses. But success is hardly guaranteed for the next generation. In America, many children of business owners don't leverage the lucky circumstances of their birth and instead tumble down the economic ladder.

Only 12 percent of the children of parents in the top 1 percent in income—a group that includes many business owners—stay in the top 1 percent themselves. The average rank of such children when they become adults is the 73rd percentile, which is significantly below the 99th percentile of their parents. About 40 percent of children of the top 1 percent fall below the top fifth in income, and 17 percent fall below the median.

Why? For one thing, they're less likely than first-generation founders to reinvest every dollar of profit back into their business. Heirs tend to focus less on future company growth and more on living lavishly. Without more evidence, we cannot say that a particular heir is failing to prioritize growth. Still, it is striking how many heirs listed below own private jets and superyachts:

- Chuck and Rick McGuirk of Mount Pleasant, Michigan, the third-generation owners of an eponymous sand and gravel business. They've owned many yachts, including one called *Sassy* that was frequented by singer Katy Perry.
- Burney Jennings of Greensboro, North Carolina, who inherited his father's "Fresh. Friendly. Fast" Biscuitville restaurant chain with more than forty locations. He owns a private jet.
- Joseph Sheetz of Altoona, Pennsylvania, who owns a family grocery store chain, with over twenty thousand employees and seven hundred stores. He has a private jet, and *Forbes* estimated the family's net worth at $1.9 billion in 2015 (although Sheetz disputed the figure).
- John and Brad Boswell of the Missouri Ozarks, who own Independent Stave, a fourth-generation cooperage company (the company makes barrels). They own a private jet.
- Thomas Klein of Lincolnshire, Illinois, who co-owns the family company Klein Tools, Inc., which makes small hand tools, was founded in 1857, and employs nine sixth-generation family members. He owns a private jet.
- Robert Sands of Canandaigua, New York, a billionaire who, along with his brother Richard, inherited his father's wine business, Canandaigua Wine Company, which was founded in 1945. They are among the nation's richest beverage distributors and own multiple private jets, including a $50 million Gulfstream G550, and multiple superyachts.
- Don Leebern III of Columbus, Georgia, the third-generation owner of the Georgia Crown Distributing Company, which was founded the same year that Georgia repealed Prohibition (1938) and now does business in Georgia, Alabama, and Tennessee. He lives in a $10 million, 13,702-square-foot estate in Atlanta and owns a private jet.

With these examples of such lavish lifestyles in mind, we shouldn't be surprised to learn that, according to a study from Sweden, most heirs drain their inheritances within a decade rather than preserve them.

* * *

"The father buys, the son builds, the grandchild sells, and his son begs." It's an old Scottish proverb that speaks to a timeless story: the withering away of family fortunes as they're passed down through generations.

In his 1889 essay, "The Gospel of Wealth," Scottish-American steel magnate Andrew Carnegie argued that transferring wealth to children did them more harm than good because it reduced their work ethic, diminished their sense of purpose, and encouraged a culture of entitlement and dependency among them.

Not surprisingly, children of the ultrawealthy do a bit better than typical heirs in preserving their inheritance. They're better able to finance their lifestyle from the annual returns on their inherited investments without having to dip into the underlying principal.

Whatever the size of their inheritance, however, heirs in general tend to consume more and work less than those who haven't yet received their inheritance. Someone who inherited $450,000 in 2024 dollars was four times as likely to leave the labor force as someone who inherited less than $75,000, one study estimated. Of those who do work, the study also found, heirs with bigger inheritances tend to work less and generate lower earnings growth.

Firms that have family CEOs perform less well than others that don't, a study from Denmark found. They suffer an average 4 percentage point deficit in profits as a share of assets. Family CEOs also perform worse in dynamic industries with fast growth, skilled workforces, and high wages. U.S. studies have produced similar findings, especially when heirs do not attend selective colleges.

Along with their conspicuous consumption, the children of wealthy business owners fall down the income scale because of what's known as "mean reversion" in talent. That is, talent does not necessarily pass down through generations. As Warren Buffett put it, "Choosing the 2020 Olympic team by picking the eldest sons of the gold-medal winners in the 2000 Olympics [would be] absolute folly in terms of athletic competition." Why should running a business be any different?

In addition, children of wealthy business owners likely fall due to mean reversion in grit. To be sure, some children of wealthy business owners capitalize on that wealth, taking risks as entrepreneurs because they have a family safety net protecting them. But a cushy early childhood may make children of the wealthy less resilient than others in the face of business challenges.

Many firms face challenges around the time of generational transition. Competitors emerge. Key employees and partners leave. Many heirs are not prepared to adapt to market changes. Annette Lareau, a University of Pennsylvania sociologist who interviewed over a hundred wealthy families for her forthcoming book on inherited wealth, gave us a dramatic take: "If given the choice between inheriting $40 million or not, I would choose the latter for my family."

Even for heirs who don't fall, inheriting a family business can still be more stressful than you might think. Just ask Sam Walsh.

* * *

Sam Walsh (all names in this story are pseudonyms) never wondered whether he'd join the family business. Around 1970, his father started Street and Sewer Company (SSC) (also a fictitious name), selling street sweepers. Sam joined a few years later, straight out of high school.

Today, the firm sells, rents, and services garbage trucks, street sweepers, and sewer suckers for municipalities and municipal contractors in the greater metropolitan area of a major northeastern American city. SSC, which started out selling to just a single customer, did about $50 million in sales in 2024.

But it didn't always enjoy such robust financial health. For decades, the company didn't make much money—but it made enough to provide a comfortable living for Sam and his three siblings who worked there.

When their father retired, he left his oldest son, Terry, in charge. As Sam sees it, his father didn't think deeply before deciding.

"He's the oldest brother," his father reasoned. "He should be in charge"—regardless of the brothers' distinct attributes or what the business needed.

* * *

Profitable in the equipment business, the brothers assumed they could make more money by also running truck dealerships and, in the late 1990s, they bought into a couple of local ones. "We were profitable in the equipment business," Sam explained, "and we thought, Oh, we must be good at this."

Now, there were two family businesses, owned by four brothers who were trying to vote on everything equally. They had poured a lot of their personal wealth into the truck dealerships to try to make them work. But this expansion spread them too thin and put great strain on the original business of SSC, which itself was under serious stress. It all crumbled in the early 2000s, and the family business went into receivership. The brothers, each with joint and several liability for the company's debts, were in financial jeopardy.

But no one was more at risk than Sam.

* * *

Sam had saved carefully, while his brothers had spent more of their wealth.

Now, he feared that his financial prudence would come back to haunt him. If the business was foreclosed, he worried, the bank would come for his assets first. "They're going to take everything from me because I have cash," he thought, leaving him to try to recoup his losses from his brothers.

The bank forced the brothers to hire a turnaround consultant to try to stop the bleeding. The consultant soon concluded that the trucking business might not be salvageable. By then, the brothers had invested at least $7 million of their own money into it, even dipping into their 401(k)s.

With the consultant's encouragement, Sam gave his brothers an ultimatum: "Buy me out or put me in charge. I'm not going through this any longer. The bank will close us. They will take our homes."

The consultant gave Sam the confidence to stake his claim, telling him that he was the only one who could lead the company out of crisis.

"I'm not sure if I believed in myself enough to run the place, but he kind of put it to me," Sam said.

* * *

No one could buy Sam out, so the brothers agreed to put him in charge.

As the consultant recalled to us, "We worked with their bank to close [the trucking business] down, sell off land, sell off equipment, do it in a fairly orderly fashion, and also protect [SSC] because they were putting both businesses at risk."

Sam was wrangling with the bank in one arena and his brothers in another. The brothers hired a business industrial psychologist to help smooth relations among them, but conflicts continued to emerge.

Amid the desperate financial straits of their business, "two of my brothers wanted to raise their own pay," Sam told us, although they lacked the needed support to do so. "It was not anything about the business, it was about them, and I really came to realize that was one of the biggest negatives in family business . . . it's got to be a business owned by a family as opposed to a family business"—that is, a business that focuses on the bottom line and not a piggy bank for family members. "If it's a family business, they all think it's about their lifestyle."

Sam secured a few big sales contracts that helped keep the firm alive. But when the 2008 financial crisis hit, SSC needed to cut expenses. Sam said his brothers wanted to lay off employees without cutting their own pay, but Sam insisted otherwise. "It was a big battle," he recalled, but he eventually prevailed.

Brotherly relations were tense at best. If a bank document needed signing, SSC's lawyer would review it and then two of the brothers insisted that their own lawyers review it as well—at SSC's expense—before they'd sign. Sam was technically in charge, but the brothers remained equal partners. Terry and another brother, Ernie, often overruled him or otherwise complicated his decision-making.

"I had to be a bully," Sam recalled to us. "I would have to be very forceful on things. I was kind of put in a bad position. It just made it painful."

His view of management was simple. "Slay a dragon a day," he explained. And that's what he tried to do, chipping away at wasteful practices and pushing for better margins by improving operations.

* * *

The firm started writing down used equipment while reorganizing the parts and service business. Profit margins started to improve.

Sam and Ernie bought out and split Terry's share of the business in 2015, and Sam began to feel freer to make decisions. Sam, Terry, and Ernie each had owned 30 percent. Now, Sam and Ernie each owned 45 percent. A fourth brother, Steven, retained 10 percent of the business, but Sam was closely aligned with Steven and, together, they could overrule Ernie.

Then, COVID forced SSC to do business in new ways that boosted profits over the long term. The company stopped its deliveries and started shipping parts with common carriers. "Each driver with a truck [costs] about $200,000 a year," Sam explained, "as opposed to putting it on a truck and the customer pays for freight."

Also, with traffic unpredictable, customers grew less willing to come to SSC's downtown location to repair equipment. So, SSC sold its headquarters and land for a hefty profit and relocated to just outside the city, making life easier for its customers.

Profits from selling the original real estate gave Sam the resources to buy out Ernie's share of the business. Steven still owned 10 percent, and Sam's son Mike joined the firm as an employee. But the family business as it was previously constituted was all but dissolved.

* * *

With Sam firmly in control, the company performed impressively, with revenues growing nearly 25 percent a year since 2020. The rental business found its footing and boosted the company's overall margins.

Firing on all cylinders, Sam was even talking to two other companies about acquiring them. But, in 2023, his advisers offered some surprising counsel at their annual meeting. It was time for him to sell the company. He was startled but open to their perspective.

"They saw something in me that I didn't see at the time," he acknowledged. "I'm not the same person I was fifteen years ago."

Sam hired the investment bank that was affiliated with the turnaround consultant to sell the business, which they did for $40 million. As of this writing, Sam plans to spend his time consulting for the new owners and to stay active through business support organizations that helped him over the years.

He wants to help others avoid the struggles that tore his family apart. Though it ended cleaner than it began, he sees his family's journey as a cautionary tale. "I firmly believe no father or mother should pick their child as their successor," he said. "They should have a third party involved."

Along with the travails that Sam was forced to endure, nepotism can prove costly in other ways—such as by prompting a high-performing non–family member to leave the business and become a superstar elsewhere.

* * *

A University of Utah dropout, Larry Miller started his career in the auto industry in 1964. He was a twenty-year-old $1.10-per-hour counterman at American Auto Parts, a mom-and-pop shop in Salt Lake City, where he grew up.

He answered phones, helped customers, cleaned floors, delivered goods, and stocked shelves, according to his autobiography, *Driven*. He developed innovative inventory and customer service processes that enabled him to handle nearly two-thirds of all customer traffic himself. Working eighty-three hours a week, he sought a raise based on performance, didn't get it, and left after a year.

After a few more odd jobs, he wound up at Gresh and Jerry's Chevron, where he was promised forty-hour weeks but worked seventy-two-hour weeks instead, doing mechanical work, managing parts inventories, and pumping gas. He then moved to Peck and Shaw's GMC-Toyota dealership, where he managed parts, developed the wholesale parts business with independent service and body shops, and built a strong reputation for problem-solving and efficiency.

At age twenty-five in 1969, he was appointed the parts and service director of a Salt Lake City dealership that Peck and Shaw had bought, where he managed twenty employees and helped turn around an operation that was losing $40,000 a month. It was profitable within five months, in part because he developed inventory management systems.

By 1971, Miller had established himself as an exceptional performer in auto parts management. After several successful positions of increasing responsibility, he joined Chuck Stevinson's Toyota dealerships in Lakewood, Colorado, where he worked for eight years.

* * *

At Stevinson Toyota, Miller engineered a dramatic turnaround.

Hired to revitalize the parts department, he took the dealership from 961st nationally in parts sales to first in just twenty-eight months. With the typical parts department averaging about $80,000 in annual sales, Miller's became the first to reach $1 million, then $2 million (before any competitor reached $1 million), and then $3 million.

He was promoted to general manager in 1974 and tripled store profits in his first year on that job. Three years later, he became the operations manager for all of Stevinson Toyota's five dealerships.

Despite his stellar record, his career at Stevinson Toyota came to an abrupt halt over breakfast at a Denny's restaurant in February 1979. Chuck Stevinson told him that, rather than expand his role as they had previously discussed, he was demoting him to manage a single store while installing his eight sons in leadership positions across the dealership network. The owner also wanted Miller to mentor these sons, effectively asking him to train his replacements.

"I was blindsided by this," Miller wrote in *Driven*. "I thought I was going to be doing this for the rest of my career, but in reality, he had planned to give the business to his sons and never told me."

Stevinson's decision to prioritize family over merit propelled Miller into entrepreneurship.

* * *

"What would you say if I told you I spent one million dollars today?" Miller asked his wife, Gail, the high school sweetheart he married in 1965.

"I didn't know we had a million," she replied.

Within months of his departure from Stevinson Toyota—and with only $88,000 in savings—Miller bought a Toyota dealership in the Salt Lake City suburb of Murray for $3.5 million. He borrowed $1 million himself and relied on seller financing and investment from a family member.

In his first month at the helm, the dealership, which usually sold 30 cars a month, sold a whopping 172. From that one dealership, he went on to build an empire of fifty-four new-car dealerships, seven used-car dealerships, and eleven collision centers, generating $5.7 billion in annual sales and making him one of the nation's largest car dealers.

He also became one of Utah's wealthiest and most influential business leaders, expanding his empire beyond auto sales to encompass nearly ninety other businesses. Before his death in 2009, he owned the NBA's Utah Jazz, multiple movie theater chains, a $50 million community college, a TV station, a radio station, and many other ventures. His auto group employed seven thousand people over seven western states.

In 2021, the Asbury Automotive group bought the dealerships from the Miller family for $3.2 billion.

* * *

The Walsh and Miller stories illustrate the perils of keeping Main Street Millionaire businesses in the family across generations. Such firms struggle to keep up with their competitors and with changing industry dynamics.

America's economy is the world's strongest in part because family firms play a smaller role in the United States. Across eighty-five countries in 2012, around 40 percent of larger companies were "family-controlled"—that is, the family owned more than 20 percent of them. In the United States, only 20 percent of larger companies were family owned.

Countries with higher family firm shares tend to report lower per capita incomes, smaller firms, and fewer publicly traded firms. Those countries tend to have weaker protections for external investors in financial markets. Inherited firms are less dynamic and innovative, and they draw from a smaller pool of talent. The heirs who run them often are more reluctant to take big risks, develop new products, enter new markets, and restructure their companies.

To be sure, inherited firms have some potential advantages over others. Family members, for instance, may more fully subscribe to the company's long-term goals than new owners who come in from the outside, and family members also often have industry- and firm-specific experience.

In some cultures, family firms have found creative solutions to the challenge of succession. In Japan, parents who own businesses sometimes arrange marriages for their daughters and, in the process, choose the appropriate son-in-law to inherit the business. "You can't choose your sons," a classic Japanese adage advises, "but you can choose your sons-in-law."

And, heirs to Japanese businesses performed remarkably well compared to heirs in other countries, a large-scale analysis found. The difference is largely because of how well these "non-blood heirs"—sons-in-law or adopted sons, chosen more for managerial talent than love—do their jobs.

In a lot of other countries, family firms dominate because there are few good options for exiting the business. Capital markets in the United States, however, offer creative and lucrative ways to cash out.

Main Street Millionaires often decide that keeping their business in the family isn't worth the aggravation and, when they make that decision, they frequently turn to private equity to take over.

9

Cashing Out and Cashing In

After business school? Ah, I'm joining a prestigious private equity firm in San Francisco, to run their plumbing company in Mississippi.

—Matt Levine, Bloomberg columnist, musing about what graduates of the nation's top business schools are thinking these days, June 2024

Chris Sullivan opened the first Outback Steakhouse in Tampa, Florida, in 1988 with three friends, hoping to develop a modest restaurant chain that would give them time and money to play golf.

Their success, however, undercut their plans.

Their company, OSI Restaurant Partners, grew to over nine hundred Outback locations and three hundred other restaurants. Driving that rapid expansion was a unique organizational model that Sullivan and his partners had developed, giving ownership stakes and decision-making authority to restaurant managers. Those managers would invest $25,000 of their own money to run restaurants, receive restricted stock, and earn 10 percent of their restaurant's cash flow.

Outback prioritized people—including suppliers, partners, customers, employees, and local community members. To make life easier for its cooks, servers, and other staff, it built large kitchens that occupied half the restaurant floor plan, assigned servers only three tables instead of the industry standard of five or six, and did not serve lunch. Sullivan credited its employee-first philosophy for industry-leading customer satisfaction and loyalty.

The more money that Outback's restaurants made over time, the more private equity (PE) firms viewed them as an investment opportunity. In 2007, Bain Capital, of Boston—which former Republican presidential nominee Mitt Romney cofounded and which is now one of the world's largest PE firms—and partner L Catterton, of Greenwich, Connecticut, bought OSI Restaurant Partners.

The deal valued the business at $3.5 billion and, with Sullivan owning 3.3 percent of the shares, he got a juicy $115 million out of it, finally giving him the time to work on his golf game at his home in Pebble Beach, California.

What happens when Main Street Millionaires cash out? Like Sullivan, they often sell to PE investors. Why is PE infatuated with Main Street Millionaire–owned businesses, and what does selling to PE do to these firms, their workers, and their communities?

* * *

PE's interest in Main Street Millionaires and their businesses has never been higher, with around 60 percent of PE deals in 2023 involving founder-owned firms.

PE refers to firms that take capital from institutional and individual investors (think pension funds, university endowments, and very wealthy people) and use it to buy, manage, and then sell companies, with each deal typically playing out over the course of five to seven years. PE deals are known as leveraged buyouts, or LBOs, because each deal combines invested capital with borrowed funds to leverage the returns and allow investors to buy bigger companies.

PE is distinct from venture capital. PE investors buy established businesses, which tend to need more capital because they are more mature, with settled owners and substantial assets already in place. Venture capital, by contrast, looks for new businesses, such as in software and tech, that might achieve extraordinary growth with low up-front investments.

Because the PE model doesn't require as much growth to satisfy its investors, it works well in a much broader set of industries. As a result, PE firms increasingly target Main Street Millionaire–owned businesses in diverse sectors and geographies. Examples abound:

- Kodiak Building Partners of Englewood, Colorado, targets lumberyards, steel fabricators, drywall distributors, and kitchen-interior companies.
- John Loud gets calls almost daily from PE firms that want to buy his alarm installation firm, Loud Security Systems, based in Kennesaw, Georgia. With sixty employees, his company generates $7 million a year in revenue. But he finds the interest from PE less tempting than annoying. "If you want job security," he told his workers, "save me from these calls and these emails."
- PE firms have been hounding Jay Cunningham, who owns Superior Plumbing, a sixty-employee plumbing business in the Atlanta area that generates $12.5 million a year in revenue. And he's no more pleased by all the attention than John Loud is.

For Loud, Cunningham, and other targets, however, the hounding from deal-hungry PE firms likely won't stop anytime soon.

* * *

The PE sector has soared from under $5 billion in 1980 to a whopping $3 trillion today, making it more than two-fifths of the over $7 trillion private capital markets in North America. PE's rise, in turn, has shaped what are the most coveted jobs in finance, what the top students want to do after business school, and how the richest and most sophisticated investors choose their investments.

Changes in pension rules played a key role in PE's rise. The 1974 Employee Retirement Income Security Act (ERISA) enabled pension funds to invest in a broader range of ventures beyond blue-chip stocks as long as they diversified their portfolios and chose their investments prudently. Pensions and other sophisticated institutions like Yale University started looking for new asset classes to boost their returns and meet their long-term investment horizons. This capital flow spurred a new generation of PE firms, including Blackstone, Bain, Carlyle, and KKR, to enter this exploding market in search of companies to buy.

In addition, in the late 1970s and early '80s, economic conditions and the tax code helped spur PE's rise. Corporate income tax rates, interest rates, and inflation were all high, making the "debt tax shield" an important source of value in early PE investments. Here's how it works:

PE investors borrow money to buy companies. Investors can deduct the interest payments on their debt to reduce their federal taxes. The combination of high interest rates (and thus high interest payments) and high taxes (which make deductions more valuable) meant that lots of borrowing could leave investors with little tax to pay on their big investments.

The tax shield became less important in later decades when interest rates and tax rates fell. To make more money on their investments, PE investors were forced to focus more on improving operations and cutting costs at the companies they bought.

* * *

Yale was a pioneer investor in the shift to PE, steered by a native of Ames, Iowa, who became its chief investment officer in 1985 and, over the next four decades, a legend in the world of investing.

David Swensen created what became known as the "Yale Model," shifting the university's portfolio from stocks and bonds into alternative assets that offered higher returns. He believed that less efficient markets offered greater opportunities for skilled investors. As of 2024, nearly half of Yale's $41 billion endowment was allocated to PE and venture capital (more the former than the latter).

Under Swensen's leadership, Yale's endowment grew from about $1 billion in 1985 to $31 billion in 2021, consistently outperforming peer institutions. His PE strategy drove the bulk of this growth.

Endowment distributions grew to cover a third of the university's annual budget, which means that after accounting for these distributions, Swensen and his team actually generated around $46 billion in gains—making them arguably the most important benefactors in the history of any university.

But if PE firms do well for themselves and investors like Swensen, how do they do for the Main Street Millionaires who sell their business?

* * *

PE can help business owners who are approaching retirement and want to sell part of their businesses and use the profits to diversify their savings.

Some owners see less promise than, say, Ken Karns (whom we met in the last chapter) in transferring their businesses to their kids. And a sale to a PE firm can work out well for everyone involved.

In 1917, Italian immigrants Peter Domenici (not the namesake future senator) and Enrico Parducci founded the San Francisco Sausage Company, making whole-muscle artisanal salumi in a two-room flat in the North Beach neighborhood of San Francisco. They expanded the business over decades and retired after thirty years. In 1946, they passed the business on to their friends—brothers John, Tony, Luis, and Victor Devencenzi—who sold it in 1957 to six local friends and family members.

In 2006, the owners at that time decided on a different kind of succession plan by partnering with the PE firm Endeavour Capital. Founded in 1991 and based in Portland, Oregon, Endeavour pursues a regional investment strategy that focuses on family businesses in the western United States.

The transaction with Endeavour gave the owners of the company—by now known as Columbus Manufacturing—more cash in their pockets as well as funding for an expansion plan. Under Endeavour's ownership, the company acquired new facilities, established new co-packing relationships, and built a state-of-the-art slicing facility. Endeavour also replaced most of the family management with experienced executives.

When, in 2011, Endeavour started looking to sell the company, Columbus's progress and growth in prior years set the stage for a profitable exit. Annual revenue had grown to $200 million. Columbus's ownership remained committed to finding a new partner that could continue its growth while preserving its legacy and unique culture.

Endeavour sold the company in 2012 for $220 million to Arbor Investments, a mid-market PE firm based in Chicago. For the next five years, Columbus faced cost shocks to turkey prices from the avian flu and the World Health Organization's classification of deli meat as a possible carcinogen. Nevertheless, Columbus doubled its sales force and added more than thirty thousand new retail customers, raising revenues by 50 percent while increasing its profit margins. By 2017, the business was large enough to attract strategic interest from the Hormel Foods Corporation, which bought it for $850 million.

As a general matter, Main Street Millionaires grow their businesses slowly and steadily over decades without relying on external finance. PE, however, uses a combined infusion of financial and human capital to try to shrink that multi-decade process to fit within a five-to-seven-year investment horizon.

* * *

Before Main Street Millionaires are ready to cash out, PE can provide what investors call "growth equity" to help them expand more quickly.

At age thirty-seven in 1986, Tom Stemberg founded Staples after he was fired as vice president of a supermarket chain called Jewel.

His inspiration came during a July Fourth weekend when he couldn't find a printer ribbon, learning firsthand how hard it was to buy office supplies. He partnered with Leo Kahn, a seventy-year-old former grocery industry executive, to create an office supply superstore selling products at about half the price of traditional stationery stores.

In 1986, Stemberg and Kahn secured $600,000 to $700,000 in funding from Bain as part of an overall initial investment of $4 million. The first Staples opened in Brighton, Massachusetts, in May of that year, with Romney and his team providing nonfinancial support such as strategic guidance.

Within two years and with expansion capital from investors, Staples had opened sixteen superstores along the Boston–Washington, D.C., corridor. By the time Stemberg retired as chairman in 2005, Staples had grown to nearly eighteen hundred stores worldwide, with seventy thousand employees and $16 billion in annual sales.

When Romney was running for president in 2012—and Bain faced sharp attacks from President Obama's reelection campaign for allegedly destroying jobs at companies it bought—Stemberg defended PE. Because Bain helped firms like his expand, he said on Bloomberg's "Political Capital," "these things had redeeming social value, in addition to making Mitt and his investors a lot of money."

But not every PE deal, financed by Bain or otherwise, works out nicely. Some load firms with substantial debt that makes them vulnerable to economic shocks, and some cost workers their jobs, lower their pay, or exacerbate their working conditions.

Consider, for instance, what happened after Bain and a partner firm bought Bloomin' Brands, which then owned Outback.

* * *

Before the deal, Chris Sullivan's successor at Outback, Bill Allen, told his ninety-five thousand employees that "no jobs will be cut if the privatization is completed."

With fewer customers dining out during the Great Recession of 2008–9, however, Bain broke that promise to keep the business out of bankruptcy. As sales fell, Outback faced growing pressure to cut costs, close underperforming restaurants, and make interest payments on its debt from the LBO.

Outback cut its employee rolls by 26 percent between 2006 and 2011. In 2011–12, Bloomin' Brands' leaders strongly backed a Florida bill to cut the state's minimum wage for tipped employees from $4.65 an hour to the federal minimum of $2.13. Also in 2011, a group of Outback servers in Illinois filed a class-action suit against the company, claiming that management forced employees to do non-tipped work at tipped pay rates and withheld proper compensation.

In August 2012, as Romney ran for president, 175 protesters

gathered in front of the headquarters of Bloomin' Brands in Tampa. They waved signs that read DON'T LET BAIN CAPITAL DESTROY THE MIDDLE CLASS and chanted "How many millions do you need? We've got hungry mouths to feed."

Workers weren't the only stakeholders left with bad tastes in their mouths. When the deal had been announced, Chris Sullivan said reassuringly that "this company was built around a set of principles and beliefs that emphasize consistently high-quality food and service, generous portions at moderate prices, and a fun, casual atmosphere. Bain Capital and Catterton share our commitment to this philosophy and, as we return to private ownership, will support our people in achieving our long-term goals."

Bain's cost-cutting measures, however, conflicted with Outback's founding principles by reducing portion sizes, replacing Swiss cheese from Switzerland with a cheaper substitute, and prohibiting chefs from making salad dressing in-house—all part of what's known in the industry as "value-engineering the menu."

Bain took Bloomin' Brands public five years later at essentially the same valuation as when investors initially invested. The company's profits had shrunk over this period, and it still carried more than $2.1 billion in debt. The deal was a bad one for investors, who didn't come close to reaping their expected rewards, and for customers and others whom Outback's founders had prioritized.

* * *

Stories like Outback's, along with Romney's political prominence, helped to nourish PE's notorious reputation, illustrated by the titles of two best-selling books of 2023—*Plunder: Private Equity's Plan to Pillage America* and *These Are the Plunderers: How Private Equity Runs—and Wrecks—America*.

PE can be especially problematic in sectors with important social functions. When, for example, PE invests in health care, its aggressive sales tactics, procedure-pushing, and cost-cutting can reduce service quality and even endanger lives.

Dr. Ira Fieldman (a pseudonym) is a world-renowned physician who's made groundbreaking contributions to medical practice in his area of specialization. But he's clear-eyed about what he doesn't know about business: "I'm probably, like most physicians, an absolute business knucklehead."

Back in 2010, Fieldman and his partner joined forces with a larger medical group, with sixty physicians operating under the same corporate umbrella but with separate business units. They shared IT support, a surgery center, radiation centers, and pathology services. The partners split the profits based on the work they brought in.

Years later, after hearing how other practices had cashed out to PE, the group began looking for a partner entity that was more business-oriented and hired its own investment bankers to help find a suitable match. They settled on Solaris Health Partners, a conglomerate of seven hundred medical providers in fourteen states (as of 2025)—which was funded by the PE firm Thomas H. Lee Partners and which bought the group in 2023.

The deal came with strong financial advantages for the doctors, but also with surprises that left Fieldman with some regrets.

* * *

He reaped about $3.7 million for his share, but 30 percent of it went back to Solaris for an ownership stake, leaving him about $2.5 million before taxes.

In his early seventies as of this writing and still working, Fieldman told us that he believes his payout was fair. But he and several of his old partners were surprised by a Solaris-directed change in accounting procedures that meant he wouldn't receive any additional profit from the deal for nearly two years.

Under the change, he needed to kick in $75,000 a year and make that amount back before he'd receive any profits, "even though I was taking a ridiculously low salary. I haven't seen a salary like that probably in twenty-five years."

He hopes that, over time, the advantages of being in a big, well-run conglomerate will help make up for the lower current pay. But it didn't start out that way, and Fieldman wasn't fully prepared for the new realities.

"Now, I got a nice chunk of dough up front so, you know, shut up, Ira. I think that's their perspective," he said of Solaris's leadership. "They say I'm a valued individual that keeps the business going. But what they also say is, 'You're just an employee now.' So when we try to bring up certain things that are uncomfortable or we're not happy with, it's sort of like, 'Fuck off.'"

Fieldman still believes he has the freedom to provide the best possible care for his patients. But he said he now faces additional pressures to also consider what treatments will be most profitable.

"They just say, 'Hey, look, this is a method that can be highly profitable,'" he said of, for example, radiation treatments. "A bunch of literature came out to support that it was actually a good way to go in a lot of ways, mostly for the patient. And so I think a lot of us felt, Okay, let's do this for a while and see how the patients do and how we do. But there was a lot of pressure in a sense by emails and things of that sort to utilize this technology.

"There is no effort to control how I practice medicine whatsoever," he went on, "other than saying, 'Hey, look, we have a surgery center. Let's use this surgery center.' It's a great surgery center and I use it a lot. But there are some individuals in our group, I would say 20 percent, who hardly use it at all. And yet they benefit from it financially because we're dividing up the profits and some of that falls to them. So there's a little bit of disappointment or complaining that's going on within our organization that not everybody is pulling on the rope the same way."

Such procedure pushing and value maximization is hardly unusual in health care. PE-acquired nursing homes, for instance, increased their Medicare billing by 8 percent, according to a study of 12,400 nursing homes from 2000 to 2017, including 1,674 that PE firms bought. PE firms also raised management fees, suggesting that money that could have gone to patient care went to PE investors and to service debt.

Moreover, mortality rose by 11 percent at the PE-owned homes compared to others, the study found, while patient well-being and the quality of care declined.

* * *

As with most PE investments, rolling up a firm like Fieldman's into a larger entity is not the ultimate goal.

The next step, what Fieldman calls "the second bite of the apple," will come when Solaris is sold, presumably to an even larger organization. That's not likely to happen right away, which means that he and other doctors his age must keep working to secure their future payout.

Without the sale to PE, Fieldman believes he would be earning more each year in the short term than he is now. But his accountants convinced him that it was smarter to bet on the long game.

"If I hadn't joined Solaris, you know, I'd be making $400,000 to $500,000 *more* a year" on a pretax basis, Fieldman said. (The average annual income of a procedural specialties doctor was $815,000 in 2024 dollars, and half of those doctors were in the top 1 percent in income.) "But . . . let's say in five years down the line, when I decide to shut the office, I turn the lights out and nobody's giving me anything for it. So they gave me something for it [up front]. It's not free money. I'm paying it back."

He feels better off overall under the deal. "They paid a lot, a whole bunch of money," he said. "I am grateful for getting that dough and actually being in this position. I just feel as though the transparency of a lot of the stuff wasn't as good or wasn't as clear as we would have liked."

As in Fieldman's case, PE changes the employer-employee relationship. Employee satisfaction tends to fall after PE acquisitions because work-life balance and firm culture suffer, according to a study of employee reviews of more than three million workers at 271,000 companies on the website Glassdoor. Average pay does not change, but investors shift compensation toward performance-based pay to prompt employees to work harder. The closer tie between pay and performance causes more intra-firm inequality because executives and managers, but not janitors and secretaries, get performance bonuses when the firm does well.

PE deals in manufacturing in particular improved productivity, according to another study, potentially making the economy more efficient while driving small declines in overall employment.

Intriguingly, PE apparently is having an even larger effect in the market for top business school students; it's become the go-to path for these students to "cash in" on Main Street Millionaire wealth.

* * *

Matt Perelman and Alex Sloane grew up three blocks from each other on the Upper East Side of Manhattan.

Perelman graduated from Washington University in St. Louis in 2009 and worked for Citigroup as an investment banker for two years before spending two years in PE at L Catterton. Sloane graduated from Harvard in 2009 and worked for two years in banking at Goldman Sachs before spending two years in PE at Apollo Global Management, of New York. After four years in the banking-to-PE pipeline, they found themselves in September 2013 as first-year students at Harvard Business School (HBS).

During that first year, Perelman and Sloane tried to buy five Kentucky Fried Chicken outlets in Vermont. They were rejected because they were too young and didn't have enough money or restaurant experience.

To boost their knowledge, they moved the following summer to Henderson, North Carolina, to take on a mentor in Ray Meeks, an experienced Burger King franchisee, and through his tutelage they were able to acquire 23 struggling Burger Kings. They grew the portfolio to 166 Burger Kings and 55 Popeyes before selling their restaurant group for $238 million in 2019.

Perelman and Sloane's firm, Garnett Station Partners, which they named after the train station housing the first franchises they bought, has invested in a range of Main Street Millionaire–owned businesses, including funeral homes and car washes. They now manage $3.5 billion in assets.

The banking-to-burgers path isn't widely advertised, but it's far from rare. Writing about Perelman, Sloane, and other Harvard MBAs who leverage their training and ambition into acquiring and expanding fast-food operations, *Financial Times* columnist Sujeet Indap wrote an article under the title, "Harvard Burger School."

Nor are Perelman and Sloane the only HBS grads to have their paths shaped by the rise of Main Street Millionaires.

* * *

Tracy Britt Cool's journey to become one of Warren Buffett's trusted lieutenants began with remarkable initiative.

In 2009, with an HBS degree at twenty-four but little formal work experience, she mailed a letter to Buffett asking to work for him and arrived at his office with corn and tomatoes from her family's Kansas farm—a nod to their shared Midwestern roots. Buffett created the position of "financial assistant to the chairman" for her, and she quickly became part of his inner circle. Buffett affectionately called her and investment managers Todd Combs and Ted Weschler "the three T's."

During her time at Berkshire Hathaway, Britt Cool developed a reputation for reviving struggling businesses, earning her the nickname "fireman" and Buffett's praise that "she thinks like I would." She served as CEO of cookware company Pampered Chef, chair of paint maker Benjamin Moore, and board member of various Berkshire subsidiaries. She became a close and invaluable aide to Buffett, who walked her down the aisle in 2013 after she had lost her father.

Britt Cool left Berkshire in early 2020 to cofound an investment firm targeting midsize businesses with $5 million to $50 million in earnings. Her new firm, Kanbrick—so named to connote the combination of Kansas and the notion that building enduring businesses is a brick-by-brick process—sought opportunities to invest in the gap between tech start-ups and large public corporations. Kanbrick viewed solid but straightforward family or founder-owned businesses as an underserved market that was too small for Berkshire but perfect for a boutique investment firm.

Kanbrick, for which Britt Cool raised $220 million, combines operational expertise with long-term capital for businesses that need growth support but want to preserve their culture and legacy. Rather than plan to exit these businesses after five years, Kanbrick invests for longer. In contrast to traditional PE, the firm seeks to avoid chopping up companies or laying off employees.

Two of Britt Cool's first deals were with Main Street Millionaires—one a maker of boat covers in the Lake of the Ozarks called Marine Concepts, the other a servicer of industrial calibration equipment in Louisiana. She's not worried about running out of investment opportunities because, she estimates, the nation is home to about thirty thousand businesses with profits between $10 million and $50 million.

* * *

Another indication of how the rise of Main Street Millionaires is influencing elite MBA programs is the birth of *searchers* and the *search funds* they create to support their work.

At HBS in 1983, lecturer Irv Grousbeck created this alternative career path to consulting and banking for his students. The searcher identifies a company to buy and earns a share of the company and its profits by running it.

Searchers raise money and create their own search funds in two stages. In the search stage, investors contribute a small amount of capital to cover salaries and expenses related to finding a target company for up to two years. In the investment stage, the initial investors who contributed that early capital have the right of first refusal to participate in a particular target acquisition. To fund the purchase, searchers typically pool about $5 million in equity from a dozen investors with about $7 million in debt, making the resulting structure look like a mini LBO.

But unlike an LBO, in which PE firms hire managers, the searchers *are* the managers and they run their companies for up to ten years. If they hit financial targets, searchers can take home part of the proceeds when they sell their businesses. Along with the experience of doing a deal and running a company right out of business school, a successful searcher typically takes home several million dollars as part of a sale; many searchers bring home more than $10 million.

The searchers' targets are classic Main Street Millionaire–owned companies. The median target has thirty-four employees and is owned and operated by a white male in his fifties. Targeted industries include, among others, medical records and storage, home health care, invasive plant and mosquito remediation, and nonhazardous liquid waste treatment. Searchers have done deals in nearly every state. And once their business grows large enough to attract attention from PE investors, they often cash out to PE too!

While many searches do not end in deals, the investments perform tremendously well on average. That's because investors only lose a small amount of money when a deal does not arise. On average, the 681 search funds formed since 1984 enjoyed astonishing returns on investments of 35 percent a year.

Jim Southern founded one of the first search funds in 1984, with funding from professors and former colleagues. He sought out business owners who wanted to sell their companies and discovered Uniform Printing, which printed business forms and had $40 million in revenue and 750 employees. After ten years of growing and managing the company, Southern sold it for twenty-four times his initial investment.

After big successes like Uniform Printing, search funds have been steadily growing in popularity. Around thirty searchers raised funds between 1984 and 1999, and the pace quickened this century. Around one hundred searchers raised funds in 2023 alone, five times the annual number of a decade earlier. Thus, search funds constitute a rapidly growing niche within the broader PE ecosystem.

Notwithstanding the successes of search firms in general, a search is not necessarily a walk in the park.

* * *

Jennifer Braus spent a year shopping for a company to buy.

She cold-called business brokers and small firms, "scouring the earth trying to find something" to acquire and run, she recalled to us. She finally settled on Systems Design, a small ambulance billing company based in Poulsbo, Washington, nestled between Seattle and the Olympic Mountains. As CEO, Braus has boosted annual earnings from $650,000 to $4 million in less than a decade.

Braus was neither an executive nor an investor. At the time of the purchase in 2015, she had no money. What she had was the support of two of her HBS professors who became her business partners.

Braus hadn't planned to be an entrepreneur. Strong in math and science, she attended the Rose-Hulman Institute of Technology in her home state of Indiana, graduating with two engineering degrees. Her parents, both engineers, warned her that she would hate being one herself. "I did hate it," she confirmed. "I could not get jazzed about a machine part. It was just not for me."

At HBS, she approached Royce Yudkoff and Richard Ruback, the two professors who taught her course in Entrepreneurship Through Acquisition, and who she learned were planning to invest in a search. (The two wrote a book, *HBR Guide to Buying a Small Business: Think Big, Buy Small, Own Your Own Company*, and have a podcast called *Think Big, Buy Small.*)

The professors were interested but said they would not discuss it with Braus until after she graduated. She came back after a year and started searching in 2014 from Portland, Oregon, where her sister-in-law lived.

Only around 20 percent of searchers are women, so Braus was a bit of an outlier from the start.

* * *

It was lonely and often disheartening.

"I probably looked at ten thousand deals in my year of searching," she told us, "and every day was just no, no, no, not that one. And then you get one that's a maybe, and it turns into a no. There's never a good day because you are just seeing a lot of things that aren't going to work until you find one that might work, and you see it through up until the point where it doesn't."

The search took her to some dreary corners of the economy. She briefly considered a slaughterhouse in New Jersey, which made lots of money—some of it in bags of cash from a storefront meat business. Braus says all the other searchers she knew at the time looked at that business. "They all saw the same thing. The company had really high margins," Braus said. "But you would have to spend your days working in a slaughterhouse. Who wants to live that life?"

Because she would be a first-time CEO in her twenties, Braus and her partners agreed that she needed a company that was stable and predictable, with a rock-solid revenue stream that would continue even in the face of an economic downturn. She also needed a big enough company to enable her to make money off a 20 percent stake, which is what her investors were offering.

"It wasn't going to be something where I was going to buy the company and it was going to fail for reasons beyond my control," she explained. "This was my first time out of the gate, and my first general management position as CEO. I didn't want to mess it up. So I was looking for the stable, predictable, frankly boring business where it had been in business for a long time."

Systems Design offered such a model.

* * *

The firm provides ambulance billing, EMS billing, and accounting services for ambulance service providers.

Braus's visit to look at Systems Design marked her first time in Washington State. Poulsbo, a 4.5-square-mile city of 13,010 residents on Liberty Bay, is known as "Little Norway" because of its Scandinavian heritage. But its small size and somewhat remote location didn't deter her because, she recalled, "I didn't own a house. I didn't have kids. I didn't own hardly anything at all. I was open to picking up and moving and uprooting because I had no roots at the time."

Though it was a much smaller company than Braus had hoped to find, the renewal rate of its customers was staggeringly high, ensuring that it had a recurring base of revenue. "It was just the best business we had seen, even though it was very small, and it had been in business since 1989," she said. "I could come in and do nothing and be pretty reasonably assured it would be a going concern."

Once an ambulance provider transports a patient, it sends Systems Design the documentation. "We do everything in the revenue cycle management process from there," Braus explained. "The source of our growth is just how many people are calling 9-1-1 and getting transported."

When she was buying the company, Braus asked the previous owner how he had grown the business. "I sit around and wait for the phone to ring," he told her. Success without the need to market made the business very alluring.

As the deal came together, the owner was about to get married. "There was no transition time," she recalled to us. "We closed the deal on August twelfth and he was getting married on Labor Day, and he never came back after his wedding. It was truly just like, 'Here's the bills. Here's the Quickbooks file. Have fun.'"

That was nine years before we talked to Braus. She's run the company ever since, expanding its market share across Washington and into Oregon.

* * *

Systems Design still has no sales team.

"What we have are very satisfied customers," she said. "When a fire department is unhappy with its EMS billing or wants to start EMS billing or is thinking about transports, the first thing they do is they call their [neighboring fire department]. They're not in some competitive industry where they're gonna hesitate to call all their neighbors and ask what they're doing."

"If the answer is, 'Oh, we use this company in Poulsbo, they're great,' then I get a phone call, and then they don't want to shop around. They're just like, 'Yeah, sounds good. Send me the contract.' And that's how we've grown. My sales effort is truly just making people aware that we exist."

As a CEO and now the parent of two young children, Braus appreciates the predictability of what's largely a Monday-to-Friday desk job. "I'm not traveling all over the country," she noted. "You know, I've got little kids. I'm at home with them. I like to go to the gym. I play in a soccer league."

With a large share of her personal wealth tied up in the company, her partners worked with her to provide an advance on future cash flow distributions. Structured as a loan, the advance helped remove some of the personal risk of having most of her assets concentrated in the business.

Braus was very fortunate. "Cashing in" can be risky and challenging to begin with. Moreover, it's especially hard to find a company that's located in a place where you want to live, doing something you'd be willing to do for a decade, and already performing quite well.

Besides, PE may be hungry for high-quality Main Street Millionaire–owned businesses, but it's often not easy to persuade the owners to sell.

* * *

Remember Damon Chandik, the investment banker who finally convinced Dick Portillo to sell his hot dog empire to the PE firm Berkshire Partners? That $1 billion deal remains one of the most unusual of Chandik's twenty-five-year career.

Chandik can't remember where he first learned of Portillo's. "I'm from the West Coast, so the hot dog thing didn't really make a lot of sense to me," he told us. But he kept hearing about this iconic Chicago business with tremendous sales volume and decided to check it out when he was in Chicago.

Chandik had worked with PE clients as an investment banker at Piper Jaffray for twenty years, and his business relies heavily on relationships, introductions, and perseverance. But no matter how much he asked around, he couldn't find anybody who could introduce him to Portillo. "People kept telling me, 'Oh my God, Portillo is a phenomenal guy.' He's got a phenomenal reputation," but nobody ever saw him. "He didn't go to conferences. He never went to industry events."

Chandik connected with Portillo's CFO, Karen Peterson. "He doesn't want to talk to bankers," she told him. As Chandik kept pressing for a meeting, Peterson finally said a store was opening soon and he could stop by and maybe see Portillo there. "And so I did that . . . a bunch of times."

Portillo loved his business and didn't want to sell it to anyone. But he knew he was getting older and needed to plan for the future, Chandik said. Portillo was seventy-four at the time of the sale. He had a son working with him, but he wasn't planning to give him the company. "It wasn't a family business," Chandik observed. "It's Dick's business."

Typically, a founder helps with the transition after a sale and, with a sale to a PE fund, the owner often retains 10 or 20 percent of the business and the buyer gets the rest. That gives investors some comfort that the business won't unravel right away when its leader departs.

But Portillo told Chandik he wanted no such thing. "He was like, 'Look, I can't be one foot in, one foot out. I'm gonna sell 100 percent.'" Chandik agreed but thought Portillo would change his mind. He did not.

Even with these unconventional terms, investor interest was unusually strong. A call for initial bids yielded twenty-four potential offers from PE firms, more than double what you would expect for a similar sale. And that was before the prospective buyers could take a close look at Portillo's finances.

As Chandik peeled away the layers, he realized that Portillo's success was even better than he had imagined. "All the metrics were off the charts," Chandik said. "The craziest thing about it is they had no idea" how successful they were. "He just is focused on doing as much business as possible as well as possible."

A successful McDonald's, which serves breakfast through dinner, would have about $3 million in annual sales. A Jack in the Box would probably do a little over $1 million. Portillo's was doing $9 million in a single store. Nobody was doing that out of a fast-food place at the time.

* * *

The twenty-four bidders were salivating.

PE firms generally love a strong brand because it protects them from competition and has loyal customers. And they like steady, profitable businesses with stable cash flows and high profit margins because high profit enables PE firms to borrow money to buy the business, cover the interest costs on the debt, and pay down the principal before selling.

Chandik whittled the twenty-four first bidders down to about ten and pushed them to raise their offers. "This is extremely competitive," he said. "You're going to have to move, even if you were at the top." Restaurants generally trade at a value of six to eight times cash flow. Bidding for Portillo's was more than ten times, reflecting its highly unusual profitability and growth prospects.

Chandik invited the finalists to a meeting. "You want to keep as many as possible because you want competition," he explained. "That's how you drive up the price." But entertaining too many buyers would drag out the process. "We try and fit these into a two-week period. Once you select your bidders, you want to run as quickly as possible."

When Chandik issued a call for final bids, three buyer groups were ready to sign a deal. Portillo liked Berkshire Partners the best, but bidding continued between two buyers. The price was rising by increments of about $25 million. Chandik had already gone back to the bidders two or three times, and he knew he was running out of chances by asking for higher and higher bids.

And now Chandik found himself up against an unusual deadline. Portillo had commissioned a yacht and when it was ready, he was getting on it.

"Dick," Chandik told him, "you've got to put this off. I can't hold this together for friggin' six weeks. While you're on a friggin' boat, you know?"

"I'm not gonna wait an extra day," Portillo answered. "I'm getting on this boat." When he got to port, he said, he would have some cell phone reception and could call in. He was adamant.

"I think at the end of day, that helped because it created a sense of urgency where people were just like, 'Oh, shit, you know what, I gotta do this if I'm gonna do it.'"

The deal with Berkshire was announced just in time and, while details remain private, Chandik confirmed that, at $1 billion, it was the largest "multiple" at the time for a business of its kind—"multiple" meaning the sales price relative to a profits measure called EBITDA (i.e., earnings before interest, taxes, depreciation, and amortization). With no debt and no one else with equity in the business, Portillo realized all the profit.

"It created a huge splash in the industry. People were just like, 'Oh my God, a restaurant can trade for this,'" he recalled. The deal continues to raise expectations for what a good restaurant chain can fetch.

* * *

As PE's reach continues to grow in the middle market, it will continue to provide succession plans for business owners and needed cash for their businesses, helping them prosper well into the future.

Main Street Millionaires love their businesses. Most don't want to sell. But when they do, they command top dollar because there is more capital looking to buy these businesses than there are people willing to sell them. Cashing out is the last way that Main Street Millionaires amass extraordinary wealth.

At the same time, the Age of Millionaires will continue to transform finance as investors, portfolio managers, and top business school graduates focus on the businesses that Main Street Millionaires have created.

Who goes to business school with plans to buy a bunch of Burger

Kings? As it turns out, the best and the brightest of the financial world do.

With their wealth, Main Street Millionaires are not just transforming the world of finance, however. Wealth brings power, and Main Street Millionaires are using it at the federal, state, and local levels to fend off potential competition and further expand their businesses, as we will discuss next.

PART III

How They Shape Society

10

Stealthy Politics

In most elections . . . we don't get a say in something important: whether we're governed by the rich. By Election Day, that choice has usually been made for us. Would you like to be represented by a millionaire lawyer or a millionaire businessman?

—Nicholas Carnes, political scientist, 2012

Chicago has one of the nation's highest property tax rates and, not surprisingly, many property owners appeal the assessments they receive from the Cook County Assessor's Office.

Many of these property owners hire lawyers to help with their appeals. From 2011 to 2016, no law firm won more commercial property tax appeals before the Assessor's Office, the Board of Review, the Circuit Court, or the Illinois Property Tax Appeal Board than Madigan & Getzendanner. In the six-person firm, Vincent "Bud" Getzendanner and four other staff attorneys handled the appeals, while Michael Madigan Jr. brought in the clients. Until 2021, Madigan also was the state's most powerful politician.

Born in the spring of 1942, raised on Chicago's Southwest Side, and a graduate of Notre Dame and Loyola Law School, Madigan served as speaker of the state House of Representatives for four decades—longer than any leader of a state or federal legislature in U.S. history—and chaired the state Democratic Party for more than twenty years. His positions as House Speaker, party chair, ward boss, and private businessman added up, in the words of a former Cook County official, to the "Madigan Political Industrial Complex."

It was a lucrative mix of positions. When Madigan stepped down in 2021, the salary for a state House member was just over $69,000; as speaker, he received another $16,000. But that was hardly the bulk of his annual income. In fact, during a 2015 debate over a ballot referendum for a millionaires' tax, Madigan told a reporter, "In a good year I would be subject to this [tax]."

How did he generate so much business for Madigan & Getzendanner and so much income for himself? With a soft but clearly understandable touch. Consider, for instance, the case of Anthony Rossi, a developer of high-end apartment buildings. After the city approved a project for him, he received a cold call from Madigan and, at Madigan's request, met with him and a partner to go over Rossi's list of buildings to find appeals work. Naturally, Rossi agreed to the meeting because, as he put it, "Nobody wants to piss off the Speaker of the House."

Madigan—who was sentenced to seven and a half years in prison and fined $2.5 million for corruption in the summer of 2025—is just one of tens of thousands of rich business owners who have run for, and often won, federal, state, or local office in recent decades. Most of the victorious candidates don't end up in prison, but many of them use their political positions to steer more business to themselves or to enact laws and write regulations to help their firms or those of their rich benefactors.

During Madigan's trial, in *Snyder v. United States*, the Supreme Court revisited the definition of the word "corruptly" and narrowed it considerably in the context of federal bribery law. The Court argued that after-the-fact rewards known as "gratuities" did not qualify as bribes. Madigan subsequently hired nationally renowned attorneys to appeal his conviction on the grounds that his behavior would no longer qualify as illegal. Of anyone, he should know the value of hiring the right appeals lawyer.

And, when they're not running for office, many Main Street Millionaires are donating huge sums to political campaigns in hopes of protecting their businesses or securing even more tax, regulatory, or other benefits.

In parts I and II, we explained who Main Street Millionaires are and how they amassed their wealth. Through that wealth, they have also amassed considerable power. In part III, we show how they wield it and why that matters for the rest of us.

* * *

Business owners are very well represented in elective office. They comprise just 3 percent of the U.S. population, but they hold seats in far higher percentages, at every level of government, all across America.

At the federal level, members of Congress are much richer than the general population. The mean wealth of a House and Senate member in 2018 was $7 million and $10 million, respectively.

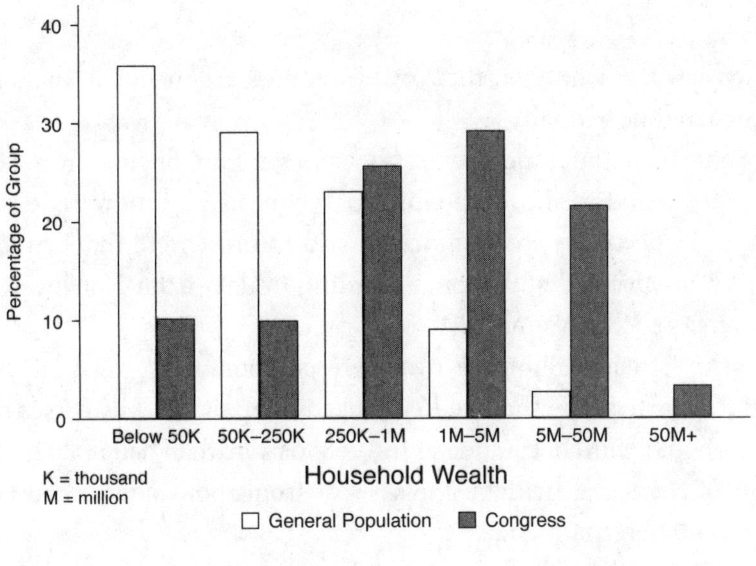

In other words, decamillionaires are more than ten times as likely to sit in Congress than their share of the population would suggest, while centimillionaires are sixty-two times as likely to hold congressional seats. These wealthy politicians are predominantly Main Street Millionaires.

From the 106th to the 110th Congress—that is, from 1999 through 2008—about 25 percent of federal lawmakers owned businesses.

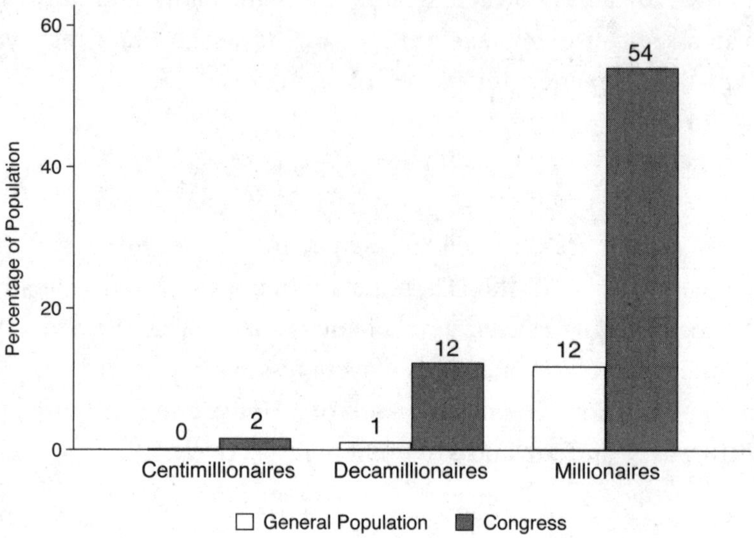

When lawyers who own their own practices are included, the share approaches nearly half.

Some forty thousand business owners ran for Congress from 1968 to 2022 (including those who lost), of whom 52 percent were Republicans, 42 percent were Democrats, and the rest were independents or of non-specified affiliation, according to data from Northwestern University's Silvia Vannutelli.

Main Street Millionaire overrepresentation has grown in both political parties. The share of Republicans who owned businesses rose from about a third of candidates in 1968 to more than half in 2022. The share of Democrats with businesses rose from about a quarter in 1968 to over 40 percent in 2022.

Of note, business interests are well represented on the House Ways and Means Committee—the committee where the process of rewriting the nation's tax laws and, in turn, significantly reshaping the bottom lines of potentially every business in America traditionally begins. In the 118th Congress of 2023–24, nearly a quarter of its forty-three members owned businesses.

The business-owning members of the committee, their business interests, and their self-reported net worth included:

- Vern Buchanan (R-FL)—auto dealerships, reinsurance companies, $157 million;
- Don Beyer (D-VA)—auto dealerships, $125 million;
- Kevin Hern (R-OK)—McDonald's franchises, banking, publishing, $61 million;
- Brad Schneider (D-IL)—consulting, insurance, $27 million;
- Mike Kelly (R-PA)—auto dealerships, $12 million;
- David Kustoff (R-TN)—law firm, $3 million;
- Lloyd Smucker (R-PA)—commercial construction, $3 million.

While business owners are overrepresented on Capitol Hill, especially on key committees, other types of Americans are underrepresented—in some cases, starkly so. Throughout the twentieth century, more than half of Americans had working-class backgrounds (working in manual labor or the service sector). But less than 2 percent of lawmakers came from those backgrounds.

* * *

Wealth concentration among politicians is even more pronounced in states and localities. In 2023–24 state legislatures, 40 percent of legislators came from business backgrounds—and that figure rises significantly if we include lawyers and doctors who own their own practices.

Business ownership is clearly a bipartisan pathway to elective office, even if two-thirds of business owner–legislators are Republicans. Twenty-one state legislators across the country were auto dealers in 2023–24; a car dealer was ten times as likely to sit in a statehouse as a factory worker.

At the local level, Patricia Kirkland conducted the most comprehensive study ever of mayoral candidates, covering forty-two hundred candidates who ran between 1950 and 2020 in 273 cities across forty-four states. Business owners and executives accounted for 32 percent of all candidates. Were we to add doctors and lawyers who own their own practices, the share would rise to about half.

Nor was the mayoralty the first office in which most business owners who ran for mayor actually served. About 70 percent served on city councils, in county positions, in state legislatures, or in other positions.

Why do business owners run for federal, state, and local office, and why are they elected in such large numbers?

* * *

Business owners enjoy distinct advantages when they run for office, including the luxury to consider running in the first place. Their wealth gives them the means to run that non-wealthy candidates do not have. Public office at any level doesn't pay well, which weeds out lots of would-be candidates.

At the federal level, congressional salaries are a growing impediment to enticing talented individuals to run. Lawmakers set their base pay at $174,000 in 2009 and have since repeatedly rejected proposals to raise it. While a superficial nod toward fiscal responsibility, this freeze makes it likelier that the job of a member will attract people with substantial means.

The problem is far more serious at the state and local level. A factory worker who earns $50,000 a year cannot afford to take a $30,000 job as a state legislator. A teacher supporting a family cannot afford to spend half the year away in the state capital while the legislature conducts its business.

In 85 percent of local governments in 2011, a mayor's job was part-time. Even in larger cities, three-quarters of mayoral positions were part-time. That creates a natural filter favoring those with lots of other income—precisely the business owners and professionals who dominate candidate pools.

Moreover, unlike employees with fixed schedules, business owners can attend weekday meetings, travel for campaigns, and manage the irregular demands of political service far more effectively than, say, a factory worker who can't leave the assembly line for a 2:00 p.m. city council meeting.

While the salaries of elected officials are modest, the private returns can be huge, especially for business owners like Madigan.

* * *

Modern political campaigns demand substantial up-front investment that favors candidates with personal wealth or access to affluent networks.

Campaigns for a U.S. House seat routinely cost more than $2 million, while a competitive state legislative race can cost $80,000 to over $300,000. Candidates often must front some of these costs before their fundraising efforts bear fruit, creating an immediate barrier for working-class aspirants.

Additionally, wealthy business owners can self-fund their campaigns altogether, avoiding the time-consuming and politically compromising process of soliciting donations. When they do fundraise, their professional networks provide ready access to other affluent individuals who can contribute generously.

Day-to-day, business owners cultivate relationships with other affluent professionals—lawyers, local bankers, accountants, contractors, suppliers—who become natural donors when they run for office. These relationships often span multiple industries, providing broader networks than most workers can access.

Running a political campaign also may bear some resemblance to running a business. For instance, each involves making sales, managing employees, and securing financing. Entrepreneurship requires comfort with risk, and running for office is an inherently risky venture. Business owners are accustomed to investing their own money for uncertain returns.

Now, let's meet some Main Street Millionaires who capitalized on their wealth and business accomplishments to run successfully for office.

* * *

When Bob Corker won a U.S. Senate seat from Tennessee in 2006, the Chattanooga-based developer became one of the wealthiest members of Congress (as of 2015, his net worth was about $70 million).

Born in Orangeburg, South Carolina, in August 1952, Corker moved with his family to Tennessee when he was eleven and, in his youth, displayed an entrepreneurial streak. He collected trash and bagged ice at thirteen and then worked as a construction laborer at Western Auto. After graduating from the University of Tennessee in 1974, he joined a development company and, when his boss was transferred, he wound up at age twenty-three in charge of building a large shopping mall.

Two years later, he invested $8,000 of his savings and leveraged his labor market experience to start a construction company, Bencor. After his firm landed a contract to build drive-through windows for the Krystal restaurant chain, Bencor built projects in eighteen states and grew at a blistering 80 percent annual rate.

Corker sold Bencor. In 1999, he bought two of Chattanooga's largest property companies and amassed a portfolio of commercial buildings. A downtown office tower proved especially fruitful because its tenants included a law firm that later became Corker's top campaign donor while simultaneously paying him millions in rent.

After Corker lost his first race—for the Republican nomination for a Senate seat—in 1994, Governor Don Sundquist appointed him the state's commissioner of finance and administration. In 2001, he won election as Chattanooga's mayor.

By 2006, Corker's local successes—both political and commercial—and deep pockets made him the ideal GOP contender for an open Senate seat. His Republican rivals cast him as insufficiently conservative, but Corker pumped $1.7 million of his own money into his primary campaign war chest on top of the $1 million he raised from donors. His opponents raised barely $500,000 each. Corker won the nomination and then the general election.

Corker served two Senate terms, from 2007 to 2019, chairing the Foreign Relations Committee for four years and holding seats on the Housing and Urban Affairs and Banking committees. He developed a reputation for bipartisanship, working, for instance, with Virginia Democrat Mark Warner on financial and mortgage reform in the wake of the Great Recession.

He decided to support President Trump's huge tax cuts in 2017 only after lawmakers inserted a provision—later dubbed the "Corker kickback"—from which he was destined to benefit greatly due to his rental income from real estate–related LLCs.

* * *

Whether they're car dealers or real estate brokers, people know the names of successful business owners. Their private-sector success, moreover, lends them a certain legitimacy when they seek public life. Many voters assume that business success will translate into governing competence.

William J. "Bud" Starker, the mayor of Wheat Ridge, Colorado, believes his decades of work as a commercial builder enabled him to appreciate what it takes to get things done in his Denver suburb of 33,000.

After college, Starker partnered with a friend and set roof trusses on four-plex apartment buildings. The firm did lots of insurance work, and he became an estimator, learning the business end of the operation and eventually managing its commercial division.

He left that job in 1983 to launch the Starker Construction Company and later paid back the friends who lent him start-up capital. The company financed its own growth and, at its peak, employed up to twenty people. It built schools and federal and state government buildings as well as retail projects and shopping centers for developers.

Starker then met Steve Ells, who had founded the Chipotle restaurant chain in Denver in 1993. "He had built one store and was looking to build a second store, so he came to us and we ran some numbers, and then he walked out," Starker told us. But Ells came back. Over the next fifteen years, Starker's company built about eighty Chipotle restaurants from southern Wyoming to northern Mexico.

Starker's construction business all but dried up during the deep

2008 economic slowdown, but a shabby storefront about two blocks from his home caught his eye as a place to build a restaurant. "It's on a good street that I had driven by a hundred times, and it seemed to be vacant."

This struck Starker as a good way to ride out the recession. "My workload had sort of been worked off," Bud recalls. "Things were looking awry. And here was an opportunity to put my staff to work and my crew to work building this restaurant."

He remembers thinking, "I know how to build restaurants for other guys and I've built a lot of those. I'm sure I can find a restaurateur that will be my partner." Starker never found a partner. "So I said, 'Well, I'll hire a manager and we'll hire a cook staff and run a restaurant.'"

His West 29th Restaurant and Bar opened in 2013. With one hundred seats, a European-style menu, and two patios, it's a popular and well-loved spot that nourished his image and boosted his visibility. "It harkened back to when I was in Europe as a young boy," he said of his place, "and my image of having sort of a community hub in the middle of small towns where people felt friendly, gathered for a meal and a good beer."

By the time he opened his restaurant, Starker had already begun his political ascent.

* * *

In the late 1980s, he became an active member of the Associated General Contractors of Colorado, serving on its board for more than thirty years and as its president in 1999. In the early 2000s, he joined the State Board of Licensure for architects, professional engineers, and professional land surveyors, staying on for eight years and chairing it for two.

As he was building the restaurant years later, Starker befriended a city councilor at the gym who encouraged him to run for an open council seat. At first he said no, but then it started to appeal to him. "I was a leader in Boy Scouts. I was a leader in my school government and a leader in my business enterprises," he explained, so running for local office was a natural next step.

He won, serving for four years before losing his seat to a challenger in 2015. When then-Mayor Joyce Jay decided not to seek reelection, Starker ran and won that seat in 2017.

"There's a fair amount of overlap," Starker said after comparing his roles as builder and mayor. "Because you really understand things from a technical aspect. Cities do a lot of building."

Among its projects, Starker's construction company expanded city hall and worked on park and recreation sites. So, he knew what it was like to do business in Wheat Ridge. "Why does it take my permit so long to happen?" he wondered at the time. "Or when I call city hall, I don't really get a sympathetic ear."

Of the successes during his mayoral tenure, he's particularly proud of a hundred-acre development that includes a state-of-the-art hospital that opened in 2023. In a part of town where residents had once fought off big-box stores, the hospital is now the city's biggest employer.

"I think it's the best job in government, being the mayor," Starker said.

Business owners like Starker often bring practical experience with arcane details of government to their political roles, giving them concrete areas to work on to improve the functioning of government.

But Main Street Millionaires who enter office also bring their particular worldview, which means some constituents have leaders who don't understand their plight. And some have leaders who abhor them.

* * *

In the Rio Grande Valley of South Texas, Othal Brand, the "Onion King," built a produce empire and then one of the most durable political machines in Texas.

Born in August 1919 in Grayson, Georgia, Brand (and his older brother) dropped out of high school to start a family produce business to provide for their mother and her six children during the Great Depression.

Griffin & Brand was America's largest onion shipper for several decades and, in the mid-1980s, was valued at $77 million (more than

$200 million in 2025 dollars). The company farmed 40,000 acres of onions, melons, citrus, and vegetables across Texas, Colorado, Idaho, and California and shipped produce to forty-eight states and seven countries.

During its peak spring season, the company could pack eighty thousand bags of onions daily—over four million pounds loaded onto more than a hundred semitrucks that were bound for markets across the country. Its annual revenues approached nine figures while providing "one of the largest single payrolls in the Rio Grande Valley," employing thousands during peak harvests.

The Onion King's business philosophy was total control. Vertically integrated "from seed to shelf," Brand owned the farms that grew the crops, the packing sheds that processed them, the cold storage facilities to store them, and the distribution networks that sold them.

A tall, barrel-chested Southern Baptist who taught Sunday school, Brand had a booming voice, a short temper, and an iron will. He served six years on McAllen's school board and then four as a city commissioner before beginning his two-decade mayoral reign in 1977. Known for tantrums during school board meetings, he once punched a fellow board member who opposed him.

* * *

As mayor, Brand outspent opponents and showcased his distaste for organized labor.

He staunchly opposed farmworker unions. When melon pickers surrounded his car during a 1975 wildcat strike, he stepped out with a pistol, later boasting that he "stopped them with the necessary equipment."

ACLU attorney James Harrington, who sued Brand "countless times on behalf of farmworkers," publicly labeled him "a bully, a racist . . . who can be very vindictive," claiming that "farmworkers in the Valley fear Brand" as almost a feudal lord.

During his bitter (and successful) 1981 reelection campaign, Brand ran newspaper ads insinuating that his opponent was captive to César Chávez and his farmworkers' union. Alleging voter fraud, he dispatched camera crews to polling places on Election Day to photograph voters—a move critics blasted as an effort to intimidate newly registered Hispanic voters. In an era when McAllen grew rapidly and became overwhelmingly Hispanic, Brand—a white Republican—dominated city politics.

He consolidated power through patronage. City contracts and appointments went to allies. Locals joked that nothing happened in town without his blessing—he toured street repair projects, conferred with police chiefs, and even called judges about friends' traffic tickets.

An infamous political cartoon from the era depicted Brand as a bloated octopus, each tentacle clutching dollar bills while entangled in different sectors of the community—agriculture, police, city government, banking, and media.

By the 1990s, changing demographics and organized opposition finally caught up with the Onion King. In 1997, when he was seventy-eight, voters unseated him. His farming operations ceased soon thereafter in the wake of the North American Free Trade Agreement, which opened markets to cheaper Mexican imports.

* * *

Wealthy business owners wield political influence not just through seeking office but also through behind-the-scenes power brokering, lobbying, and campaign contributions.

The saga of Glant Havenar shows what can happen when that behind-the-scenes dealmaking spills into plain view.

Havenar built her life in Palmer Lake, a small Colorado town of 2,500 residents that sits between Denver and Colorado Springs, as a residential real estate broker and public servant. She "served in nearly every key leadership role in Palmer Lake's local government" over the course of twelve years, including two terms on the Palmer Lake Board of Trustees before she ran successfully for mayor in 2022.

In late 2024, Buc-ee's approached Palmer Lake with plans to build a giant center "on the outskirts of the tiny town"—a Beaver Aplin–approved 74,000-square-foot convenience store with sixty fuel pumps and parking for eight hundred cars that would be open twenty-four hours a day. Under the plan, Palmer Lake would extend the city's limits to the proposed Buc-ee's location. Buc-ee's said being part of the town was necessary to ensure water rights for the travel center.

Analysts projected that the new Buc-ee's site could generate $38 million in annual taxable sales, yielding $1 million a year in new tax revenue in its first year (a 30 percent increase for the town) and hundreds of jobs.

Havenar presented the proposal to the town's trustees, who would have to rule that the site was eligible for annexation, and most of them seemed enthused.

Many locals, however, recoiled at the scale of the project, for Palmer Lake is a quiet mountain town of natural scenery and mom-and-pop shops that many cherish. Some, with reference to the Buc-ee's beaver mascot, displayed "Heave the Beave" lawn signs.

Criticism morphed into scandal. Havenar was seen dining with Mark Waller, a Buc-ee's lobbyist, a day after the town board held a confidential executive session. In addition, a watchdog group sued Havenar and other officials, charging that they violated the state's open meetings law.

Then, Havenar's former close friend, Darcy Schoening, released dozens of pages of text messages that purportedly came from the mayor's group chats. They revealed plans to manipulate the process, her apparent contempt for constituents, and references to riding a private jet.

The mayor created social media accounts under false names to "engage with people online" and sway public opinion in favor of the annexation. She referred to some vocal opponents as "terrorists" and "losers" and criticized some of their appearances, calling one resident "a cow" and another "unfortunate looking."

Facing a firestorm, she resigned in June 2025. Her sudden exit midway through her second term came just days after the text leaks and as pressure mounted from the lawsuit and a potential recall.

As of this writing, the Palmer Lake project remains uncertain, as other supportive trustee members face recall votes.

* * *

Main Street Millionaires are also donating huge sums to help elect candidates who will cater to their needs.

Consider who donates to members of Congress's tax-writing committees. The top industries for campaign contributions mirror the top industries of Main Street Millionaires in general. For House Ways and Means Committee members who were elected or reelected in 2022, the top twenty donating industries included:

- Real estate ($5.6 million);
- Health professionals, including doctors ($5.0 million);
- Lawyers ($3.1 million);
- Automotive ($1.6 million);
- Beer, wine, liquor ($1.3 million); and
- Accountants ($1.3 million).

Similarly, for the Senate Finance Committee, the top twenty donating industries included:

- Lawyers ($27.9 million);
- Real estate ($21.4 million);
- Health professionals, including doctors ($16.7 million); and
- Business services ($7.1 million).

At the state level, this pattern is even more pronounced. All state lobbying totals about half of all federal lobbying, indicating that state and local influence is a high priority for business owners, even if it draws much less media attention.

Based on data from 2017 to 2019 in twenty-seven states from economists Sarah Moshary and Cailin Slattery, the top five industries in terms of state lobbying are:

- Business, professional, labor, political, and similar organizations ($900 million);
- Legal services ($540 million);
- Agencies, brokerages, and other insurance activities ($540 million);
- Offices of physicians ($470 million); and
- Management, scientific, and technical consulting services ($440 million).

Systematic data that link specific donors to their businesses are not available. Dark money super PACs make it hard to paint a comprehensive picture. Nevertheless, the more we learn from the incomplete data, from news stories, and from other sources, the more we find that Main Street Millionaires are having a massive influence on the political process.

* * *

In recent years, two of the biggest Main Street Millionaire donors at both the federal and state levels have been Dick and Liz Uihlein.

Dick Uihlein comes from the German American family that owned Milwaukee beer giant Schlitz. His family strongly supported right-wing causes—from Charles Lindbergh's America First Committee to George Wallace's campaigns to the rabidly anti-Communist and segregationist John Birch Society; for the latter, Dick's father served on its National Finance Committee.

Born in 1945 and raised outside Chicago, Dick attended Phillips Academy–Andover and Stanford University and then worked for his father at General Bindings Corporation for thirteen years before quitting to launch his own venture.

In 1980, he and Liz founded the shipping company Uline, which makes shopping bags, mail-order boxes, and other shipping supplies that are so ubiquitous that they're almost invisible; you likely have a Uline packaging product in your home. The company remains under tight family control, with Dick as CEO, Liz as president, three sons as vice presidents, and a daughter as corporate planner.

The billionaire couple has given hundreds of millions to far-right candidates and causes, planting them firmly among the nation's most prolific Republican donors.

* * *

From the 2016 election cycle through the 2024 cycle, the Uihleins spent more than $300 million for local and national candidates; for "dark money" super PACs that buy attack ads, including against Republicans they think are too moderate; and for groups that organized the January 6 "Stop the Steal" rally.

For 2022, they were the largest federal campaign donors for Republicans and the second-largest political donors overall, behind George Soros, spending more than $121 million on state and federal races. For 2024, it is estimated that they gave more than $140 million to GOP candidates and causes, including more than $60 million to pro-Trump super PACs. That year, they donated as much as half of the nearly $300 million that Elon Musk donated while attracting far less public scrutiny.

For the 2023–24 election cycle, Dick also funneled nearly $22 million to the Club for Growth Action, which works to elect and reelect ultraconservative House and Senate candidates, and $9.6 million to Fair Courts America, which works to elect far-right judges to state supreme courts.

Dick Uihlein is also one of the two biggest financial supporters of Ron Johnson, a Republican senator from Wisconsin. Johnson declared that he would vote against then-President Trump's 2017 tax cut unless it cut taxes more for pass-through businesses. Johnson later claimed credit for the sweeteners that secured his approval.

Those sweeteners netted the Uihleins a cool $43.5 million in tax savings in the first year alone.

* * *

While the Uihleins were wielding power and influence in Republican circles, a Main Street Millionaire who had founded an insurance company was doing the same in Democratic circles in southern New Jersey.

"In the end," New Jersey power broker George Norcross said in a 2021 conversation, the recording of which came to be known as the Palmyra Tapes, referring to the Garden State's most important elected officials, "the McGreeveys, the Corzines, they're all going to be with me. Not because they like me, because they have no choice."

Born in Camden in 1956, Norcross, a Rutgers University dropout, landed a government job at twenty-two. His well-connected father arranged for the city's mayor, Angelo Errichetti, to appoint him to run the Camden Parking Authority. From that position, he started learning about local politics and stitching together a network of labor and political allies.

A year after his appointment, Norcross founded an insurance firm, which later became Keystone National Insurance, and started selling insurance from a card table in a basement office in Camden. Keystone began winning contracts with Camden and other public entities, tying him directly into the machinery of local government. He sold insurance to school boards, local towns, and utilities. His growing wealth, access to elected officials, and donations to political campaigns enabled him to rise quickly within southern New Jersey's Democratic establishment.

"Over the last two decades," a prominent journalist wrote in 2011, "the Norcross organization has steadily expanded its hold on the region and extended its reach across the state. It's not written down anywhere, but it's acknowledged by everyone (privately, of course): You don't run for office as a Democrat in South Jersey unless George is OK with it—and you don't win in the fall without him."

You also didn't do business in South Jersey without feeding the machine. Contractors would receive invitations to expensive fundraising events, with the number of tickets they were expected to buy already set. Those who ignored the invitations might find their government contracts canceled or their permit applications delayed. Politicians who took Norcross money could operate independently, as long as they voted with him on issues he cared about.

Though a Democrat, Norcross built a strategic partnership with then–New Jersey Republican governor Chris Christie. That alliance culminated in the 2013 Economic Opportunity Act, a sweeping overhaul of state corporate tax subsidies. The bill was cosponsored by George Norcross's brother Donald, then a state senate member, and shaped in part by his brother Philip, a lobbyist. It was designed to draw investment into struggling cities, and Camden emerged as the biggest winner.

Of the $4.9 billion awarded statewide, Camden alone received $1.6 billion—and about $1.1 billion of that $1.6 billion flowed to entities tied to Norcross and his extended network, according to a joint investigation by WNYC and ProPublica. His insurance brokerage received $245 million, while clients of his brother Philip's law and lobbying firm secured $770 million. Major beneficiaries included Holtec International, Subaru of America, the Philadelphia 76ers, and Cooper Health System, for which both George and Philip served on the board.

In June 2024, New Jersey attorney general Matt Platkin announced a thirteen-count racketeering indictment against Norcross and five close associates, alleging that he led a criminal enterprise that used intimidation and insider access to commandeer Camden's waterfront redevelopment for personal gain. Eight months later, Superior Court Judge Peter Warshaw dismissed the case, acknowledging that Norcross's conduct may have been "boorish and indecorous" but finding that it did not meet the standard for criminal extortion or coercion under state law.

For Norcross, it was vindication. His brand of politics was aggressive but, in the eyes of the court, not illegal.

* * *

Beyond the Uihleins and Norcross, what do we know about the partisan leanings of other Main Street Millionaires?

Generally, they lean farther right than the U.S. population writ large. In an article in the *British Journal of Political Science*, Neil Malhotra, Yotam Margalit, and Saikun Shi argue that "the experience of being a small business owner causes them [owners] to become more skeptical of government regulation" that they encounter in their everyday working lives.

In a large-scale 2024 survey of small business owners, 32 percent identified as Republican, 23 percent as Democrats, and 36 percent as independent—compared to 35 percent Republican, 38 percent Democrat, and 27 percent independent for the general population. When independent small business owners were forced to lean toward a party, they were 10 percentage points likelier to lean Republican. Within occupations such as doctors, Main Street Millionaires who own a business were around 5 percentage points likelier to vote for or donate to Republicans. That said, plenty of business owners identify as Democrats.

Republicans tend to own businesses in more complex industries, such as construction, health care, and manufacturing. Those businesses are likelier to face labor laws or health and safety regulations.

The variation in political affiliation appears in federal donation data from 2020, which lists self-reported occupations. Focusing on those who are likely to be business owners, the most Democratic-leaning occupations include psychologists (93 percent of whose donations go to Democrats), producers (93 percent), lawyers (86 percent), architects (85 percent), and publishers (84 percent). The most Republican leaning are auto dealers (86 percent of whose donations go to Republicans), contractors (79 percent), farmers (78 percent), CEOs (68 percent), and chiropractors (60 percent).

Even within industries, political affiliation varies widely. Among doctors, more than three-quarters of orthopedic surgeon donations, but less than a quarter of pediatrician donations, go to Republicans.

* * *

When Main Street Millionaires sway the political process for themselves, the rest of us are left holding the bag. For New Jersey taxpayers, that bill amounted to around $1 billion in Norcross-linked projects that provided little if any widespread local benefit. For federal taxpayers, the price tag can be much larger.

In response to COVID and the economic nosedive that it spurred, federal lawmakers enacted the Paycheck Protection Program (PPP), providing $800 billion in forgivable low-interest loans to small businesses. Firms with fewer than five hundred employees were eligible, and most Main Street Millionaires qualified for loans that totaled the lesser of 2.5 times their monthly payroll or $10 million.

Beneficiaries were the types of businesses that wealthy politicians own: professional services firms, real estate operations, car dealers, and mid-market family businesses. In theory, a loan was meant to support a firm's payroll and other necessary expenses. In practice, most firms operated the same way they would have in the absence of the loan, leaving the benefits to firm owners.

No fewer than twenty-eight members of Congress (or their spouses) collectively obtained $27 million in these loans. Rep. Mike Kelly (R-PA), Congress's thirty-ninth-wealthiest member, with a net worth of $12.4 million, secured between $150,000 to $350,000 in loans for his auto dealerships. Kelly claimed he was "not involved in the day-to-day operations" of his businesses, but he was listed as president of three dealerships on his House financial disclosures.

Rep. Roger Williams (R-TX) secured over $1.4 million for his north Texas car dealership. He had previously criticized government subsidies, telling *The Epoch Times* in March 2020 that "a socialist wants you to get a check from the government . . . a capitalist wants you to get a check from the place that you work."

Other PPP beneficiaries from Congress, and their affiliated businesses, included:

- Sen. Markwayne Mullin (R-OK, plumbing);
- Rep. Vicki Hartzler (R-MO, tractors);
- Rep. Nita Lowey (D-NY, law firm);
- Rep. Devin Nunes (R-CA, farms and wineries); and
- Rep. Kevin Hern (R-OK, McDonald's franchises).

Hern owned ten franchises as of 2018 and reported an estimated net worth of more than $60 million. He pushed for a PPP provision that enabled a business owner to receive a loan even when the business was part of a conglomerate with total employment that exceeded the five hundred–worker threshold. "'McCongressman' Gets a Large Order of PPP," read a Bloomberg headline about Hern.

* * *

In Chicago, where Mike Madigan shaped the property tax process to benefit his appeals firm, a *Chicago Tribune* and ProPublica Illinois investigation revealed the broader social costs—massive inequities in effective property tax rates.

Wealthy North Siders paid far lower rates than poorer minority households on the South Side, as assessments historically gave beneficial valuations to the former. The appeals system that benefits tax-lawyer-politicians in Chicago like Madigan further tilts the scales in favor of wealthy individuals and businesses. The wealthy and well-connected are likelier to hire the best-connected attorneys to appeal, win appeals, and receive large tax reductions when they do.

This story is one example of a widespread phenomenon. Main Street Millionaires use their political influence to protect their businesses and enrich themselves across a range of industries.

11

Market Power in a Million Markets

> *Large coalitions of small businesses are more evil than small coalitions of large businesses.*
>
> —Former Treasury Secretary Larry Summers, 2023

As John McCain accepted his party's nomination for president at the Republican National Convention in the summer of 2008, sporting a gold tie and flashing his high-wattage smile before thousands of politicos, journalists, and a TV audience of nearly forty million, his journey from combat hero and prisoner of war to charismatic senator was the stuff of folklore.

Far fewer of those watching knew that Cindy Lou McCain, who joined her husband onstage in a double-breasted teal skirt suit, with pearls around her neck and wrist, was at least as important to her husband's political ascent as his compelling story. For McCain's rise in Arizona was powered in large part by the wealth of his wife's family, who owned one of America's largest distributorships of Anheuser-Busch beer.

Beer is the nation's most popular alcoholic beverage—the lifeblood of American leisure and, as brewers like to say, the "drink of moderation," because it's less intoxicating than full-proof spirits or wine and more egalitarian than either.

Among the industry's happy beneficiaries of its popularity are beer distributors. The industry's "middle tier," distributors take beer from brewers and deliver it to stores, bars, and restaurants. When Cindy

McCain's father, James Willis Hensley, launched his Phoenix distributorship as Hensley & Co. in 1955, he had a $10,000 loan and two federal felony convictions for falsifying records and conspiring to conceal illicit liquor deals for the Arizona mob. By the time Hensley died in 2000, the *Phoenix New Times* estimated his net worth at $200 million. In 2008, *The New York Times* reported annual company revenues of $300 million.

While bankrolling John McCain's political ambitions, the family fortune helped the McCains acquire eight properties, including a vacation compound in Sedona and a $4.7 million condo in Phoenix. (Oblivious to their holdings, the senator made an embarrassing gaffe in the 2008 campaign when—during the housing market collapse—he couldn't recall how many homes he owned.) Cindy was the registered owner of eleven of their thirteen vehicles, and her driver at the time chauffeured her in a Lexus with the license plate MS BUD.

The Hensleys, along with many other Main Street Millionaires, grew rich not just by outcompeting rivals but also by writing the rules of the game. From beverage distributors to auto dealers, Realtors to physicians, business owners consolidate and entrench their local market power. Their political influence protects them and, in turn, so do the laws and regulations they shape. Over decades, they've restricted entry and blocked power grabs by other market players, amassing extraordinary wealth while pushing up costs for the rest of us.

* * *

To be sure, the evolution of each industry over the last century, the rules under which it operates, and the political organizations that wield its influence are peculiar to that industry.

Nevertheless, the operational strategies of each are strikingly similar: Limit entry to its market, restrict access to its products, and raise prices. The economic and political effects are strikingly similar as well.

That beer distributor who's been "the only game in town for decades"? His stranglehold on local beer sales didn't come just from operating more efficiently—state laws guarantee it by preventing breweries from selling directly to retailers and requiring that all beer flow through a middleman with exclusive territorial rights.

That Chevy dealer who's been "serving this community for three generations"? He didn't earn his place in the market just through better service—state franchise laws make it nearly impossible for GM to close his dealership or for competitors to encroach on his turf.

That Realtor who "knows this market better than anyone"? Her monopoly on home listings isn't due to expertise—the Multiple Listing Service cartel protects it by blocking competitors from accessing listing information, and the National Association of Realtors imposes contracts to ensure that all Realtors comply with the standard, exorbitant commission structure.

That doctor who's "cared for generations of local families"? His high income isn't only the product of superior medical practice—laws protect him from competition by limiting how many doctors can be trained or certified, and medical boards restrict what services non-MDs can provide.

In thousands of regional markets across America, the result is market power for Main Street Millionaires—enriching for owners, bad for business dynamism, costly for customers, and far less publicly scrutinized than the market power of megacorporations like Alphabet and Amazon.

Let's take a closer look at each of these industry examples. Main Street Millionaires are dominating local markets everywhere. How did their market power arise? And how do they keep protecting it?

* * *

No beer distributor in America is likely wealthier than J. Christopher Reyes, founder of Reyes Holdings, the country's largest beer distributor as of this writing and sixth-largest privately held company. He and his brother Jude, the company cochair, are each worth $12 billion, *Forbes* estimated in 2025.

In 2024, the company listed fifty-two facilities across eleven states and Washington, D.C. By expanding into Texas in 2022, it acquired sixteen million cases' worth of business from Capitol Wright Distributing—"roughly equivalent to the total volume of Miller High Life sold in the U.S. in the first nine months" of that year. The company is the preferred distributor of Constellation Brands, which sells Corona and Modelo, in each of the twelve states in which it owns distributorships.

In the mid-'70s, the Reyeses bought a Schlitz distributorship for $740,000 in Spartanburg, South Carolina, where Jude had attended Wofford College. It was their first middle-tier acquisition in what, over time, would become dozens.

In 1989, the Reyes brothers acquired Harbor Distributing in Huntington Beach, California. They then began to expand their footprint across the state, which was at the time the nation's largest single beer market. While other distributors in California were buying ski houses and yachts, the Reyes brothers began buying the distributors themselves.

But if Chris and Jude Reyes are the nation's richest beer distributors, they're hardly the only ones with oodles of money. After *Beer Business Daily* held its annual "Beer Summit" in San Antonio, Texas, for the first time in the early 2010s, publisher Harry Schuhmacher received a call from the city's mayor, Julián Castro.

"He found out who I was, and he called and thanked me," Schuhmacher recalled to us. "I was wondering why and he said, 'We've never had that many private planes at the San Antonio airport at one time before.'"

How did all those beer distributors grow so rich?

* * *

When you see a big truck double-parked outside a bar or restaurant with a giant graphic of, say, Miller Lite on its side, look closer.

Virtually without exception, you'll also see a smaller graphic, usually on the door of the truck's cab, of a company you've probably never heard of. The truck doesn't belong to Molson Coors Beverage Company, the country's second-largest brewer and the maker of "The Original Lite Beer." It belongs to an independent firm—typically a family-owned pass-through that's been passed down at least one generation—that buys Miller Lite from the brewery and sells it to the retailer that then sells it to you.

Beer distributors owe their position in the market to the industry's hierarchy that was established in the aftermath of Prohibition. By the early 1930s, even pro-temperance zealots recognized that Prohibition had failed. Thirsty for new tax revenues, a reprieve from gang violence, and (for many) the freedom to again drink on the right side of the law, the public clamored for the end of the Eighteenth Amendment that had triggered Prohibition.

Just after midnight on the day Prohibition ended in the spring of 1933, a "shiny new beer truck, swifter if less picturesque than the brewers' big horses of ante-bellum days," rumbled down Pennsylvania Avenue to deliver two cases of beer to the White House. "The truck," *The New York Times* reported, "bore a huge sign announcing: 'President Roosevelt, the first real beer is yours!'"

The Twenty-First Amendment, which ended Prohibition, returned alcohol's regulation to the states. But what would it look like?

Not many lawmakers wanted to again entrust the regulation of alcohol to the federal government. Nor did they want to green-light a return of the so-called tied-house system that emerged by the late nineteenth and early twentieth centuries, under which brewers controlled the entire supply chain, enjoying enormous leverage over the comparatively tiny independent bars and shops that sold their brews.

In the aftermath of Prohibition, the fortune of the big beer manufacturers rose considerably. Anheuser-Busch and Schlitz couldn't buy saloons thanks to a 1935 federal anti-tied-house law but, with their staggeringly large resources, these heavyweights were consolidating power over their distributors.

States moved to protect the market (and their excise tax revenues) from the growing power of macrobrewers by dividing the industry within their borders into three discrete levels of responsibility: manufacturing (brewers), distribution (distributors), and sales (retailers). In state after state, lawmakers enacted their own tied-house laws to prevent a return to the old days. These laws often prohibited producers and distributors from owning retailers, thus keeping each level of responsibility distinct.

Thus was born the middle tier, through which brewers (and, similarly, distillers and winemakers) must pass to get their liquid wares to market.

* * *

The 1970s. Texas. A disgraced vice president, a Hall of Fame Dallas Cowboy, and America's first astronaut walk into a bar—or, more precisely, tried to sell beer to one as a distributor.

When, in 1975, the Adolph Coors Brewing Company announced plans to expand in Texas, it received more than four thousand applications for twenty-nine distributorships. The hopefuls included Vice President Spiro Agnew, Dallas Cowboy defensive tackle Bob Lilly, astronaut Alan Shepard, and baseball's Ken and Bob Aspromonte. "Never in the history of Texas business," marveled one observer, "would so many try so hard to win something so ostensibly ordinary as the opportunity to sell beer." (As it turned out, Lilly, Shepard, and the Aspromonte brothers secured distributorships; "adverse publicity" from his alleged political corruption and tax evasion convinced Agnew to withdraw his application.)

By the '70s, the number of breweries nationwide was shrinking as macrobrewers gobbled up regional players; that number would bottom out at just eighty-nine in 1978. Gone were the days when brewers handed out distributorships to family and friends. With most territories already spoken for, and fewer beer brands to distribute, distribution rights became highly coveted assets.

At the same time, distributors became ripe for de facto capture by the large, sophisticated breweries against which they were meant to serve as bulwarks. The fortunes of distributors in this era depended above all else on the good graces of their brewing partners. Anheuser-Busch lavished its well-performing distributors with gifts, such as fine cutlery and chafing dishes with gilded engravings of the company logo and pomp-and-circumstance visits from the iconic Budweiser Clydesdales. The Coors family, raised on frontier stoicism and libertarian politics, reacted far differently when its distributors prospered.

"With Coors the biggest-selling beer everywhere it was sold, the distributors were fabulously rich—many times richer, for example, than Bill Coors," journalist Dan Baum said. "One distributor in Texas had just hosted a wedding party for his daughter, and had filled his mansion's swimming pool with ice and champagne. When Bill—who lived in a modest subdivision house—heard about it, he was livid."

But even if some individual distributors grew wealthier than some individual brewers, the increasingly corporatized, increasingly national breweries reigned over their middle-tier counterparts. If distributors crossed their heavyweight brewing partners, they often got the stick in return.

Big brewers could make life hell for distributors by slow-walking deliveries, throttling ad purchases in their market, or making surprise visits to their warehouses to look for evidence of sloth. More terrifying, breweries could cut their out-of-favor distributors off from the tap entirely. "If they wanted to terminate, we were screwed," recalled Joe Thompson, a beverage industry veteran.

In response, distributors learned how to save their skin by leveraging the political system to their advantage.

* * *

Across the country, distributors sought protection from their state's elected leaders, and their push was wildly successful.

By the end of the '70s, eighteen states had enacted laws that restricted brewers from canceling or not renewing contracts with their distributors. Today, forty-seven states have laws that provide such franchise protection. Distributors successfully pitched politicians on the notion of protecting small, family-owned businesses and the jobs they represented from the corporate greed of large breweries. (Wine and spirits distributors enjoy similar protections from around half of the states.)

In nearly every state, political organizing helped distributors secure the vital second half of what Thompson calls their "double-whammy . . . Basically, you have a contract, and [starting in the '60s and '70s] you have franchise protections, in most states," he said. "That's what makes distribution rights extremely valuable. That's where the wealth is created."

The rules vary by state, but they all address the conditions that brewers must meet to terminate a distributor. As far as distributors are concerned, the holy grail provision of these laws prohibits brewers from pulling their distribution rights without "good cause" and fair-market value compensation. Of forty-seven states with franchise protections, thirty-six feature that stipulation, which deters termination by threatening brewers with a large financial hit.

Through their national association, distributors wield quite a bit of political power in Washington as well.

* * *

"Why do we come here to D.C. to advocate every year?" Craig Purser asked a ballroom audience in April 2024.

At the Hyatt Regency Washington, just 1,287 steps from the U.S. Capitol, Purser was speaking to more than six hundred beer distributors who had flown in from around the country to attend the annual legislative conference of the National Beer Wholesalers Association (NBWA)—the three-thousand-member political behemoth for which Purser has served as president and chief executive since 2005.

In 1994, at just twenty-seven, Purser quarterbacked Jim Inhofe's successful campaign for a U.S. Senate seat from Oklahoma. Three decades later, his salt-and-pepper scruff and "hey-how-are-ya?" charisma had long endeared him to the industry's trade press, which affectionately calls him "Beer Dad."

Why do distributors come to Washington every year, as Purser asked rhetorically? Because they're highly sensitive to the machinations of Capitol Hill. And they spend accordingly. By 2024, Purser was making over $1.5 million a year in salary and other compensation. His job was to protect the interests of beer distributors while reinforcing the regulatory system under which they operate. Only two other political action committees outspent the NBWA's PAC on House and Senate races for 2022.

Most beer distributors are still local, family-owned businesses, employing hundreds or thousands of people in nearly every congressional district in America. They have skin in the game and boots on the ground. Their local stature nourishes political capital more discreetly, and more directly, than political spending.

"My dad was friends with [Arizona's] Senator [Dennis] DeConcini, Senator McCain, Congressman [Mo] Udall," Kimberly Clements, former owner of Tucson's Golden Eagle Distributors, recalled to us. "Beer distributors have been doing this for a very long time, and they are friends [with politicians]. When I say friends, they could go golfing with a senator . . . These are very, very well-connected people."

The NBWA's political power often shocks Washington outsiders, who assume that beer trucking would leave distributors without the sophistication and savvy to lobby effectively. The truth is far different. The distributors are "the toughest lobby you've never heard of," according to Jeffrey Birnbaum, a former *Wall Street Journal* Washington correspondent and author of several books on lobbying.

Consider two good examples of their power—in the first, defeating the president of the United States and Mothers Against Drunk Driving (MADD); in the second, defeating the world's second-largest food conglomerate.

* * *

In 1993, President Clinton was trying to gin up support for universal health care, and he envisioned an increase in federal excise taxes (FET)—which are imposed on alcoholic beverages, tobacco, gas, diesel fuel, aviation, and other items—to help pay for it.

Anheuser-Busch launched a national marketing campaign that included emblazoning its long-haul trucks with decals that read "1-800-BEER-TAX"—a hotline it established to urge consumers to demand that lawmakers not only reject Clinton's proposals but also repeal the excise tax increase on alcoholic beverages and tobacco that lawmakers enacted in 1990. Joining the effort were "local delivery trucks" that were owned by distributors like Chicago's Superior Beverage Group, which sent some of its fleet to an anti-FET rally at the Capitol Reflecting Pool in Washington.

While distributors' trucks were asking drinkers to call a hotline, the NBWA was asking distributors to call their members of Congress directly. The NBWA also "sent an Action Alert to all NBWA members[,] who lobbied the White House through letters and phone calls. When Clinton unveiled his health care reform package, it contained no mention of tax increases on beer."

In the wake of that success, the NBWA's confidence and organizational capacity continued to grow. "I want every member of Congress to look in the mirror and say, 'It's not worth messing with the beer wholesalers,'" David Rehr, NBWA leader and a former congressional campaign operative, told Birnbaum that year.

Then, a new battle erupted over whether lawmakers would allow the Office of National Drug Control Policy to include anti-drinking messaging as part of its broader antidrug efforts. MADD, a fearsome political machine, backed the proposal.

"In the days ahead," MADD president Karolyn Nunnallee declared at a news conference, "we will learn whether the members of the House Appropriations Committee see Mr. Rehr's face when they look in the mirror or the faces of thousands of young people who die each year as a result of alcohol."

Nunnallee soon learned her lesson: Lawmakers in both the House and Senate rejected the anti-drinking message.

"We worked it about as hard as any other issue I've been involved in," a MADD lobbyist later recounted, but even the mighty MADD was no political match for the mightier NBWA.

* * *

PepsiCo, the world's second-largest food conglomerate, behind only Nestlé, tried to enter the beer distribution business in 2022.

Pepsi had licensed its Mountain Dew brand to Boston Beer Company to produce a flavored malt beverage called Hard Mtn Dew. It then formed its own distributorship, Blue Cloud Distribution. Under Pepsi's plan, Blue Cloud would buy Hard Mtn Dew from Boston Beer Co. and truck it to all the supermarkets and convenience stores with which it already had strong sales relationships.

Beer distributors, however, weren't about to accept threats to their market. "Most states have a specific prohibition on large manufacturers owning alcohol distribution," Purser told the NBWA's annual convention that year. "Put simply, if Molson Coors or [Anheuser-Busch InBev] can't own distribution, how can Pepsi?"

The NBWA went to work, reportedly circulating photographs of the drinks in stores next to Hot Wheels toys and nonalcoholic drinks like Kool-Aid, suggesting that Blue Cloud was creating confusion in the marketplace. Distributors mounted lawsuits aimed at blocking Blue Cloud's licensure in each state.

The battles dragged on, and Hard Mtn Dew's rollout dragged on with them. In early 2024, with its tail between its legs, Pepsi gave up on its distribution ambitions.

"Blue Cloud took on the system and even with PepsiCo's resources still couldn't beat the middle tier," marveled Sean O'Leary, a beverage industry attorney and blogger. "They simply run the industry!"

* * *

We Americans sell cars similarly to how we sell beer. Under franchise laws, a car dealer secures an exclusive distribution right in a certain geographic territory. By controlling their local turf, auto dealers wield considerable market power against both manufacturers and consumers.

The model emerged more than a century ago. The first dealer was William E. Metzger, who secured a franchise in 1898 to sell steam automobiles from GM. Over the next two decades, manufacturers experimented with many ways to sell their cars—factory stores, mail order, department stores, and wholesale distributors. But as the market matured and competition intensified, they increasingly relied on independent dealers to provide local sales expertise, service capabilities, and the substantial capital investments needed for car inventory and facilities.

This relationship worked reasonably well until manufacturers began exploiting their leverage. In the 1920s and '30s, Ford and GM forced dealers to buy inventories of new cars they were unlikely to sell, taking advantage of dealers' sunk investments in their facilities. Even during the Great Depression, when so many Americans struggled just to survive, Henry Ford "kept his factories running at 'full tilt' and allegedly was able to 'force' dealers to buy inventories of Model Ts that they would be unable to sell, under threat of not getting any more inventory in the future if they refused delivery." Thus, manufacturers could essentially hold dealers hostage by controlling their product supplies and franchise agreements.

Spurred in part by a recession in the early 1950s that soured manufacturer-dealer relations, federal lawmakers gave dealers some recourse against the bad faith of manufacturers by enacting the 1956 Automobile Dealers' Day in Court Act. The act enabled dealers to sue manufacturers in federal court. It also established a "good faith" standard for manufacturer-dealer relations under which dealers could seek recourse, mandating damages and court costs for successful dealer claims. But, for franchisees, the more important action came at the state level.

By that same year, twenty states had enacted auto franchise laws to protect small-town dealers from the manufacturing behemoths. Today, every state has them. These laws offer several protections. First, manufacturers cannot close dealerships except for "good cause" and, importantly, "good cause" cannot relate to dealer efficiency or manufacturer profitability. Second, manufacturers must demonstrate "need" before establishing competing dealerships in dealers' territories. Third, manufacturers cannot discriminate against dealers by offering lower prices and bigger discounts to some but not others. Last, manufacturers must pay dealers generously when they do work that's covered by warranties.

Most dealer franchise laws require that car manufacturers, upon terminating a dealer, buy back unsold new vehicles, parts, accessories, special tools, and equipment. In addition, some states require that manufacturers provide even more compensation to dealers upon terminating them. Virginia, for instance, requires that a car manufacturer that discontinues a brand, thus terminating the associated dealers, also must pay those dealers the fair market value of the franchises and up to three years of rent.

Why are states so eager to grease the dealers' palms?

In large part, the answer is taxes and jobs. In 2022, the nation's roughly seventeen thousand franchised dealerships provided about 20 percent of all sales taxes that states collected, and dealerships accounted for 8 percent of America's retail employment, with 1.3 million people working at auto dealerships across the country.

In addition, auto dealers throw their weight around in other ways. The quintessential booster of the local high school football team is an auto dealer. If you've seen the TV show *Friday Night Lights*, you'll remember Buddy Garrity, who owns a Chevrolet dealership in Dillon, Texas, and tries to influence the coach and players. You can find dealers like Garrity in communities all over America. With the NCAA's recent decision to allow advertisers to pay college athletes, stories abound of dealers who offer nice cars to would-be recruits to attract top players to the local team, or who reward recruits with cars after they commit to play for the team.

For Ohio State, auto dealer Rick Ricart rewarded a top wide receiver who committed to the school with an advertising deal that gave the player free use of a Dodge Challenger 392 Scat Pack. For Arizona State, auto dealer Parker Jones cut a deal with quarterback Jayden Daniels (who later won the Heisman Trophy after transferring to LSU and then quarterbacked for the NFL's Washington Commanders) with a black 2020 Ford Mustang GT Premium. The players get nice wheels; the dealers get good publicity. Estimating that he sold at least twenty cars thanks to this deal, Jones quipped that it's "not a losing-money venture for us."

As for the political power of auto dealers in Washington, the 2008–9 financial crisis dramatically demonstrated it.

* * *

As GM and Chrysler faced bankruptcy and received unprecedented government bailouts that totaled over $80 billion, both companies announced plans to close low-volume dealerships.

GM was expected to send termination notices to up to two thousand of its roughly six thousand U.S. dealers, while Chrysler would do the same with up to one thousand of its thirty-two hundred U.S. dealers. The planned closures came in the wake of the industry's drastically reduced sales volume: Chrysler's car sales plummeted from more than two million in 2007 to 931,000 in 2009. America's dealer network was clearly bloated; Toyota sold about the same number of cars as Chrysler through just twelve hundred dealers.

In response to the carmakers' plans, the dealers' political machine sprang into action. More than one hundred members of the National Automobile Dealers Association (NADA) met with members of Congress, asking them to intervene with the Obama administration's automobile task force on planned reductions. NADA chairman John McEleney said that his organization didn't oppose consolidation but that the administration and carmakers were moving too fast.

The political pressure forced the car companies to scale back their plans. Congress established a special arbitration system for terminated dealers, and several dealers won their cases, forcing the manufacturers to reinstate their franchises. Even scaled-back plans by the manufacturers met resistance, prompting them to backtrack, with GM reversing a third of its planned closures.

The administration's task force, which had demanded aggressive restructuring by the carmakers as a condition for receiving a taxpayer bailout, yielded to the dealers' political power. Task force members "knew there might be difficulties" with accelerating dealership closings, internal memos showed, but Treasury officials nevertheless approved both companies' scaled-back approaches.

* * *

Beer distributors and auto dealers protect their positions as middlemen in their markets through territorial rights and franchise laws. Unlike them, real estate agents protect their own positions as middlemen by controlling information—who gets to see which homes are for sale and who gets to bid on them.

America's Realtors have maintained a 5 to 6 percent commission rate for home purchases for decades, generating $100 billion in commissions a year for the 1.5 million members of the National Association of Realtors (NAR).

The Multiple Listing Service (MLS), which reportedly dates back to the late nineteenth century, is a foundational piece of the Realtors' market control. Before the internet, Realtors showed Americans homes for sale on paper from their binders. Regional or local associations, typically affiliated with NAR, collected the information in the MLS and delivered it to brokers, who shared it with would-be homebuyers. Their control over access to information about homes for sale made them indispensable intermediaries in the housing market, protecting them from potential competitors.

The internet seemed poised to revolutionize home buying by enabling buyers to do their own research online, eliminating the need for brokers. As lower-cost brokerages emerged, NAR-connected listing platforms restricted what those firms could show, leaving them unable to display a full set of property listings.

While 90 percent of homebuyers now find properties online, nearly 90 percent of them still use agents to buy their homes. Realtors cultivated a "you have to use an agent" mindset with American homebuyers, as an internal NAR report of 2015 revealed. In Australia, by contrast, buyer agents participate in as few as one in one hundred real estate sales.

Brokerages coach their Realtors to accept nothing less than the standard commission rate, which comes filled in on many forms that Realtors use with clients—and that rate has remained two to three times higher than in comparable countries like Australia, Canada, and Great Britain.

Brokerages also give their agents similar scripts to use if a client asks to negotiate a commission: "I could not cut my commission because I would not offer you less than my very best," reads one script that multiple brokerages have distributed. "If I reduce the commission to agents with potential buyers, we may not be sending the message that will get your home sold," reads another. Ultimately, studies show, brokers don't show homes to their buying clients if sellers offer lower commissions, creating a powerful market mechanism to maintain high commission rates.

In March 2024, NAR settled a class action lawsuit, *Burnett v. NAR*, which alleged anticompetitive practices. If not for NAR's rule that brokers offer only standard commission rates, many buyers wouldn't use a broker or would negotiate much lower commissions as in other developed countries, economist Craig T. Schulman had testified for the plaintiff.

The $418 million settlement required that agents no longer discuss splitting compensation on the MLS databases they use to list homes. Nevertheless, NAR, which continued to deny "any wrongdoing in connection with the MLS cooperative compensation model rule (MLS Model Rule) as part of the settlement," seemed to think that it lost the battle but not the war.

"If there's one thing I know about members," NAR president Kevin Sears said in a video message after the settlement, "they will figure out how to efficiently communicate the information to see if there will be any cooperating compensation."

* * *

With around $350 million in annual revenue in 2023, NAR is larger than two of the largest lobbying groups, the Chamber of Commerce and Business Roundtable, combined.

It spent more on federal lobbying than any other U.S. company or organization during the 2024 electoral cycle—more than the senior citizens behemoth AARP, and more than Amazon, Alphabet, and Meta combined.

NAR has strategically funded stealthily named groups like the Alliance for a Better Pennsylvania to advance its agenda without leaving obvious fingerprints. It also builds its own political bench by training real estate practitioners to run for office and investing millions to help aligned candidates win.

Thousands of Realtors serve in public office. In a 2011 article in NAR's in-house magazine titled "How and Why to Get Members Elected," an Illinois real estate association official explained how securing seats for Realtors on his local village board had proven useful on matters of land-use planning, zoning, and sign-posting rules: "It makes my job a million times easier," the official said.

They also shape policy. Consider an example from Florida. *NOTUS* reported that a 25 percent rent hike in Orlando between 2021 and 2022 pushed local officials to put a rent-control proposal before voters. Because it could lower prices and reduce tenant turnover, rent control held the potential to hurt the bottom line for Realtors. The Florida Association of Realtors sued, arguing that the proposal violated state law. A PAC largely funded by NAR poured at least $2 million into defeating the Orange County proposal.

A state appellate court ruled for the Realtors, knocking down the rent control proposal, and the state supreme court then refused to take up the case, leaving the lower court ruling in place. The association then lobbied successfully for legislation to impose a statewide ban on all local rent control ordinances, which Governor DeSantis signed into law in March 2023.

* * *

While Realtors profit by enforcing the long-standing structure of commissions and limiting access to information, doctors profit by restricting access to medical care. Specifically, they maintain their market power most effectively via artificial constraints on the number of residency positions and the ability of non-physicians to treat patients.

Medicare is the nation's primary funder of graduate medical education, providing about $16 billion a year for resident training. In the

1997 Balanced Budget Act, lawmakers froze Medicare-funded residency positions at 1996 levels (about a hundred thousand slots) as a cost-saving measure.

Doctor groups lobbied for the freeze, arguing that the nation would soon face a glut of physicians, which the cap on positions could prevent. Despite a growing U.S. population and its rising health care needs, lawmakers have raised the cap only once since then, and only by one thousand positions. By 2017, the number of doctors per thousand people in the United States was 2.6, nearly 30 percent lower than the average of 3.5 in other advanced economies.

Beyond controlling their own numbers, physicians shape regulations to limit competition from other health care professionals. State medical boards, typically dominated by doctors, have historically interpreted their authority broadly to restrict non-physician providers.

For example, nurse practitioners (NPs) face varying practice restrictions across states, with only twenty-six states and Washington, D.C., granting NPs "full practice authority" to diagnose and treat patients without physician supervision. In restricted states, NPs must maintain formal supervision agreements with physicians, often requiring that they pay for the supervision. Physician assistants (PAs) face even stricter limitations, with no state permitting fully independent PA practice.

Care costs substantially less when NPs or PAs provide it rather than physicians, studies indicate, and delivers the same health outcomes. Residents of geographic areas with more relaxed "scope-of-practice" laws (about what NPs and PAs can do) also have more access to care. The Federal Trade Commission has repeatedly warned that excessive scope-of-practice restrictions harm competition.

In most states, dentists also benefit from scope-of-practice protections, promulgated by state dental boards often comprised of practicing dentists. While dental hygienists can perform routine cleanings and X-rays, for example, they usually cannot perform diagnostic work without dentist supervision. Only Colorado and Oregon allow hygienists to do so.

* * *

Doctors and dentists wield extraordinary political influence through their professional organizations and local prominence.

The American Medical Association (AMA) and specialty medicine societies operate at both the federal and state levels, coordinating campaign contributions, grassroots mobilization, and direct lobbying.

Physicians often hold prominent positions in their communities as respected professionals and major employers. They serve on hospital boards, in local health departments, and sometimes in elected office.

So, too, do dentists. In 2022, the 162,000-member American Dental Association lobbied successfully against President Biden's proposal to include dental coverage in Medicare, despite its popularity with voters and potential to leverage Medicare's size to reduce dental costs.

The dentists, who tend to be more conservative than most other Americans, feared the lower reimbursements that Medicare would likely provide compared to what dentists ordinarily charge.

* * *

In the mid-1990s, lawmakers grew concerned that Medicare spending on physician services was rising at unsustainable rates; costs had risen an average 13.4 percent a year throughout the 1980s.

In response, the 1997 Balanced Budget Act—the same act that capped the number of residency positions—established the Medicare Sustainable Growth Rate (SGR) formula to reduce physician payment rates if total Medicare spending exceeded predetermined targets.

The SGR was designed to prevent doctor payments from growing faster than the economy. When the formula would have triggered a 4.8 percent cut in Medicare's base payment rate for doctors in 2002, and another significant cut loomed in 2003, the doctors mobilized an extraordinary lobbying effort to prevent the cuts, arguing that, without such action, they would no longer participate in Medicare.

They testified before congressional committees; met with individual lawmakers; flooded congressional offices with calls, faxes, and emails; wrote op-eds and letters to the editor; and encouraged their senior citizen patients to urge Congress to protect access to their doctors.

Due to the intense lobbying, lawmakers responded with the first installment of what became known as the "doc fix"—a temporary postponement of the mandated cuts. They enacted it eleven straight years, repeatedly postponing SGR-mandated cuts. With all the accumulated postponements, by 2015 the formula would have required a 21 percent cut to physician payments.

That year, President Obama signed the Medicare Access and CHIP Reauthorization Act, permanently scrapping the SGR. The doctors had blocked a bipartisan cost-control mechanism for over a decade and then killed it altogether.

* * *

Main Street Millionaires, of course, don't win all their political battles, whatever their industry.

Around 2006, mall kiosks and salons in North Carolina started offering quick, cheap teeth-whitening services. Using over-the-counter peroxide gels, the procedure posed little medical risk, but it undercut the hefty prices that dentists charged for in-office whitening. North Carolina's powerful State Board of Dental Examiners, comprised mostly of dentists, moved fast to shut down the upstarts.

The board sent at least forty-two cease-and-desist letters to non-dentist teeth whiteners across the state, ordering them to stop their service because they were practicing dentistry without a license. In some cases, board agents warned mall owners to evict the kiosks, chilling the business by threat of legal action.

The dentists might have succeeded if complaints by the non-dentist teeth whiteners hadn't reached federal authorities, who grew interested in the issue. The Federal Trade Commission (FTC) sued the board in 2010, arguing that dentists conspired to stifle competition for their own gain.

After years of legal battles, the U.S. Supreme Court in 2015 affirmed an appellate court ruling that the board violated antitrust laws. The decision forced the board to stop policing teeth-whitening by non-dentists.

* * *

Meanwhile, years before Elon Musk's foray into politics, Tesla (along with start-ups Lucid and Rivian) began selling electric vehicles (EVs) directly to consumers, bypassing dealerships. At the same time, traditional car manufacturers began making plans to do the same thing with their own EVs, with the Ford CEO announcing plans to sell its EVs "online with a fixed price."

In response, not surprisingly, dealers have been defending their role in car selling and fighting threats to their exclusive terrain.

"The dealer franchise system is the most consumer-friendly, efficient, and effective model of distribution for motor vehicles in the U.S.," outgoing NADA chairman Mike Alford said in 2023. "Dealers are truly essential to the future of ICE [internal combustion engines] and EVs . . . only a local dealership network can provide the personal relationship consumers want."

Battles are raging in the states. As of 2021, at least seventeen states bar direct sales to consumers, at least eighteen let manufacturers sell directly, and at least nine bar new direct sales while letting manufacturers who were already selling directly "maintain a certain number of sales locations" in their states.

But while Main Street Millionaires will continue to fight threats to their monopolies across various industries, waves of consolidation in some industries have further boosted their market power.

* * *

Across industries, federal regulators review proposed mergers to assess whether they would undermine competition. But most Main Street Millionaires often escape public or regulatory scrutiny when they seek to merge their business with another one by acquiring it.

That's because Main Street Millionaire–owned businesses tend to be too small to face the federal requirement that an acquiring firm notify antitrust regulators of a proposed merger. Those unscrutinized mergers enable firms to accumulate more market power and generate juicier profit margins while raising prices for consumers and lowering wages for workers.

In 2000, lawmakers raised the threshold—based on the assets that the acquiring firm will hold after the merger (among other standards)—for when companies must notify the Federal Trade Commission and the Justice Department's Antitrust Division of a proposed merger from $10 million to $50 million. That threshold rises each year in concert with economic growth.

As a result, premerger notifications to the Justice Department fell by 70 percent shortly after the law took effect; mergers between competitors rose by 20 percent. Legal services, funeral homes, auto dealerships, and pest control services were among the top sectors affected by the change.

In some markets, such as health care, "stealth consolidation"—i.e., mergers below the threshold for regulatory scrutiny—likely raises consumer prices. Stealth consolidation of anesthesiology practices by PE-backed companies, according to one study, raised prices by up to 35 percent. Stealth consolidation in dialysis, according to another study, boosted the concentration of that service in regional markets while driving worse health outcomes, including higher mortality rates.

By limiting choices, as per the health-related examples cited above, stealth consolidation enables Main Street Millionaire–owned businesses to accumulate more local market power, harming consumers in the process.

* * *

Across industries, Main Street Millionaires don't just compete; they conspire to write the rules of the game to protect their profits. Less competition means less innovation and higher prices, all to the detriment of consumers.

- In the case of Realtors, higher commissions translate into higher housing costs, as sellers raise home prices to cover those fees. Commissions also create skewed incentives: Buyer brokers have no financial incentive to get the best deal for their clients. Instead, both buyer and seller brokers share an interest in selling homes at higher prices and making higher commissions.
- With auto dealers, financing and repair costs are higher than they should be because dealers largely control financing and warranties. And dealers restrict competition by limiting the number of franchises in any geographic area.
- Regarding beer distributors, breweries must work through the middle tier to access customers, the cost of which passes to beer drinkers in the form of higher prices and less variety.
- The cases of doctors and dentists represent a broader pattern of professional guilds and occupational licensing rules that induce scarcity in the market for skilled services. That means longer wait times and higher prices for patients, and a less efficient health care system.

In each case, the harms are diffused among millions of consumers. The benefits, however, are concentrated among a distinct number of "large coalitions of small businesses," in the words of former Treasury Secretary Larry Summers.

When Summers coined the phrase that opens this chapter, he was reminiscing about a series of policy battles during his career, including the Obama administration's clash with auto dealers during the government's rescue of the auto manufacturers. But he was also reflecting on an even more bruising episode during the Clinton administration, when the small business lobby first sought to repeal the estate tax.

Nowhere is the stealthy power of Main Street Millionaires more prominent than in rewriting America's tax code.

12

The Loophole Lobby

I just have in my heart a real affinity for these owner-operated pass-throughs.

—Senator Ron Johnson (R-WI)

Thirty miles west of Fort Worth lies Weatherford, the self-proclaimed cutting horse capital of Texas, where farms grow the state's "biggest, sweetest, juiciest" peaches. The town is named for Thomas Jefferson Weatherford, a sawmill operator who pushed for secession as a state senator before the Civil War.

There, on Interstate 20 across from the Cracker Barrel, lies a totem of American enterprise: a car dealership with a platoon of Dodge Rams and Jeep Wranglers. As with most dealerships in north Texas, a majestic American flag, large enough to enshroud one of the megatrucks below it, towers over the lot of the Roger Williams Chrysler Dodge Jeep Ram auto dealership.

Williams, a tall, athletic man in his seventies, parts his thick silver hair down the middle, speaks with a deep Southern drawl, and extols the virtues of Main Street America. On the campaign trail, he wears a navy suit with a bright red tie over a crisp white shirt. Like many politicians, he essentially dresses as an American flag.

Born in September 1949 in Evanston, Illinois, and raised in Fort Worth, he played center field for Texas Christian University's baseball team, was named to its All-Decade Team for the 1960s, and was drafted by the Atlanta Braves. He suffered a career-ending injury, however, so he went to work for his dad, who operated the dealership that he inherited and still runs.

In his late forties, Williams started to raise money for the state's Republican politicians, including Governors George W. Bush and Rick Perry. After securing some state-level appointments, including as secretary of state, he ran for the U.S. House in 2012 and has represented Texas's Twenty-Fifth District ever since.

He uses sports analogies to talk about policy. For instance, he says, "We're playing defense" on tax policy and need to compete more aggressively against foreign rivals. He romanticizes Main Street America, characterizing America's small businesses as its greatest assets.

Williams's greatest financial asset is his auto dealership, which accounts for most of his $85 million net worth. His other assets include a $12 million mansion and a $4 million lake house. In that sense, he's merely one of the thousands of wealthy car dealers and millions of rich business owners in cities and towns from coast to coast.

But as a member of Congress, and one whom we heard from directly when we visited Washington in the fall of 2017, Williams personifies how Main Street Millionaires shape the laws and regulations that govern our society. Largely through the influence of these millionaires, lawmakers have built a two-track tax code that favors business owners over wage labor and gives them advantages at every point of taxation—from income and payroll taxes to estate planning.

"I am a second-generation small business owner, and my daughters are third-generation," he declared in a House floor speech in the spring of 2017, promoting a tax reform plan he wrote called Jumpstart America. "I understand, firsthand, the impact that unfair, job-killing taxes and regulations have on Main Street. I know what it's like to nearly lose a family business that was built from the ground up, just because the federal government believes in a death [i.e., estate] tax."

Lawmakers passed President Trump's tax cuts later that year, enacting the largest business tax cuts in U.S. history. Known as the Tax Cuts and Jobs Act, the legislation cut the top tax rate on corporate income from 35 to 21 percent, let firms write off their equipment purchases immediately rather than over several years, and created a new regime for taxing foreign source income. They also showered pass-through businesses with a big new tax cut, making many Main Street Millionaires even richer.

Then, with many of those tax cuts from 2017 set to expire at the end of 2025, Trump signed into law his One Big Beautiful Bill Act on July 4 of that year, making several key expiring provisions permanent—including the big new tax cut for pass-throughs. It also provided additional tax perks for businesses such as Williams's.

The act culminated a multi-decade effort by lawmakers to tilt the tax code to the benefit of Main Street Millionaires. Whether as legislators or lobbyists, these business owners have won new tax breaks to grow their businesses, keep more of their profits, and pass on wealth to their heirs tax-free.

* * *

Early in the postwar era, entrepreneurs faced two options in structuring their businesses.

They could form traditional C corporations, which would give them liability protection but force them to pay both corporate taxes on their earnings and dividend taxes on their payouts to owners. Or they could create partnerships or sole proprietorships to avoid that double taxation, but they wouldn't have liability protection and would have to pay higher individual income tax rates.

With the 1986 Tax Reform Act, lawmakers cut both individual and corporate tax rates but, for the first time in U.S. history, set the top individual rate (28 percent) below the corporate rate (35 percent). In ensuing years, lawmakers continued cutting taxes for individuals and businesses and also for estates, capital gains, and dividends. In addition, they gave business owners still more tax breaks.

Pass-through owners benefited greatly. In recent decades, federal lawmakers gave pass-throughs a 20 percent income deduction, meaning that they don't pay taxes on a fifth of their business income. They enabled pass-through owners to avoid paying Medicare payroll taxes.

They made it easier for these owners to classify their businesses as pass-throughs, and they ruled that limited liability companies could be taxed as pass-throughs rather than as corporations. Meanwhile, many states enabled pass-through owners to sidestep the federal limit on how much they can deduct in state and local taxes.

That's not all. Employers report the incomes of their employees to the IRS, but business owners have flexibility to hide their own incomes. At the same time, IRS audit rates for S corporations and partnerships have fallen by more than 40 percent since 2010. Now, the IRS audits fewer than one in five hundred of them each year. Audit rates have declined dramatically in large part because lawmakers have sliced the IRS budget, forcing sizable staff cuts.

More than at any recent time, the tax code for pass-throughs runs on the honor system, with predictable results. The IRS estimates that the "tax gap" (the taxes owed that taxpayers haven't paid) totaled $600 billion in 2022, and the income and self-employment taxes that pass-through owners haven't paid accounted for 44 percent of it.

* * *

What businesses can write off from their income greatly shapes the bottom line of Main Street Millionaires.

These millionaires have long benefited from special investment provisions, Section 179 expensing and bonus depreciation, which enable them to write off the cost of equipment and capital investments far more quickly—and generously—than ordinary accounting rules would suggest.

Take, for example, a plastics manufacturer. It might invest heavily each year in new equipment: precision extrusion machines, industrial packaging systems, and forklifts for the factory floor. With the tax code's investment incentives, it can deduct most of the cost of these purchases immediately.

Section 179 is a supercharged incentive that lets firms write off the entire cost of their eligible investments. It has always excluded the largest companies from eligibility, but the definition of "small" has grown more generous over time. Initially in the 1990s, it was targeted to very small firms, with a maximum write-off of $17,500 in eligible investments. Lawmakers gradually raised that threshold to make it much more generous for mid-market companies and, in 2025, boosted it to a whopping $2.5 million. A business doing that much investment would typically be worth more than $10 million and perhaps more than $100 million.

Promoting investment is economically useful, but depreciation incentives highlight the difficulty in maintaining what tax insiders call guardrails to prevent private business from finding new ways to avoid taxes. Consider the Hummer tax loophole. In 1984, lawmakers prohibited business deductions for cars but not heavy-duty vehicles, hoping to exclude nonbusiness consumption while ensuring that farmers and construction workers could deduct the cost of heavy vehicles. In response, many Main Street Millionaires bought Suburbans, F-250s, and Hummers, which qualified for the deduction—and which are hard to monitor in terms of their business and nonbusiness usage.

More broadly, lax rules and incomplete enforcement enable business owners to buy a long list of items through their company; they can, for instance, deduct their home office, phone bills, business travel, continuing education, medical reimbursement plans, and retirement accounts.

"Owning a small business," says Mitchell Baldridge, cofounder of Better Bookkeeping, "is the best tax deal in America."

That "best tax deal" did not happen by accident. Rather, Main Street Millionaires have been working for decades to secure it.

* * *

No battle better illustrates Main Street Millionaires' political influence than their long and successful campaign to eviscerate the estate tax.

Established in 1916, the estate tax was designed to prevent wealth concentration across generations. For most of the twentieth century, it affected a substantial number of business-owning families. In 1976, estates worth at least about $60,000 (about $340,000 in 2025 dollars) faced taxation, with rates reaching as high as 77 percent on the largest fortunes.

But a carefully orchestrated campaign, funded by wealthy pass-through owners like the Mars family (candy) and Fred Meijer (supermarkets) fundamentally transformed public perceptions of this tax. Frank Blethen, owner of *The Seattle Times*, created a website called deathtax.com to help rebrand the estate tax as the "death tax"—portraying it as an unfair penalty on hardworking Americans when they die rather than a check on intergenerational wealth concentration.

As Michael Graetz and Ian Shapiro detail in *Death by a Thousand Cuts: The Fight over Taxing Inherited Wealth*, the campaign proved remarkably effective. In 2001, President George W. Bush signed legislation that gradually increased what was then the $675,000 threshold for facing the estate tax and cut the top rate, culminating in a one-year full repeal in 2010. That year, Dan Duncan, a Houston pipeline tycoon worth $9 billion, died and thus became perhaps the wealthiest American in more than a century to pass on his entire fortune without paying a penny in federal estate taxes.

The estate tax returned in 2011, but the exemption threshold has continued to rise. By 2025, individuals could pass $15 million ($30 million for married couples) to their heirs entirely tax-free—amounts around ninety times higher than the inflation-adjusted exemptions from the 1970s.

Main Street Millionaires also developed sophisticated strategies to minimize even these reduced tax obligations. As tax law scholar Daniel Hemel has argued, a host of techniques with complex names—e.g., family limited partnerships, grantor retained annuity trusts (GRATs), installment sales to intentionally defective grantor trusts—serve a simple purpose: to transfer wealth while avoiding or minimizing taxes on it. These strategies are particularly effective for transferring family businesses. As it turns out, the Karns family, whom we met in chapter 8, are hardly alone when it comes to transitioning a business to an heir and minimizing the tax impact.

These sophisticated strategies remain the domain of the wealthiest Americans, requiring teams of high-priced attorneys, accountants, and wealth managers. Due to the elevated thresholds and avoidance strategies, only about 0.1 percent of all estates now face any estate tax at all.

Or, as Gary Cohn, former Goldman Sachs executive and Trump's top economic adviser in his first term, put it: "Only morons pay the estate tax."

* * *

The Meijer family illustrates how Main Street Millionaires preserve their fortunes across generations.

Hendrik Meijer, a Dutch immigrant barber, founded the grocery chain by opening his first store in 1934. His son Fred expanded the business into a retail empire across the Midwest that was worth billions. To ensure beforehand that much of Fred's fortune would pass to his heirs with minimal taxation when he died, the Meijer family established a complex web of trusts. By assigning slices of the business to different legal owners, these trusts also enabled the family to claim that the business as a whole was worth less than it really was—perhaps by 30 percent or more (due to minority owner discounts).

Heirs of Main Street Millionaires also enjoy the crucial tax-law advantage of "stepped-up basis." When business owners die, the tax basis of their businesses and other assets is "stepped up" to the value of those assets at the time of their death. That enables their heirs to avoid taxes on decades or even generations of unrealized capital gains on that higher value of their assets. When combined with strategies to avoid the estate tax, heirs can sell their inherited assets immediately without paying a penny in capital gains tax or continue watching those assets appreciate in value even more. Main Street Millionaires benefit the most from this policy: two-thirds of unrealized capital gains among households with at least $50 million in wealth comes from their private business wealth.

The wealthiest Americans pass on around $200 billion a year to their heirs without triggering the estate tax, driving a dramatic shift in who bears tax burdens in America. Wage earners, meanwhile, face inescapable taxation through withholding on every paycheck.

"You have an army of well-trained, brilliant people who sit there all day long, charging $1,000 an hour, thinking up ways to beat [the estate] tax," tax expert Jack Bogdanski observes. "Don't expect anyone in Congress to stop this."

Especially when so many in Congress are set to benefit personally from these tax changes.

* * *

When President Trump and Republican congressional leaders began crafting their big tax cut in 2017, they initially focused most heavily on cutting the corporate tax rate from 35 to 20 percent.

The corporate tax dates back to 1909, when lawmakers imposed a 1 percent levy on corporate income above $5,000. Over the years, presidents and congresses gradually raised the rate so that by 1968, it sat at 52.8 percent and generated around a quarter of federal revenues. In ensuing decades, lawmakers cut the top rate to 35 percent, where it stood until Trump and his allies went to work.

Around the world in recent decades, countries have lowered their corporate tax rates in the hope of attracting multinational businesses to establish headquarters or factories within their borders. That left the United States with a relatively high corporate tax rate—in fact, one of the highest among Western industrialized nations—raising concerns among some lawmakers and economists that U.S. businesses were struggling to compete around the world. With a lower corporate tax rate, they argued, U.S.-based multinationals not only would be more competitive but they also wouldn't be as tempted to shift their operations and jobs to low-tax countries.

With Trump and congressional Republicans destined to cut the corporate rate, the "small business" lobby—led by groups like the National Federation of Independent Business (NFIB) and the S Corporation Association—campaigned aggressively to secure comparable tax relief for pass-throughs, though it rarely noted that many pass-throughs reap millions or even billions in annual profits.

* * *

In early October 2017, as Republicans were rushing to finish their work before the end of the year, Stanford economist Ed Lazear was trying to inject some rational economic analysis into the policy process. The former chair of President George W. Bush's Council of Economic Advisers, Lazear enlisted ten tax economists to advise GOP lawmakers on how best to shape what would become the biggest business tax cut in U.S. history.

At the time—three years after our first foray into the Treasury Department basement—our research about the rise of pass-through businesses and their Main Street Millionaire owners was gaining traction in academic circles and beyond. We circulated research papers among economists, tax experts, and others inside and outside government, and we spoke about our findings on public panels. Perhaps most heartening, top policymakers in the White House and Congress were struck enough by our work to propose that government reform how we treat pass-throughs.

As the recognized academic experts on pass-throughs, we joined Lazear's delegation and returned to Washington. We hoped to learn more about the tax policymaking process and, if we could, improve tax policy itself. Then we learned who's really setting tax policy in America.

Most members of our delegation were seasoned tax policy veterans, including Stanford's Michael Boskin, the mustachioed former chair of President George H. W. Bush's Council of Economic Advisers; Donald Marron, director of the nonpartisan Urban-Brookings Tax Policy Center; and Columbia Law School's Michael Graetz, a bearded, motorcycle-riding former assistant Treasury secretary.

Lazear, a man of infectious charm and enthusiasm, had recruited Mike Franc to work as Washington director of Stanford University's Hoover Institution. Former policy director for then–House Majority

Leader Kevin McCarthy, Franc set up a full schedule of meetings for us. Over two days, we met with virtually every tax policymaker of consequence (and plenty of other lawmakers) in Washington.

When we gathered for a preliminary working dinner, Lazear asked each of us for a best guess of how much the emerging Republican tax plan would boost the economy. The forecasts ranged from 0.1 to 2.0 percentage points of annual GDP growth, a range wide enough to encompass all plausible outcomes. He then asked each of us for one concrete policy idea to improve the plan.

* * *

We first met with Trump's top economic team in the Roosevelt Room of the White House, across the hall from the Oval Office.

President Nixon gave the room its name to honor Teddy and Franklin Roosevelt, who were fifth cousins of each other, and portraits of each adorn the walls. One chair, built slightly taller than the others, is reserved at the center of the conference table for the president. He did not attend that meeting, but his two top economic advisers did. Steve Mnuchin and Gary Cohn were both former Goldman Sachs executives who were now serving as, respectively, the Treasury secretary and the National Economic Council director.

Cohn outlined the administration's priorities for the corporate rate cut: the lower, the better. Our delegation suggested ways to design the tax cut narrowly and avoid creating massive new loopholes for pass-through business owners. Mnuchin proudly announced their plan to build guardrails to prevent such tax avoidance. The old guard within our delegation—seasoned by decades of tax policy written by overconfident policymakers—expressed skepticism. Cohn then asked all of us to help enact the rate cut by writing supportive op-eds (some did; we did not). It seemed as though what the administration wanted was not advice so much as support for its existing plans.

The day after our chat with Cohn and Mnuchin, we were on Capitol Hill from morning to evening, hearing the concerns of Republican lawmakers while trying to impart some tax policy wisdom.

* * *

"All bills for raising revenue shall originate in the House of Representatives," the U.S. Constitution dictates. In that chamber, those bills are drafted by the Ways and Means Committee—Congress's oldest committee, established in 1789, the first year of George Washington's presidency.

We met with about a hundred Republican lawmakers and staff in Room HC-5, a conference room in the basement of the Capitol where the House Republican conference met every week as a group. Lawmakers and staff from Ways and Means were heavily represented, but plenty of other Republicans with a keen interest in the pending tax bill were on hand as well.

Our delegation sat up front and Kevin Brady—the bald, stocky Ways and Means chairman who worked for more than one local chamber of commerce in Texas before running for Congress—introduced us to the throng. Lazear then skipped to the lectern and called on a few of us to offer our thoughts. Among other things, the two of us said that lawmakers should not shower pass-throughs with more tax breaks, since the benefits would flow overwhelmingly to wealthy business owners. Lazear then opened the floor for discussion.

Roger Williams, the rich auto dealer from Weatherford, loudly objected to the pending bill as a threat to his business, and by extension, the auto industry. He explained to us that his family dealership borrows lots of money to finance his fleet. The impending tax proposal would have scaled back some business tax write-offs to reduce its overall cost, such as by limiting the ability of businesses like his dealership to deduct their interest expenses.

Williams was hardly the only House Republican to express his concerns, nor was this the only meeting during which we would hear them.

* * *

At a dinner that evening at the Capitol Hill Club, a Republican hangout, Rep. Devin Nunes, a farmer and businessman who represented

California's Twenty-Second District, near Fresno, told us that he couldn't go back to his district and say that he got a big tax cut for big companies like Facebook but nothing for "the little guy." Other representatives expressed similar concerns.

But which "little guy" were they talking about: the "little guy" who runs a mom-and-pop shop or a local "small business" owner who owns a very successful pass-through? The two are hardly equivalent in their ability to pay taxes. But our discussions in Washington indicated that many lawmakers consider all pass-throughs to be "small businesses"—including multibillion-dollar companies like Fidelity, the investment manager; Hobby Lobby, the retail chain; and Mars, the maker of M&M's, Skittles, and other well-known candies.

At that dinner, when we noted that many of these "small" businesses actually are not small, no one wanted to talk about it.

We reminded them that, based on the Treasury Department's definition of businesses with incomes below $10 million, less than 20 percent of pass-through income is really earned by small businesses and that 70 cents of every dollar that pass-throughs earn accrues to America's top 1 percent in income. But these facts didn't seem to carry much weight with the assembled lawmakers.

If Nunes and his colleagues really wanted to help "the little guy," we knew several ways to do it without giving away the store to huge companies like Fidelity and Mars. For starters, they could permit firms to write off investments only up to a certain dollar amount, so that the big companies with the means to invest substantial funds would not benefit disproportionately from the write-off.

* * *

"If they can pass it without me, let them," Wisconsin's Republican senator Ron Johnson told *The Wall Street Journal* in November 2017 after Senate Republicans unveiled their version of the tax legislation.

With Republicans controlling just fifty-two seats in the hundred-member chamber, and with a few other Republicans expressing their own concerns, Johnson's suggestion could help kill the bill.

Republican leaders were stunned; the business community was panicked. And across Wisconsin, Johnson's wealthiest donors waited to see whether their investment in his political career would pay off. What few people understood was that Johnson's stand was most likely less about principle than profits—the profits of pass-through businesses like the one that had made him rich.

Born in 1955 and raised in Mankato, Minnesota, Johnson studied business accounting at the University of Minnesota, earning his degree in 1977—the same year he married his college sweetheart, Jane Curler. Jane's father, Howard Curler, was a well-known plastics industry executive. Johnson moved to Oshkosh, Wisconsin, a manufacturing hub on the western shores of Lake Winnebago, in 1979 to help his brother-in-law, Pat Curler, launch a new polyester plastics company, Pacur (named for Curler and for the NFL's Green Bay Packers).

Pacur set up shop adjacent to the Bemis packaging plant that Howard Curler was overseeing. For the first few years, Bemis was Pacur's only customer. Johnson started out as Pacur's accountant—running extrusion machines on the factory floor when needed—while brother-in-law Pat served as its president. "It was an opportunity for [Pat Curler] to get into business for himself, and I just kind of came along for the ride as the accountant," Johnson recalled.

Through the 1980s, Pacur grew into a profitable maker of specialty plastic sheeting. After Pat Curler sold Pacur to a larger plastics manufacturer in the mid-1980s, the company retained Johnson as chief executive to oversee the company's growth. In 1997, he bought the business back, returning it to family ownership.

After thirty years in business, Johnson's free-market, small-government philosophy propelled him into politics in 2010.

* * *

Johnson "would not have run for the U.S. Senate," he said in an interview with CNS News, "had Obamacare not been passed."

Johnson's first child, Carey, was born with a severe heart defect that required innovative surgery to save her life. He believes that it was America's excellent private health care system—the "miracles of modern medicine"—that saved her, and he worried that a government takeover of health care would stifle the innovation that helped his family. More broadly, he was alarmed by what he viewed as excessive federal spending and regulation in the wake of the 2008 financial crisis.

Johnson began speaking at Tea Party events, where his criticism of "federal overreach" and growing budget deficits resonated with audiences. In 2010, he launched a Senate campaign, styling himself as a straight-talking businessman determined to clean up government. He stepped back from day-to-day management of Pacur, giving the reins to his younger brother, Barry, and other longtime employees so he could run for office. That November, Johnson rode the Tea Party wave into the Senate, stunning the political establishment by upsetting incumbent Democrat Russ Feingold.

In the Senate, Johnson portrayed himself as the guy from the Oshkosh plastics plant, and he cultivated a reputation for bucking party leaders if a Republican proposal didn't meet his commonsense, cost-conscious standards. As of 2018, he was the Senate's sixth-richest member, worth around $40 million.

In 2017, his demand for supporting the tax bill was straightforward: It must significantly reduce taxes for pass-through businesses. "I just have in my heart a real affinity for these owner-operated pass-throughs," he told *The New York Times*. He neglected to mention what was tugging on that heartstring—the millions at stake for both his family and his top campaign donors.

* * *

Johnson's most generous donors stood to benefit handsomely from his ultimatum.

Dick and Liz Uihlein of the shipping company Uline, whom we met in chapter 10, and Diane Hendricks, cofounder of the building products distributor ABC Supply Co., contributed about $20 million to pro-Johnson groups during his 2016 reelection campaign. The Uihleins gave more than $8 million to political committees that blanketed Wisconsin with pro-Johnson ads, prompting the *Milwaukee Journal Sentinel* to dub them "the Koch brothers of Wisconsin politics." Hendricks provided around $12 million to committees supporting Johnson.

The senator also acted as a conduit for other wealthy business owners seeking changes to the legislation. "Dear Ron," Wisconsin developer and Johnson donor Ted Kellner and a colleague wrote to him, "I'm concerned that the goal of a fair, efficient and growth oriented tax overhaul will not be achieved, especially for private real estate pass-through entities." Johnson forwarded the letter to top House and Senate Republicans and added his own note: "Yesterday, I received this letter from very smart and successful businessmen in Milwaukee," noting that the bill as it stood gave pass-throughs "widely disparate, grossly unfair" treatment. "Senator," House Ways and Means Chairman Kevin Brady replied, "I strongly agree we should continue to improve the pass-through provisions at every step. You are a *great* champion for this."

Within two weeks of Johnson's ultimatum, Trump called the senator to lobby for his support and Republicans drafting the Senate bill raised the tax cut for pass-through businesses—from their original proposal to let owners deduct up to 17.4 percent of their profits to a new proposal of 20 percent. That 2.6 percentage point increase would mean tens of millions more in tax savings for some of the nation's wealthiest business owners.

This provision, which became a new Section 199A of the tax code, created a lower tax rate for business profits than for wages that employees earn by doing the same work. The owner-manager of a pass-through would pay much less tax than the salaried CEO of an identical C corporation. It would cost the federal government an estimated $415 billion in lost revenues over 10 years.

After securing these changes, Johnson helped Senate Republicans pass the final bill along party lines. "I was not a big fan of the Tax Cuts and Jobs Act," Johnson later recalled, "especially as it came out of the House where all they were doing was cutting taxes for C corps, [which are] 5 percent of American businesses. Ninety-five percent of

American businesses would have been completely hosed . . . so I'm the guy that screamed about that and dug my heels in and made sure that not only the 80 percent smaller pass-throughs got a tax cut, but also that all the pass-throughs got a tax cut."

The administration championed the provision as tax relief for small businesses, but the reality was quite different. Those making more than $1 million in annual income reaped more than a third of the billions in tax savings, a Treasury study found, and most of that went to the top 0.1 percent.

Consider the Uihleins. Uline generated nearly $1 billion in profits in 2018. On their 2018 taxes, they reported more than $700 million in income, took a $118 million deduction as a pass-through, and reduced their taxes by $43.5 million. Also that year, Hendricks reported $502 million in income and took a $97 million deduction, saving $36 million in taxes.

In 2018, just eighty-two ultrawealthy households collectively walked away with tax savings of more than $1 billion. Special tax benefits for pass-through businesses, however, didn't end with Section 199A.

* * *

In the final days of crafting the tax bill, Republican lawmakers inserted language that specifically benefited real estate investors with few employees but significant property holdings.

The provision was not included in either the House or Senate versions of the bill; GOP drafters inserted it in the final negotiated legislation. It let owners of income-producing real estate holdings take advantage of the pass-through deduction even if they didn't pay significant wages to employees—thus creating a special tax break for landlords and real estate investors.

Tennessee's Bob Corker, the only Republican senator to vote against the Senate version of the bill due to concerns that it would increase budget deficits, changed his mind and supported the final bill after this provision was added. The timing raised eyebrows because Corker, a commercial real estate mogul himself, stood to benefit personally from the change. In 2016, federal filings showed, Corker earned between $1.2 million and $7 million of rental income from real estate–related LLCs whose properties were valued at around $26 million.

Days before his switch, Corker had been "summoning administration officials and economists to his office" to see whether they could convince him to support the legislation. Asked about his change of heart, he said, "On one hand, you had the deficit issue. On the other hand, you had the economic growth issue. I took a long walk on Friday morning and just decided that from the standpoint of, if I were the deciding vote on this . . . is our country better with this or not better with it? And I feel that we are."

Critics dubbed the controversial provision the "Corker kickback," but he insisted, "I had obviously nothing whatsoever to do with that and I think that's part of the public record." Both Brady and Orrin Hatch, chairman of the Senate Finance Committee, stood by him. "To claim that Sen. Corker had anything to do with it, in my view, is baloney," Brady said, while Hatch said he was "disgusted" by news reports to the contrary.

Corker wasn't the only senator with real estate interests who benefited from the new tax break. So, too, did Senator Steve Daines, a Montana Republican who co-owns a real estate development company with Governor Greg Gianforte.

Whether or not GOP drafters specifically designed the Corker kickback to win his vote, it represented yet another tax break for wealthy business owners at the expense of the nation's fiscal health—a break that directly benefited those with the power to rewrite the tax code.

* * *

While creating the new 20 percent deduction for pass-throughs, Republicans also expanded the substantial tax advantages that were already in place for Main Street Millionaires.

Most working Americans have Medicare payroll taxes withheld from every paycheck. Most workers pay 1.45 percent of their wages in Medicare payroll taxes, while high-income earners pay that and another 0.9 percent. In addition, Medicare imposes a 3.8 percent surcharge on net investment income or adjusted gross income above certain income thresholds, whichever is lower.

Even before the 2017 tax cuts, wealthy business owners created a sneaky way to reduce their Medicare payroll tax burden. Dubbed the "Gingrich-Edwards loophole" after the politicians who exploited it—former House Speaker Newt Gingrich and former Senator John Edwards—the owners of S corporations classified their income as business profits to avoid paying those taxes. These owners pay themselves an artificially low "reasonable salary" and take the rest of their earnings as business distributions.

Consider Gingrich, who organized his media empire, Gingrich Productions, as an S corporation. While the company generated more than $3 million in income in 2010, Gingrich paid himself a salary of just $450,000 and treated nearly $2.5 million as S corporation profits, saving him an estimated $69,000 in Medicare taxes that year alone.

Edwards was a personal injury attorney before he ran for office. In the mid-'90s, he incorporated his practice as an S corporation, "John R. Edwards, P.A.," with himself as the sole shareholder. His firm earned nearly $27 million over four years before his election to the Senate in 1998, but he paid himself only $360,000 a year. He characterized the residual—more than $25 million—as business profits, saving around $600,000 in taxes.

The 2017 tax cuts made this loophole even more beneficial to pass-through owners. With the new 20 percent deduction on pass-through income, pass-through owners have even more incentive to reclassify their earnings as business profits; they not only pay less on their pass-through earnings but they also escape Medicare payroll taxes on whatever they classify that way.

For 2000, Treasury Inspector General for Tax Administration Pamela Gardiner found, 36,000 single-shareholder S corporations each reported profits of $100,000 or more (totaling $13 billion) on which they didn't pay any Social Security or Medicare taxes. In our own analysis, we found that after switching from C corporation to S corporation status, businesses in capital-light sectors like lawyers, doctors, and dentists increased their profit margins by 4 to 6 percent of sales while reducing their wage payments by the same amount. So, by transforming their practices into S corporations, doctors avoided paying Medicare taxes even as Medicare paid them for treating Medicare beneficiaries.

When, under President Biden, Democrats tried to close this loophole in 2021 as part of their Build Back Better bill, business groups launched an aggressive counterattack. The National Federation of Independent Business ran radio ads to pressure West Virginia's Democratic senator, Joe Manchin, to oppose the measure, claiming it was "a brand-new tax on West Virginia small businesses" and warning it "would have a devastating impact on Main Street and threaten jobs."

In the Inflation Reduction Act, which Biden pushed through Congress a year later along party lines, the proposal to close the loophole was nowhere to be found. In what Jason Furman, who had chaired President Obama's Council of Economic Advisers, called "100 percent political fear," lawmakers deferred to business owners over fiscal responsibility and tax fairness.

* * *

The effort to shower pass-throughs with more benefits extended beyond Washington and into the states.

Seeking to limit the cost of their 2017 tax cuts, Republicans included a provision to put a $10,000 cap on federal deductions of state and local taxes (SALT)—raising taxes on high-income taxpayers in high-tax states. Such tax increases on well-to-do taxpayers were beyond the pale for many state lawmakers.

Connecticut was the first state to let pass-through owners (but not individuals with wage income) sidestep the cap, pioneering an approach that spread nationwide. Other states quickly followed. By 2023, thirty-six out of the forty-one states with a state income tax had implemented

SALT work-arounds. Conservative states like Utah and Kansas joined liberal states like California and New York. In essence, state officials gave their high-income constituents federal tax relief without reducing state revenues. The approach became so popular that business associations lobbied the remaining states to adopt similar provisions.

Meanwhile, the Trump Treasury Department officially sanctioned these work-arounds for pass-throughs in late 2020, giving states carte blanche to maintain them. The work-arounds, the Tax Policy Center estimated, would cost the federal government $20 billion a year in lost revenue. Meanwhile, high-income wage earners remained subject to the $10,000 cap; they received no comparable tax relief.

Consider the case of two Illinois anesthesiologists who each make $900,000 a year. One earns it all as salary; the other owns a pass-through. Both doctors owe $44,550 in Illinois state income tax, given the state's 4.95 percent income tax rate.

- Under the federal SALT cap, the salaried W-2 doctor can deduct only $10,000 of this amount on her federal return, costing her about $12,778 more in federal taxes (assuming she's in the 37 percent tax bracket).
- The business-owning anesthesiologist, by contrast, can pay the Illinois pass-through entity tax (PTET) through her S corporation, shifting the $44,550 in state tax liability to her business return, where it becomes fully deductible. She still receives a credit on her personal state return. She deducts all $44,550, and she doesn't pay the $12,778 in additional federal taxes that her counterpart pays.

* * *

In the 2017 tax cuts that Congress eventually passed along party lines, big corporations got their tax cut. But, notwithstanding Mnuchin's assurances, so did the little (and not so little) guys. Mnuchin's guardrails prevented high-earning lawyers and doctors from securing massive new tax cuts, but not millions of pass-through owners in other industries. The guardrails bent—and in many cases broke—under pressure from the very business owners they were meant to constrain.

And tucked in the bill was another indication of the power of pass-through business: a carve-out to protect interest deductions for floor-plan financing for auto dealers like Roger Williams.

Eight years later, many of the tax breaks that Main Street Millionaires secured in 2017 were set to expire. A newly emboldened Republican congressional majority, buoyed by Trump's return to the White House, pushed through a package of tax cuts and spending cuts in the One Big Beautiful Bill Act (OBBBA). The act spent around $4 trillion over ten years, extending and expanding individual income tax cuts. It spent another $1 trillion on business provisions as well as on other new tax cuts and spending. To offset some of these cuts, OBBBA reduced spending on Medicaid and food stamps by a little over $1 trillion.

The act made permanent the centerpiece of the tax breaks for Main Street Millionaires—the 20 percent deduction for pass-through business income. It also doubled the estate tax exemption and the enhanced expensing provisions for business investment. The expiration of these provisions would have ended a set of policies that quietly transferred hundreds of billions of dollars to the wealthiest business owners.

The House-Senate negotiations to iron out a final bill in 2025 required some shabby dealmaking on both tax and spending provisions. Alaska's Republican senator Lisa Murkowski, whose vote was decisive, called the process "awful" and the result flawed. Yet she still voted yes after securing some new tax perks for her constituents—such as a "supersized deduction for business meals, though only for employees at certain Alaskan fishing boats and processing plants."

The 2025 debate showed who's really powerful among the wealthy, and who isn't. The media and public rightly scrutinize Elon Musk's controversial role in the Trump administration but, on the tax bill, his power was vastly overstated in comparison to that of Main Street Millionaires.

OBBBA scaled back electric vehicle benefits and clean energy credits drastically, making Musk a clear loser. Car dealers meanwhile received tax cuts through the lower top tax rate, the pass-through provisions, the SALT cap work-arounds, and a new deduction for people who borrow to buy a new car.

* * *

After the House passed its version of the tax bill in the spring of 2025, House Speaker Mike Johnson appeared on NBC's *Meet the Press* to promote the legislation.

When host Kristen Welker asked Johnson why lawmakers needed to make permanent the 2017 tax rate cut for the nation's wealthiest individuals, the speaker's response was revealing:

"This is not giving tax cuts to millionaires, it's the opposite," he said. "The people in the tax bracket that you're referring to, many of them are small business owners. They are the people that provide the jobs in every community in America. They use pass-through taxation, and we don't get in the weeds, we don't have time to get in the complications of it."

Were Johnson to "get in the weeds," he'd discover that the owners of most pass-through firms are not small business owners. They're Main Street Millionaires who hardly needed more tax cuts to get by. But Johnson may well have known all that.

In his financial disclosure form, the Louisiana Republican listed a negative net worth in 2018, telling *Fox News* viewers, "I'm a man of modest means."

While in Washington in 2025, however, Johnson lived in a six-bedroom, $3.7 million town house that sat just steps from his office on Capitol Hill. It was owned not by him but by Lee Beaman, a Republican donor from Nashville who reaped millions when he inherited an auto dealership empire.

Epilogue

The Age of Millionaires

Are we in a new Gilded Age?

—Rep. Mark Sanford (R-SC), former governor of South Carolina, October 2017

In Newport, Rhode Island, a walking trail stretches three and a half miles around the southern cliffs of the picturesque waterfront, from Easton's Beach to Bailey's Beach. Turn to the east and you look out over Easton Bay as it feeds into the Atlantic Ocean. Turn to the west and you face a series of multi-acre estates that feature summer "cottages" from the Gilded Age.

In 1885, thirty-six-year-old William Vanderbilt inherited $55 million (around $1.9 billion in 2025 dollars) and set out to build the "very best living accommodations money could buy." Three years and a half-million cubic feet of marble later, his $11 million "Marble House" was completed in Newport. (Not to be outdone, William's older brother Cornelius, who inherited $70 million, would commission an even larger mansion, now known as The Breakers.)

To enter the Marble House, you must open sixteen-foot glass doors that each weigh one ton. Images of Greek and Roman gods abound. Some rooms are literally gilded: the "Gold Room" was hand-painted with 24-karat gold. When it was in operation, a staff of thirty-six served residents and guests.

The house was spectacular enough to serve as the setting for *The*

Great Gatsby, the 1974 movie adaptation of F. Scott Fitzgerald's iconic novel that starred Robert Redford, Mia Farrow, and Sam Waterston. Its architect, Richard Morris Hunt, incorporated classic signatures of the Beaux Arts style, which he learned while training in Paris at the École des Beaux-Arts.

It is the mansions of Newport, built by the Vanderbilts and other superrich Americans more than a century ago, that best exemplify the massive wealth, architectural grandeur, and ostentatious displays of that period.

Those mansions, however, reinforce notions about wealth in America that, while once true, no longer are—that wealth is concentrated in relatively few hands, that the rich live almost entirely on the coasts, and that the path to wealth and power most assuredly runs through finance and technology.

* * *

"Are we in a new Gilded Age?" Mark Sanford, the former South Carolina governor who was then a House Republican member, asked us when we met with House Republicans in the fall of 2017.

By then, many journalists, pundits, and scholars had long answered in the affirmative. Way back in 2000, *The New Yorker* wrote a series of essays about the "New Gilded Age." Eight years later, political scientist Larry Bartels titled his book *Unequal Democracy: The Political Economy of the New Gilded Age*, describing how inequality affects politics. "The first Gilded Age saw massive wealth inequalities, hyperpartisanship, virulent anti-immigrant sentiment and growing concern about money in politics," historian Edward O'Donnell intoned in September 2023. "Sound familiar?" he asked.

Reviewing Thomas Piketty's landmark bestseller, *Capital in the Twenty-First Century*, *New York Times* columnist Paul Krugman wrote in 2014, "It has become commonplace to say that we are living in a second Gilded Age." Krugman, also a Nobel laureate and longtime Princeton professor of economics, reiterated this conventional wisdom in a 2025 essay.

At first blush, you might think that all those commentators were right. Just as in the Gilded Age, our age has witnessed widening inequality as well as exorbitant and growing wealth at the top.

In the 1910s, the 37,000 households in the highest-earning 0.1 percent (those with at least $640,000 in annual income in 2022 dollars) earned nearly 10 percent of the nation's total income. Households in the top 1 percent (with at least $100,000 in 2022 dollars) earned 18 percent of all income. That left the bottom 90 percent (with less than $34,000 in 2022 dollars) with just 60 percent of all income.

Similarly, in 2022, the 180,000 households in the top 0.1 percent (those with at least $2.3 million in annual income) earned nearly 10 percent of total income. Households in the top 1 percent (with at least $550,000) earned 20 percent. That left the 160 million households in the bottom 90 percent (with less than $155,400) with only half of all income.

Beyond inequality, however, the differences between the Gilded Age and today are as striking as the similarities. After comparing the Gilded Age with ours, we concluded that the nation is now living not in a second Gilded Age but in its first Age of Millionaires.

In this Age of Millionaires, the American Dream remains alive but achieving it is harder than it used to be. High-profile billionaires who get so much attention have less political power than you might think, while Main Street Millionaires wield far more.

We can take steps to reduce inequality and expand opportunity. We also can and should hold Main Street Millionaires accountable when they wield their power unfairly.

* * *

The end of the Civil War in 1865 ushered in the Gilded Age, an era of grand opulence and enormous political influence at the top.

Domestic peace helped expand the Industrial Revolution. Business leaders made the most of new opportunities, new markets, and new technology to amass great fortunes. The top wealth reflected the economy of the time, dominated by capital-intensive industry, transportation, natural resources, and real estate. As heavy industry sought to finance its expansion, the banking sector grew as well.

Rising globalization nurtured the need to transport goods and people across large distances. In stepped Cornelius "the Commodore" Vanderbilt, who built a shipping and then a railroad empire, creating a coast-to-coast transportation network. Meanwhile, the growing energy demands of both families and factories made oilman John D. Rockefeller the richest American of the era.

Rockefeller consolidated control of the booming oil industry through acquisition. By 1890, Standard Oil controlled nearly 90 percent of the nation's oil market. At its peak, Rockefeller's wealth may have amounted to as much as $650 billion in 2025 dollars. (To put that figure in perspective, the wealth of Elon Musk—the world's richest man—was reportedly around $840 billion in February 2026.)

In his 1889 book, *The Owners of the United States*, Thomas Shearman listed the nation's richest people and concluded that wealth concentration rivaled or exceeded the levels in Great Britain and other European aristocracies. Along with Vanderbilt and Rockefeller, members of the Astor family (sometimes called the "landlords of New York" due to their real estate holdings) figure prominently. Also included are the Morgans, whose banks stepped in to steady the economy during financial crises before policymakers created the Federal Reserve in 1913.

It wasn't just famous industrialists and real estate titans who grew rich. Lesser-known manufacturing moguls also built fortunes. O. C. Barber, "America's Match King," owned the Diamond Match Company, which controlled 85 percent of the match market. Chicago "Gum King" William Wrigley Jr. founded the eponymous chewing gum company in 1891, bought a minority stake in the Cubs in 1916, and died in 1932 with an estate valued at $450 million in 2025 dollars.

Meanwhile, the Gilded Age opened a new era of money in politics. Wealthy industrialists and financiers dominated the political sphere through relations with, and donations to, politicians.

When William McKinley ran for president in 1896, the *New York Journal* listed forty-five of his financial backers. Their combined net worth was around $19 billion in 2025 dollars, and it read like a who's who of the Gilded Age, with names like Rockefeller and Vanderbilt at the top.

Of the $3.5 million that McKinley raised during his campaign (a little over $130 million in 2025 dollars), roughly 86 percent came from New York City and its surrounding areas.

* * *

Today, top income and the political power it brings have far more to do with Main Street Millionaires than industrial billionaires.

Where did all these Main Street Millionaires come from?

- With the rise of the service economy, entrepreneurs launched new kinds of businesses that required less up-front investment and gave more flexibility to operate them.
- Globalization opened new markets for business owners to sell their goods overseas.
- Deregulation at home enabled them to sell more of their goods across state lines.
- The decline in interest rates over the last four decades made their businesses more valuable.
- And tax reforms in 1986 and subsequent years boosted the post-tax gains of these business owners even more.

To be sure, car dealers, law partners, doctors with their own practices, and many other successful business owners have been around for many decades (in some industries, even centuries), and they've often done quite well. But, in the last forty years, their prosperity and power have grown dramatically.

Let's dig a bit deeper.

* * *

In both the Gilded Age and our era, innovators have pursued new technological opportunities, but we now live in a service economy, with more economic activity involving human rather than tangible capital.

Services include everything from legal, financial, and business consulting to Uber driving, childcare providing, and landscaping. In 1900, the service sector comprised a little over half of America's economy. It now comprises more than 80 percent.

In the age of steel and rail more than a century ago, building a large business required substantial investments to marshal the land, iron, oil, and line workers for production. Today, a law partner with a laptop and a few paralegals can generate immense value for herself.

Most Main Street Millionaires started their businesses with their own savings. They relied little on external financing not only at the start-up stage but also in their businesses' growth phases. "Pocket round" funding, from family, friends, and the entrepreneur's home equity, went far. The tilt away from capital-intensive activity created new opportunities to self-finance a business.

At the same time, the scale of potential opportunities blossomed. Globalization, technology, and deregulation enabled local and regional businesses to sell their products across state and national borders and manage multiregional operations via telecommunications. In building a multimillion-dollar business, nothing can substitute for a large, growing market.

Chem-Impex started with one man making cold calls from his friends' couches. Eventually, the company would sell specialty chemicals internationally while managing workers in the United States and India. Its owners deployed technology and modern logistics to ship products and source chemicals with a lean workforce.

Coors beer was popular in the late 1970s. President Ford reportedly hoarded the stuff, and Burt Reynolds immortalized its cultlike demand in the movie *Smokey and the Bandit*. But Coors back then was only available in western states because it wasn't pasteurized and lacked preservatives, making the beverage contraband east of the Mississippi.

Deregulation—at the federal level for transportation and at the state level for beer pasteurization—opened new markets for the beer, enriching distributors by satisfying consumer demand for new products.

* * *

With so much opportunity to launch new businesses in today's economy, the path to the top is paved with hands-on equity ownership.

The income of most people—that is, the non-rich—comes mainly from wages or salaries. Most people take whatever they can save of their income and put it into pensions or brokerage accounts, where it's invested in fixed-income securities (e.g., bonds), money market funds, or public company stocks. Around 60 percent of Americans reported in May 2023 that they own stock—double the share of 1989.

The rich operate differently. "The biggest economic misunderstanding of my childhood," said Sam Altman, CEO of OpenAI, "was that people got rich from high salaries." Altman came to learn the power of ownership, a lesson Main Street Millionaires already knew: Their massive income and wealth come from the equity stake that they take in their own businesses.

Main Street Millionaires are business owners who generate income mainly in the form of profits, not wages. More precisely, their income is the profits from their businesses beyond what they reinvest in them and after they pay business taxes. They might invest in stocks or real estate as well, but their principal assets are their businesses.

Salary earners try to build wealth by spending less than they earn. Business owners try to build wealth by plowing profits back into their businesses. Successful entrepreneurs often do not pay themselves excessively, choosing instead to keep as much money as they can in their businesses. That reinvestment builds over time into huge fortunes for many Main Street Millionaires.

* * *

Over the last forty years, the dramatic decline in interest rates made these business owners even richer.

When then–Federal Reserve Chairman Paul Volcker was combating sky-high inflation in the late 1970s and early '80s by raising interest rates, the ten-year U.S. Treasury rate neared 15 percent. As it wrung inflation out of the economy, the Fed then cut interest rates gradually—and the Treasury rate has remained below 5 percent for essentially the entire twenty-first century.

The lower the interest rates, the more value a company has—for two reasons:

First, buyers of businesses often borrow money to pay for the sale. High interest rates make borrowing more expensive and reduce the price that buyers are willing to pay. Think of a business like a house. If mortgage rates are high, sellers must set their asking price low enough that potential buyers can afford the monthly cost. The same is true for selling a business.

Second, a business is more valuable "on paper" at a time of low interest rates—even if the business owner has no plans to sell. A lot of the value of a business is the income it will generate in the future. But income in the future is worth less than income today. How much less depends on interest rates. When interest rates are high, future income isn't worth as much as when they're low.

With low interest rates, business valuations boomed. Practitioners commonly value businesses based on their profits or revenues. Auto dealers, for instance, typically sell their businesses for around 25 percent of annual revenues. If dealers can sell their dealerships for, say, 30 percent because interest rates fall, the wealth of those dealerships rises. The value of an auto dealership with revenues of $100 million, for instance, rises from $25 million to $30 million.

How important are interest rates in driving wealth? For the top 1 percent of wealthy people, one study found, the decline in interest rates since 1980 contributed more than half of their increase in wealth over that period.

* * *

Soon after inflation and interest rates began their steady decline, lawmakers further drove the fortunes of Main Street Millionaires by reshaping the tax code.

Tax reform boosted their fortunes in multiple ways:

- First, many existing business owners reorganized their firms as pass-throughs to take advantage of the tax savings.
- Second, many new business owners organized their new firms as pass-throughs from the start for the very same reason.
- Third, the tax savings that these pass-throughs now enjoyed accumulated over time, making Main Street Millionaires richer than their counterparts from the 1970s and earlier.

Tax reform also enabled us, as researchers, to see what really drives inequality at the top. No longer did we have to rely on macroeconomic statistics or broad categories of income on individual tax returns.

Tax reform created the data linking business owners to their businesses, bringing the Stealthy Wealthy into view for the first time.

* * *

Unlike transformational innovation that is central to economic growth, the innovations of Main Street Millionaires are often more incremental.

Dick Portillo sold hot dogs. He learned how to steam buns by watching someone else do it. From that, he built a billion-dollar empire. His business grew because he sold a product that people wanted.

So, too, fifty years later did the founders of Dave's Hot Chicken. Three friends started it in a Los Angeles parking lot with $900 and a passion to perfect Nashville-style hot chicken sandwiches. Eight years later, they had more than three hundred locations, capitalizing on a rising worldwide demand for chicken. They sold the business in 2025 for $1 billion to Roark Capital, a franchise-focused private equity firm that planned to continue expanding rapidly.

Casual dining is the poster child industry for free competition, with businesses starting and closing all the time. Downtown streets and highway rest stops are among the places where they compete. We should encourage such healthy competition because we as consumers benefit from it, as does the economy. Incremental product improvements by one business force its competitors to respond with their own improvements if they hope to keep pace and not lose customers.

That dynamic generates a cycle of progress that translates into higher standards of living (and tastier hot chicken sandwiches) compared to those of the past.

* * *

Many of those who rise to the top go beyond growing their wealth by outcompeting their rivals. In some industries, they also position themselves to protect their interests and shape society.

Concerned about the concentration of power in a few hands, policymakers during the Gilded Age enacted the Sherman Antitrust Act in 1890, prohibiting monopolistic practices and enhancing competition. They later enacted the Clayton Act of 1914 to promote fair competition.

More recently, the Great Recession of 2007–9 prompted policymakers to increase transparency and reduce risk in the financial system. The Dodd-Frank Act increased government oversight of Big Banks and created the Consumer Financial Protection Bureau, which helps protect consumers from predatory financial practices (though President Trump and Republican lawmakers have sought to severely limit, if not eliminate, its power).

Today, activists allege that energy behemoths like ExxonMobil and Chevron—two descendants of Rockefeller's Standard Oil—undermine the transition from fossil fuels, while politicians routinely blame Big Oil for slow progress on climate change. Google and Meta, trillion-dollar companies with apps that pervade daily life, fund lobbyists to fight measures to strengthen data privacy. Congress and the Federal Trade Commission have increased their oversight of Big Tech in recent years (though lawmakers have not found consensus on major legislation to rein it in).

The obsession with Big Banks, Big Oil, and Big Tech, however, diverts attention from how much local market power Main Street Millionaires and their so-called small businesses have amassed, as well as the social costs of policies that protect their power. Franchise laws, occupational licensing rules, and anticompetitive real estate contracts all create uneven playing fields and, over time, enrich Main Street Millionaires at the expense of consumers, suppliers, and workers.

Federal, state, and local officeholders often wrote laws and imposed regulations to protect small businesses or new industries from powerful incumbents. But as these new industries matured and their market dominance grew, Main Street Millionaires leveraged these rules to ward off competition from those seeking to enter their markets.

* * *

The rise of Main Street Millionaires and the power they wield at the federal, state, and local levels raise fundamental questions about where we are as a society and where we're headed.

Nothing better encapsulates the idea of America than the American Dream—the centuries-long notion that anyone can climb the ladder of success, rising from rags to riches, by working hard. Does the rise of Main Street Millionaires prove that the American Dream is alive and well? Or are these new millionaires seizing too much of the fruits of our economic growth, squelching the hopes and opportunities of almost everyone else?

The American Dream is not dead. Hard work can still turn rags into riches. Dick Portillo scrubbed mustard out of his bathtub; Shahid Khan went from cleaning dishes to owning the NFL's Jacksonville Jaguars; and the Dave's Hot Chicken guys turned $900 into a billion-dollar business.

Many of the Main Street Millionaires whom we've met not only worked hard but also likely worked harder than if they had been born with more advantage. Most of the Main Street Millionaires who now reside in every town in America did not inherit their wealth or come from rich families.

That's not to say that everyone has the same opportunity. Clearly, many do not—and, throughout our history, many never have. Worse, the road to riches seems to be getting harder to navigate for those who start working only with rags. In 1900, kids born to poor families were roughly half as likely to become rich as kids born to rich families. Today, kids born to poor families are only about a fifth as likely to become rich as kids from rich families. The chance of making it to the top as a poor kid in the twenty-first century is about half of what it was at the beginning of the twentieth.

In 1900, moreover, prime-aged men (those between twenty-five and fifty-four) worked fifty hours per week on average, while women worked eight hours. In 2017, prime-aged men and women worked thirty-six and twenty-seven hours per week, respectively, which means that women today play a much more central role in the economy. Yet they still account for only a third of entrepreneurs.

The racial composition of business owners also has evolved. Over the last thirty years, the share of non-white business owners of midsize businesses has risen from 5 to more than 20 percent. The improvement is striking, but the non-white share is still well below that group's share of the population.

All told, far more avenues for upward mobility exist these days than conventional wisdom would suggest, especially through entrepreneurship. But the playing field could and should be much more level.

In the postwar era, better opportunities for talented individuals of all races and genders have greatly boosted economic growth, one influential study concluded. We would be well advised to expand opportunities for entrepreneurship among those from historically disadvantaged groups.

* * *

What can we do to help more Americans climb the ladder of success? What are the appropriate roles for government, the private sector, colleges and universities, and other institutions?

As we have said, early on-the-job experience, coupled with domain-specific skills, is crucial for successful entrepreneurs. So, how can we help more kids and young adults gain that experience and acquire those skills?

For starters, we should combine mentoring programs with any available financial support to help aspiring entrepreneurs. Local governments, business leaders, civic organizations, and schools all can help build mentorship networks to guide would-be entrepreneurs on their journeys. By themselves, subsidized loans for start-ups and tax incentives to encourage investment in them will mostly benefit entrepreneurs and investors who were going to succeed anyway.

Our education system should teach, and ensure that students develop, the skills that all entrepreneurs need. They need a basic fluency in math, accounting, and financial literacy for their firms to achieve even modest success. Communication skills, both oral and written, are important for generating sales and managing relationships with workers, suppliers, and other partners. Social skills are critical to enable entrepreneurs to create their networks of contacts.

A college degree is not a prerequisite for entrepreneurship, but more years of schooling generally mean more skills that help entrepreneurs succeed. A larger share of workers become entrepreneurs in industries in which the workforce is more educated. White-collar jobs, from which many entrepreneurs emerge, typically require a college degree to begin.

Successful entrepreneurs usually combine a good opportunity with needed skills, adopt relevant technology, and move with gumption to execute their plans. Industries with high levels of entrepreneurship are not especially capital-intensive, and they tend to be less hierarchical than others. In these industries, human capital is especially important, and workers are likelier to interact with business owners, learn from them, and become entrepreneurs themselves.

Another reason to want a broad group of entrepreneurs is that many founders hire people like themselves, helping to create a larger group of experienced workers who may go on to found even more businesses. That not only improves economic opportunity, it also boosts economic growth.

* * *

If the first step to becoming a Main Street Millionaire is gaining needed experience and acquiring skills, then the second step is managing the risk associated with starting something new.

The search fund model that we discussed in chapter 9 is one interesting path for potential entrepreneurs to bootstrap themselves while nourishing a wide array of entrepreneurial skills. Running a franchise is another. Both require capital, a willingness to work in sometimes unglamorous jobs, and a tolerance for the risk involved.

Just how risky is founding a business? We followed all entrepreneurs in America since 2000—eight million entrepreneurs in all—to answer that question.

Income-wise, these founders on average substantially outperformed their non-entrepreneurial counterparts. That's in large part because there are virtually no paths to becoming a decamillionaire or centimillionaire other than creating, buying, or inheriting a company.

Despite the riskiness of being a business owner, even founders who earned only median income among all founders outperformed their non-entrepreneurial counterparts. And those who underperformed as founders typically left their ventures and returned to the workforce. (They were not banished to debtors' prisons, nor did they wind up on the streets.)

So, would-be entrepreneurs can manage the risks that they'll likely face in founding a business. But they can reduce their risks and boost their odds of success by taking the following three steps:

First, save. Savings or a second source of household income can prove crucial in the early years. Many successful entrepreneurs moonlight on their businesses while they continue to work their regular jobs.

Second, profit. Entrepreneurs should focus on generating profitability early on. That requires discipline in modeling the business and not overextending its financial commitments in its early phases.

Third, reinvest. The rich often tie up most of their net worth in their business rather than spend opulently. That's one reason why many very rich Americans might not appear especially wealthy (at least early in their ventures).

* * *

Incomes have soared at the top but largely stagnated in the middle and at the bottom in recent decades, widening inequality and prompting calls to make incomes more equal across society.

Say you want to reduce inequality significantly. Would reducing the wealth of *Forbes* billionaires suffice? Absolutely not. Would reining in the rapid growth of fortunes in finance and technology? Nope.

Say you wanted to help the typical worker at a time of intense public attention on workers at Amazon, Walmart, and Starbucks. Don't lose sight of the much larger number of workers at smaller firms. More than half of American workers are employed in companies with fewer than five hundred workers. Small firms with fewer than one hundred workers account for around one-third.

We can help all workers and, in turn, reduce inequality in at least three basic ways. Here are some places to start:

First, reform health insurance. Most workers get health coverage through their employers, with employers and employees sharing the costs. The typical family plan costs $25,000. If government provided health insurance to all Americans and businesses did not have to help cover these costs, employers would likely boost wages. U.S. firms also would be better equipped to compete with businesses from other countries, most of which don't provide health insurance through employer-provided coverage. In addition, by removing this cost burden from businesses, more people from low-income backgrounds likely would feel secure enough to become entrepreneurs.

Second, raise the minimum wage. The federal minimum wage, which dates to FDR's New Deal, has fallen well behind the rising cost of living. Originally set at 25 cents an hour in 1938, lawmakers have raised it many times since then—for instance, to $1.00 in 1956, $2.00 in 1974, and $3.10 in 1980. But they last raised it in 2009—to $7.25, where it has remained ever since. Had it risen since then to cover inflation, it would now be over $11.00 an hour. A minimum-wage increase would likely prompt at least some employers to boost wages not only at the bottom but for others in their workforce, thus reducing income inequality across our society. When the local minimum wage increases, workers at pass-through firms see a boost in incomes. Firm owners manage the higher costs by raising prices and output rather than firing people.

Third, share profits. Main Street Millionaires may underestimate the benefits of sharing profits with their workers. Private equity dealmakers often set aside 10 to 15 percent of a firm's equity in an option pool for top managers, hoping to encourage workers to recognize how their effort contributes to the firm's bottom line by giving them a slice of the pie. Such arrangements are rare among Main Street Millionaire–owned firms, except when the firms are sold to ESOPs. That seems like a missed opportunity for business owners to better grow their businesses, and it would be another valuable way to boost the incomes of workers. Business owners in all closely held firms could enable their workers to realize some of these benefits.

The power of Main Street Millionaires to grow and protect their businesses, however, is a major obstacle to systemic labor market reform, and it makes even incremental reforms hard to enact. These proposals preserve the flexibility of firms to hire and fire workers, which is important for entrepreneurship.

* * *

The federal government collects far more tax revenue from rich people than it did around the start of the twentieth century—that is, back when the Sixteenth Amendment to allow an income tax was ratified and lawmakers enacted an estate tax.

Nevertheless, today's tax system has gaping loopholes that have grown ever wider for business owners. In 2021, the investigative journalism organization ProPublica reported on how little the government collected in taxes from the nation's very richest people, causing alarm and outrage. Jeff Bezos, for instance, paid no federal income tax in 2007 and 2011, nor did Elon Musk in 2018.

Less explored but just as outrageous is the two-tier tax system that shifts the burden of taxes away from Main Street Millionaires and onto everyone else. The list of tax perks for business owners is long and growing: special rates, generous write-offs, exclusions from the federal cap on state and local income tax deductions, exemptions and loopholes in the estate tax, and so on.

In theory, lawmakers set tax collections by how much we, as a society, want to spend and borrow. But, while lawmakers of different political persuasions will disagree on such matters, they all should want a level playing field for all taxpayers. Workers should not pay higher tax rates than business owners; doctors working at hospitals should not pay higher tax rates than those in private practice; and a well-heeled fifty-year-old who inherits millions of dollars should not pay zero tax on that windfall.

Main Street Millionaires work hard and contribute significantly to the economy. But they also pay less in taxes than they should, and they sometimes take shortcuts to get rich. We can admire them for their success and still think they should give more back to the country that helped make their success possible.

We also should welcome Main Street Millionaires when they step up to serve at a time when public service is less admired than it used to be. From their private-sector experience, business owners can recognize problems that others don't, and they can propose feasible solutions.

Business owners, however, also can shape policy to boost their private interests, especially on technical issues that few others know or care about. When Main Street Millionaires abuse their power, the burden of bringing that to light falls on the rest of us. With fewer local newspapers and, thus, fewer local journalists to scrutinize them, it's now harder to hold them accountable. The rise of elected Main Street Millionaires has increased the need for accountability, and we need to invest more in local media to make that happen.

* * *

Remember Bob Brockway, the auto dealer who threw his daughter, Madelaine, the wedding of the century in late 2023? Barons from the Gilded Age paid homage to the French royalty by building replicas of Versailles in Newport. The Brockways paid homage by renting out the real Versailles for an evening.

Where did they get all that money?

Bob Brockway is the grandson of Bill Ussery, who in 1953 cofounded the used-car dealership Caldwell-Ussery U-Drive-It in the tony city of Coral Gables, Florida. Four years later, Ussery Motors became one of the nation's first Mercedes-Benz dealers.

John Brockway, Bob's father, joined the dealership as a service manager in 1960. His qualifications included two years of junior college and marriage to Bill Ussery's daughter, Patricia. Five years later, John began to run the company. In 1973, he and Patricia bought the business from Bill.

Born in Coral Gables in March 1964, Bob Brockway graduated Texas Christian University with a business degree and started working at the dealership in 1986. He then attended the Dealer Candidate Academy, a boot camp run by the National Automobile Dealers Association. He worked in each of the dealership's departments and became its general manager before turning thirty.

As Brockway expanded the business, the dealership outgrew its original location, leaving customers on an average Saturday waiting an hour before they could even talk to a salesperson. So, he built a second site—180,000 square feet on ten acres off the Florida Turnpike that was large enough to fit three football fields, giving him the space for lots of new and used cars, a service department, a shopping boutique, an expansive lounge with refreshments, and a play area for children.

Brockway was doing just fine as business boomed. But his real windfall came in August 2023—three months before Madelaine's wedding. Dream Motor Group of Birmingham, Alabama, reportedly paid more than $650 million for Bill Ussery Motors. Dream Motor, which has rolled up dealerships across the South, is owned by CEO Joe Agresti, former Mercedes-Benz CEO Steve Cannon, and former University of Alabama football coach Nick Saban.

Bob Brockway is a Main Street Millionaire, just one of millions who own and run law firms, medical offices, auto dealerships, grocery stores, restaurant chains, plumbing companies, tanning salons, and many other successful businesses that you will find in every town in America.

Main Street Millionaires don't get the same attention as Hollywood stars, sports icons, flashy investment bankers, and eccentric big tech titans. But even if they're less entertaining than the billionaire class, their wealth and power to shape society deserve much more attention. Seeing them is the first step to understanding the economy and society as they really are.

NOTES

PROLOGUE: THE WEDDING OF THE CENTURY

xi **French royalty–themed soirée:** Natali Grace Levine, "The 59 Million Dollar Wedding and What We Know About It," Wezoree, March 19, 2024. https://wezoree.com/inspiration/59-million-dollar-wedding-and-what-we-know-about-it/.

xi **Eiffel Tower:** Kirsty Thatcher, "Madelaine Brockway's $89M Wedding Went Viral—Now, Her New Husband Is Facing 25 Years in Jail," *Elle*, December 13, 2023. https://www.elle.com.au/culture/madelaine-brockway-jacob-lagrone-wedding-jail/.

xi **Palace of Versailles:** Danielle Cohen, "This Really Was the Wedding of the Century," *The Cut*, December 8, 2023. https://www.thecut.com/2023/12/jacob-lagrone-madelaine-brockway-wedding-of-the-century.html.

xii **snapping selfies:** Rania Abdulla, "Madelaine Brockway Wedding: Total Cost, Epic Registry List and More," *Harper's Bazaar Arabia*, November 27, 2023. https://www.harpersbazaararabia.com/bride/madelaine-brockway-wedding.

xii **inspiration:** Lujure, "Chateau de Villette-Condacourt, France Luxury Villas-Lujure Villas," 2015. https://www.lujurevillas.com/villas/823/chateau-de-villette-condacourt-france-chateau-de-villette.

xii **first dance:** Cohen, "Wedding of the Century."

xii **car dealers:** Levine, "The 59 Million Dollar Wedding and What We Know About It"; Melissa Willets, "Madelaine Brockway's Parents Helped Her Pull Off the 'Wedding of the Century,'" distractify.com, November 22, 2023. https://www.distractify.com/p/madelaine-brockway-parents; Cohen, "This Really Was the Wedding of the Century."

INTRODUCTION

1 **familiar names:** Chase Peterson-Withorn, "The 2022 Forbes 400 List of Richest Americans: Facts and Figures," *Forbes*, September 27, 2022. https://www.forbes.com/sites/chasewithorn/2022/09/27/the-2022-forbes-400-list-of-richest-americans-facts-and-figures/.

2 **decamillionaires and nearly all centimillionaires:** Based on authors' analysis of 2022 Survey of Consumer Finances (SCF).

2 **times the wealth:** Based on authors' analysis of 2022 SCF and 2022 Forbes 400.

2 **every large public company CEO:** Based on authors' analysis of 2022 SCF and Execucomp data.

2 **number of decamillionaire business owners:** Based on authors' analysis.

4 **hundreds of communities:** Based on authors' analysis of U.S. Treasury data and 2019 *Forbes* data compiled by Americans for Tax Fairness.

4 **you drove:** Based on authors' analysis of housing data from Dataquick.

4 **commercial aluminum heat-treating:** Katherine Clarke, "An Oceanfront Compound in the Florida Keys Is Asking $42 Million," *Wall Street Journal*, February 11, 2025. https://www.wsj.com/real-estate/luxury-homes/florida-keys-islamorada-home-a85be4a5.

6 **lower tax rates:** Steve Robinson, "Historical Tax Rates: The Rhetoric and Reality of Taxing the Rich," Concord Coalition, March 1, 2025. https://www.concordcoalition.org/deep-dives/issue-brief/historical-tax-rates-the-rhetoric-and-reality-of-taxing-the-rich/.

7 **More than 1.1 million pass-through owners:** Matthew Smith, Danny Yagan, Owen Zidar, and Eric Zwick, "Capitalists in the Twenty-First Century," *Quarterly Journal of Economics* 134, no. 4 (November 2019): 1675–745. https://doi.org/10.1093/qje/qjz020.

CHAPTER 1: THE RISE OF PASS-THROUGHS

11 **"pass-through provisions at every step":** Email correspondence, December 9, 2017. https://www.documentcloud.org/documents/20744688-ron-johnson-et-al-tcja-correspondence from https://www.propublica.org/article/secret-irs-files-reveal-how-much-the-ultrawealthy-gained-by-shaping-trumps-big-beautiful-tax-cut.

11 **when he became president:** Martin Schram, "Reagan the Tax Lobbyist: An Artist at Work," *Washington Post*, August 13, 1981. https://www.washingtonpost.com/archive/politics/1981/08/13/reagan-the-tax-lobbyist-an-artist-at-work/c592a5eb-5285-456d-b7cb-0ad21bf3198e/.

11 **spur economic growth:** Chester Pach, "Ronald Reagan and Supply-Side Economics," Bill of Rights Institute, n.d. https://billofrightsinstitute.org/essays/ronald-reagan-and-supply-side-economics.

11 **all-star forward:** Bill Bradley, "Former Sen. Bill Bradley Talks Tax Reform,"

interview by Lizzie O'Leary. *Marketplace Weekend*, September 23, 2017. https://www.marketplace.org/story/2017/09/22/former-senator-bill-bradley-talks-tax-reform; Evan Thomas, "A Sense of Where He Is," *Time*, June 30, 1986. https://time.com/archive/6706459/a-sense-of-where-he-is/.

11 **special interests:** David Ignatius, "The Real Hero of Tax Reform," *Washington Post*, May 18, 1986. https://www.washingtonpost.com/archive/opinions/1986/05/18/the-real-hero-of-tax-reform/4ce6b8dc-226e-4eed-b853-b3a5c21dde10/.

12 **biggest reform of federal taxes:** Anne Swardson, "Senate Approves Tax Revision, 74–23," *Washington Post*, September 28, 1986. https://www.washingtonpost.com/archive/politics/1986/09/28/senate-approves-tax-revision-74-23/0a068f51-8078-48e7-b177-f2618951eb81/.

12 **once-arcane type of business entity:** Congressional Budget Office, "Taxing Businesses Through the Individual Income Tax," December 6, 2012. https://www.cbo.gov/publication/43750.

12 **tax on property was unconstitutional:** D. Andrew Austin, "Tariffs and Federal Finances: A Thumbnail History," Congressional Research Service Insight, January 10, 2025. https://www.congress.gov/crs_external_products/IN/PDF/IN12482/IN12482.2.pdf.

12 **top tax rate rose:** Tax Foundation, *Historical U.S. Federal Individual Income Tax Rates & Brackets, 1862–2025*. https://taxfoundation.org/data/all/federal/historical-income-tax-rates-brackets/.

12 **government also collected revenue:** Tax Foundation, *Historical US Federal Corporate Income Tax Rates & Brackets, 1909–2025*. https://taxfoundation.org/data/all/federal/historical-corporate-tax-rates-brackets.

13 **owners preferred to pay corporate:** Steve Robinson, "Historical Tax Rates: The Rhetoric and Reality of Taxing the Rich," Concord Coalition, March 1, 2025. https://www.concordcoalition.org/deep-dives/issue-brief/historical-tax-rates-the-rhetoric-and-reality-of-taxing-the-rich/.

13 **benefits like writing off:** Charles Clotfelter, "Tax-Induced Distortions and the Business-Pleasure Borderline: The Case of Travel and Entertainment," *American Economic Review* 73, no. 5 (1983): 1053–65.

13 **Reagan was elected:** Tax Foundation data (endnotes 75 and 76); CPI Inflation Calculator. "$200,000 in 1950 → 2025," 2025. https://www.in2013dollars.com/us/inflation/1950?amount=200000.

13 **transformation in the structure:** Robinson, "Historical Tax Rates."

13 **owners converted:** Scott Greenberg, "Pass-Through Businesses: Data and Policy," Tax Foundation, January 17, 2017. https://taxfoundation.org/research/all/federal/pass-through-businesses-data-and-policy/.

14 **estimates how much it will cost:** "Revenue Proposals," U.S. Department of the Treasury, n.d. https://home.treasury.gov/policy-issues/tax-policy/revenue-proposals.

15 **not to enable anyone:** "Challenges Facing the IRS," GovFacts, March 4, 2025. https://govfacts.org/federal/irs/challenges-facing-the-irs/.

15 **President George W. Bush's tax cuts:** Ben Harris and William G. Gale, "A Guide to the Fight over the 'Bush Tax Cuts,'" Brookings Institution, September 13, 2010. https://www.brookings.edu/articles/a-guide-to-the-fight-over-the-bush-tax-cuts/.

16 **blind spot:** U.S. Government Accountability Office, "Partnerships and S Corporations: IRS Needs to Improve Information to Address Tax Noncompliance," Gao.gov, May 14, 2014. https://www.gao.gov/products/gao-14-453.

16 **items required translation:** Marie Sapirie, "The Tax System Modernization Program That Would Not Die," *Forbes*, March 31, 2025. https://www.forbes.com/sites/taxnotes/2025/03/31/the-tax-system-modernization-program-that-would-not-die/.

16 **slash the IRS budget:** "Chart Book: The Need to Rebuild the Depleted IRS," Center on Budget and Policy Priorities, revised December 16, 2022. https://www.cbpp.org/research/federal-tax/the-need-to-rebuild-the-depleted-irs#irs_cant_perform_basic_government_functions.

18 **had access:** Other than the names of the individuals and businesses who submitted these forms, which is confidential information stored in a distinct database from the de-identified and anonymized data that we analyzed.

19 **first scholarly paper:** Michael Cooper, John McClelland, James Pearce, Richard Prisinzano, Joseph Sullivan, Danny Yagan, Owen Zidar, and Eric Zwick, "Business in the United States: Who Owns It, and How Much Tax Do They Pay?" *Tax Policy and the Economy* 30, no. 1 (2016): 91–128.

19 **made 1.5 times:** Based on authors' calculations using Wharton's Compustat Execucomp dataset. See "Compustat Execucomp: The Basics," Wharton School, University of Pennsylvania. https://wrds-www.wharton.upenn.edu/pages/grid-items/compustat-execucomp-basics/.

20 **identifiable owner:** Cooper et al., "Business in the United States."

20 **people grow their wealth:** Matthew Smith, Danny Yagan, Owen Zidar, and Eric Zwick, "Capitalists in the Twenty-First Century," *Quarterly Journal of Economics* 134, no. 4 (November 2019): 1675–745. https://doi.org/10.1093/qje/qjz020; Matthew Smith, Owen Zidar, and Eric Zwick, "Top Wealth in America: New Estimates Under Heterogeneous Returns," *Quarterly Journal of Economics* 138, no. 1 (February 2023): 515–73. https://doi.org/10.1093/qje/qjac033; Raj Chetty, Gaia Dossi, Matt Smith, John Van Reenen, Owen Zidar, and Eric Zwick, "Creating New Businesses in America: The Determinants of and Returns to Entrepreneurship," Working Paper, 2025.

20 **most of their income:** Based on authors' calculations from the Survey of Consumer Finances (SCF) 2022 and Smith et al., "Capitalists in the Twenty-First Century."

21 **requires an expert staff:** "Survey of Consumer Finances," NORC at the University of Chicago, 2016. https://www.norc.org/research/projects/survey-of-consumer-finances.html.

21 **Interviewers often struggle:** Arthur B. Kennickell, "The Role of Over-Sampling of the Wealthy in the Survey of Consumer Finances," Federal Reserve Board, SCF Working Paper, 2025. https://www.federalreserve.gov/PUBS/oss/oss2/papers/isi2007/index.html.

21 **cannot publish information:** Arthur Kennickell and Julia Lane, "Measuring the Impact of Data Protection Techniques on Data Utility: Evidence from the Survey of Consumer Finances," Federal Reserve Board, SCF Working Paper, 2025. https://www.federalreserve.gov/pubs/oss/oss2/papers/Disclosure3/.

21 **they don't ask:** Juliana Menasce Horowitz, Ruth Igielnik, and Rakesh Kochhar, "Methodology," Pew Research Center, January 9, 2020. https://www.pewresearch.org/social-trends/2020/01/09/methodology-27-2/.

22 **issue on the richest four hundred:** Our discussion of the making of the Forbes 400 list draws heavily from Chase Peterson-Withorn, "Birth of the Forbes 400: The Story Behind Forbes' First Rich List," *Forbes*, September 19, 2017. https://www.forbes.com/sites/chasewithorn/2017/09/19/birth-of-the-forbes-400-the-story-behind-forbes-first-rich-list/?sh=2078dff05db2.

22 **inflate his *Forbes* rating:** Jonathan Greenberg, "Trump Lied to Me About His Wealth to Get onto the Forbes 400. Here Are the Tapes," *Washington Post*, April 20, 2018. https://www.washingtonpost.com/outlook/trump-lied-to-me-about-his-wealth-to-get-onto-the-forbes-400-here-are-the-tapes/2018/04/20/ac762b08-4287-11e8-8569-26fda6b404c7_story.html.

23 **magazine cover listed:** Sarah Thomas-Oxtoby, "Billionaire Streakers: These 17 People Made the First Forbes 400 in 1982—and Are on the List Today," *Forbes*, September 28, 2022. https://www.forbes.com/sites/sarahthomasoxtoby/2022/09/28/forbes-400-billionaire-streakers-people-on-1982-and-2022-lists/; Peterson-Withorn, "Birth of the Forbes 400."

23 **kidnapping:** Peterson-Withorn, "Birth of the Forbes 400"; Christopher Winans, "The Rich List," in *Malcolm Forbes: The Man Who Had Everything* (St. Martin's, 1990), 117–21. https://jonathangreenberg.com/wp-content/uploads/2018/01/Forbs-Bio-Excerpt-w-Cover.pdf.

23 **Donald Reynolds:** Peterson-Withorn, "Birth of the Forbes 400."

23 **Kerry Dolan:** Willy Staley, "How Many Billionaires Are There, Anyway?" *New York Times Magazine*, April 7, 2022. https://www.nytimes.com/2022/04/07/magazine/billionaires.html.

23 **rise of the top 1 percent:** Thomas Piketty and Emmanuel Saez, "Income Inequality in the United States, 1913–1998," *Quarterly Journal of Economics* 118, no. 1 (February 2003): 1–41. https://doi.org/10.1162/00335530360535135.

24 **slogan:** "Economists Are Rethinking the Numbers on Inequality," *The*

Economist, November 29, 2019. https://www.economist.com/briefing/2019/11/29/economists-are-rethinking-the-numbers-on-inequality.

24 **Protesters raged:** David Callahan and Heather C. McGhee, "Why Occupy Wall Street?" Demos, May 1, 2012. https://www.demos.org/policy-briefs/why-occupy-wall-street.

24 **outpacing the returns:** Thomas Piketty, *Capital in the Twenty-First Century* (Belknap Press of Harvard University Press, 2014). https://www.jstor.org/stable/j.ctt6wpqbc.

24 **anyone could learn:** Steven N. Kaplan and Joshua Rauh argue that public company CEOs generate a relatively small fraction of top incomes in "Wall Street and Main Street: What Contributes to the Rise in the Highest Incomes?" *Review of Financial Studies* 23, no. 3 (2010): 1004–1050. They hypothesize that a lot of the missing top earners in their data might be successful entrepreneurs and owners of private businesses.

24 **back to the high levels:** Thomas Piketty and Gabriel Zucman, "Capital Is Back: Wealth-Income Ratios in Rich Countries 1700–2010," *Quarterly Journal of Economics* 129, no. 3 (August 2014): 1255–310. https://doi.org/10.1093/qje/qju018.

25 **accumulation of capital:** Thomas Piketty, Emmanuel Saez, and Gabriel Zucman, "Distributional National Accounts: Methods and Estimates for the United States," *Quarterly Journal of Economics* 133, no. 2 (May 2018): 553–609. https://doi.org/10.1093/qje/qjx043.

CHAPTER 2: MILLIONAIRES EVERYWHERE

26 **Senox Corporation:** "About Us," Senox, May 2, 2025. https://senox.com/about-us/.

26 **dream home:** Libertina Brandt, "An Alabama Oral Surgeon Designed His Nearly $5 Million Dream Mansion Using Home-Building Software," *Wall Street Journal*, April 10, 2024. https://www.wsj.com/real-estate/luxury-homes/an-alabama-oral-surgeon-designed-his-nearly-5-million-dream-mansion-using-home-building-software-051f80cb.

26 **eight million homes:** The first statistic is from: Dana Anderson, "Record 8.5% of U.S. Homes Are Worth $1 Million or More," *Redfin Real Estate News*, August 16, 2024. https://www.redfin.com/news/million-dollar-homes-increasing/. The following two (count of $2M+ and $5M+ houses) are based on authors' calculations using the Survey of Consumer Finances (2022).

27 **David Williams:** According to historical Census records.

27 **five acres:** See Jan Griffey, "Welcome Home: Trio of Historic Homes Welcome New Owners," *Natchez Democrat*, July 16, 2022. https://www.natchezdemocrat.com/2022/07/16/welcome-home-trio-of-historic-homes-welcome-new-owners/; "1803 Gloucester Manor Includes Private

Cemetery for $1.9M in Natchez, MS," Pricey Pads, March 13, 2021. https://www.priceypads.com/1803-gloucester-manor-includes-private-cemetery-for-1-9m-in-natchez-ms-photos/.

28 **Texas town of Colleyville:** "History of Colleyville," City of Colleyville, Texas. Accessed 2025. https://www.colleyville.com/colleyville/history-of-colleyville.

28 **mahogany-paneled staircase:** Libertina Brandt, "This $6.75 Million Texas Mansion Will Take You Back—Way Back," *Wall Street Journal*, September 23, 2023. https://www.wsj.com/real-estate/luxury-homes/this-6-75-million-texas-mansion-will-take-you-backway-back-c22d401f?st=C5DE9e&reflink=desktopwebshare_permalink.

29 **annual profits per partner:** Thomas Spigolon, "King & Spalding Sees PEP Spike 12% amid 'Solid and Even Demand' Growth," *American Lawyer*, March 5, 2024. https://www.kslaw.com/attachments/000/011/579/original/King___Spalding_Sees_PEP_Spike_12__Amid_%27Solid_and_Even_Demand%27_Growth_%28The_American_Lawyer_3.5.24%29.pdf?1709918489.

29 **Morris grew up:** "Johnny Morris: 1948–2005 Inductee," International Game and Fish Association Museum Hall of Fame. Accessed December 8, 2025. https://web.archive.org/web/20181215231500/https://www.igfa.org/Museum/HOF-Morris.aspx; Alec Harvey, "Below the Surface with John Paul Morris," *Hook and Barrel Magazine*, March 11, 2019. https://hookandbarrel.com/fishing/below-the-surface-with-john-paul-morris.

29 **tenth-tallest pyramid:** "All Bass Pro Shops Locations," Bass Pro Shops. https://stores.basspro.com/; "World's Largest Pyramid-Shaped Commercial Building: World Record in Memphis, Tennessee," World Record Academy, October 12, 2023. https://www.worldrecordacademy.org/2023/10/worlds-largest-pyramid-shaped-commercial-building-world-record-in-memphis-tennessee-423496.

29 **estimates his net worth:** "John Morris," *Forbes*, 2025. https://www.forbes.com/profile/john-morris/.

29 **Lee Hill Drive:** "335 Lee Hill Dr, Boulder, CO 80302 | MLS #1002670," Zillow, 2025. https://www.zillow.com/homedetails/335-Lee-Hill-Dr-Boulder-CO-80302/81885651_zpid/.

30 **"high-end skiwear market":** "Dave Jacobs," Roadtrip Nation. Accessed 2025. https://roadtripnation.com/leader/dave-jacobs.

30 **Spyder:** "Spyder Acquired in $100 Million Cash Deal . . ." SGB Media, 2025. https://sgbonline.com/spyder-acquired-in-100-million-cash-deal/.

30 **Kurt Larsen:** https://www.youtube.com/watch?v=2B6mWzK6bmk.

31 **Resource Management Inc.:** "Background," Resource Management, Inc., RMU, August 20, 2020. https://rminc.com/background/.

31 **not disclosed:** "Vensure Employer Solutions Expands HR Services with Acquisition of Resource Management Inc.," *Businesswire*, October 19, 2023. ttps://www.businesswire.com/news/home/20231019321052/en/Vensure

-Employer-Solutions-Expands-HR-Services-with-Acquisition-of-Resource -Management-Inc.

31 **zip code:** Internal Revenue Service, Statistics of Income Tax Statistics, "Individual Income Tax Statistics—2022 Zip Code Data (SOI)." https://www.irs .gov/statistics/soi-tax-stats-individual-income-tax-statistics-2022-zip-code -data-soi.

32 **Villa Terra Rosa:** Wendy Bowman, "Bay Area Estate Built by Married Pizza Moguls Lists for $12.5 Million," *Robb Report*, June 4, 2024. https://robbreport .com/shelter/homes-for-sale/villa-terra-rosa-petaluma-1235633151/.

33 **dabbled in several careers:** "Terrence Collins Obituary (1941–2021)—Petaluma, CA," *The Oregonian*, July 30, 2021. https://obits.oregonlive.com /us/obituaries/oregon/name/terrence-collins-obituary?id=14693377.

33 **Collins bought:** Dorothy Pomerantz, "Raw Deal," *Forbes*, December 25, 2000. https://www.forbes.com/forbes/2000/1225/6616238a.html.

33 **IPO in 2014:** For market value of equity around the IPO, see Jonathan Weil, "Even a Money-Losing Pizza Chain Can Do an IPO," Bloomberg, May 2, 2014. https://www.bloomberg.com/view/articles/2014-05-02/even -a-money-losing-pizza-chain-can-do-an-ipo. For value of debt, see Form S-1 of Papa Murphy's Holdings, Inc., Securities and Exchange Commission, March 11, 2014. https://www.sec.gov/Archives/edgar/data/1592379 /000119312514093943/d636303ds1.htm.

34 **traditional college-to-MBA track:** The following sources provide more information on Nancy Mueller: Mark Chisnell, "Lunch with . . . Superyacht Owner Nancy Mueller," *Boat International*, December 17, 2015. https://www .boatinternational.com/luxury-yacht-life/owners-experiences/lunch-with -superyacht-owner-nancy-mueller—1565; Chris Kenrick, "Nancy Mueller," Palo Alto Online, May 4, 2018. https://www.paloaltoonline.com/news/2018 /05/04/nancy-mueller/; Brian Isaeff, "QUICHE," *Peninsula Foodnews Newsletter*, May 6, 2007. https://penfoodnews.blogspot.com/2007/05/quiche .html; Elizabeth Pearson Garr, "What It's Like to Start and Run a Multi-Million Dollar Business," What's It Like To . . . Listen Notes, October 19, 2022. https://www.listennotes.com/podcasts/what-its-like-to/what-its-like -to-start-and-GeiS0bKY9hp/.

40 **leading industries:** Based on authors' calculations in Matthew Smith, Danny Yagan, Owen Zidar, and Eric Zwick, "Capitalists in the Twenty-First Century," *Quarterly Journal of Economics* 134, no. 4 (November 2019): 1675–745.

42 **six dentists:** Table 3 from "The Dentist Workforce," American Dental Association website. Accessed December 10, 2025. https://www.ada.org /resources/research/health-policy-institute/dentist-workforce.

43 **private practice to five locations:** "Meet Our Team," Charak Center for Health and Wellness, 2017. https://www.charakcenter.com/meet-us-psych.

43 **offices generate enough:** Based on authors' calculations in Smith et al.,

"Capitalists in the Twenty-First Century." For the top 0.1 percent threshold, see the March 2024 data update to Thomas Piketty and Emmanuel Saez, "Income Inequality in the United States, 1913–1998," *Quarterly Journal of Economics* 118, no. 1 (February 2003): 1–41. https://eml.berkeley.edu/~saez/TabFig2022.xlsx.

43 **market for dental services:** Sieva Kozinsky, "Building an Empire of Dental Practices—Dr. Peter Boulden," YouTube, September 18, 2024. https://www.youtube.com/watch?v=lrx2i3875DE.

43 **Total revenue from dentistry:** "Total Economic Impact and Total Number of Jobs Supported by Offices of Dentists, 2022," Health Policy Institute, American Dental Association. Accessed December 10, 2025. https://www.ada.org/resources/research/health-policy-institute/dental-practice-research/economic-impact-of-dental-offices. The underlying data, which are based on National Health Expenditure Accounts from the Centers for Medicare & Medicaid Services, are available here: https://www.ada.org/-/media/project/ada-organization/ada/ada-org/files/resources/research/hpi/economic_impact_of_dentists_2022.xlsx?rev=6f096612428e4521ba63dfbeb791111a&hash=255F5F940345138A2A3FA021A66F91B5.

43 **NFL generated:** Kurt Badenhausen, "How NFL Teams and Owners Make Their Money," Sportico, August 29, 2024. https://www.sportico.com/leagues/football/2024/how-nfl-teams-owners-make-money-1234795113/.

43 **law firm owners:** Also based on authors' calculations with data in Smith et al., "Capitalists in the Twenty-First Century."

43 **more Main Street than Wall Street:** See Figure II in Smith et al., "Capitalists in the Twenty-First Century."

CHAPTER 3: MANY ROADS TO RICHES

45 **Russell Westbrook:** Matt Craig, "Russell Westbrook Means Business," *Forbes*, May 14, 2023. https://www.forbes.com/sites/mattcraig/2023/05/14/russell-westbrook-means-business/.

45 **crowd at Texas A&M's:** From an event where Arch "Beaver" Aplin III was awarded the 2022 McLane Leadership in Business Award, by the Mosbacher Institute of Trade, Economics & Public Policy: "2022 McLane Leadership in Business Award Honoring Arch 'Beaver' Aplin III," YouTube, October 31, 2022. https://www.youtube.com/watch?v=qoMv8vyxixo.

45 **Aplin's share of the business:** For information on Buc-ee's history, see Melissa Locker, "How Buc-ee's Became the Most Popular Convenience Store in Texas," *Southern Living*, April 17, 2025. https://www.southernliving.com/buc-ees-history-11717656. For the number of locations: as of October 1, 2025, the count is fifty-four according to ScrapeHero. https://www.scrapehero.com/location-reports/Buc-ee%27s-USA/.

47 **"My dad built houses":** See "2022 McLane Leadership in Business Award Honoring Arch 'Beaver' Aplin III."

48 **land is cheap:** More on Buc-ee's strategy can be found at: Natalie Hamren, "The Buc-Ee's Effect," Playmakers, January 11, 2024. https://communityplaymaker.com/discoveries/the-buc-ees-effect/.

49 **burgeoning online resale market:** Zachary Crockett, "How One Man Created a Multimillion-Dollar Resale Market for Buc-ee's Snacks," *The Hustle*, July 29, 2023. https://thehustle.co/how-one-man-created-a-multimillion-dollar-resale-market-for-buc-ees-snacks.

49 **Chris Aarons:** Baylee Friday, Savannah Jones, and Chris Blake, "Texas Wants to Know: How Buc-ee's Built an Empire on Clean Toilets and Beaver Nuggets," NBC 5 Dallas–Fort Worth, April 15, 2023. https://www.nbcdfw.com/news/local/texas-wants-to-know-how-buc-ees-built-an-empire-on-clean-toilets-and-beaver-nuggets/3237096/.

49 **cleanest bathrooms in America:** John Gullion, "Potty Like a Rockstar: A Look Inside Buc-ee's Bathrooms (Pictures)," TheSmokies.com, December 21, 2023. https://www.thesmokies.com/bucees-bathrooms-pictures/; Megan Menchaca, "Buc-ee's Tops List of America's Cleanest Bathrooms Once Again," *Austin American-Statesman*, May 15, 2019. https://www.statesman.com/story/news/local/2019/05/15/buc-ees-tops-list-of-americas-cleanest-bathrooms-once-again/5152511007/.

49 **installed a "Tooshlight":** "Buc-ee's Legendary Bathrooms Get High-Tech Upgrade," ABC13 Houston, November 30, 2018. https://abc13.com/buc-ees-restroom-gasbuddy-survey/4796449/.

50 **values could well have doubled:** See Peter Carbonara, "How Two Texans Made Buc-ee's Convenience Stores a Phenomenon," *Forbes*, August 22, 2017. https://www.forbes.com/sites/petercarbonara/2017/08/22/buc-ees-game-of-porcelain-thrones/; "Goodyear Buc-ee's Receives Final Approval, Projected $25 Million Annual Revenue," *Daily Independent*, n.d. https://www.yourvalley.net/stories/goodyear-buc-ees-receives-final-approval-projected-25-million-annual-revenue,475151; Eric Benson, "Buc-ee's: The Path to World Domination," *Texas Monthly*, March 2019. https://www.texasmonthly.com/news-politics/buc-ees-the-path-to-world-domination/.

51 **convenience stores:** "The Brave New World of Convenience Stores," Hormel Foods, May 7, 2024. https://www.hormelfoods.com/inspired/story/the-brave-new-world-of-convenience-stores/.

51 **former Marine:** "Tom Love," *Forbes*, 2022. https://www.forbes.com/profile/tom-love/.

51 **Judy managed:** Michael Catarevas, "Love Story," *FleetOwner*, June 21, 2018. https://www.fleetowner.com/for-the-driver/on-the-road/article/21185821/love-story.

51 **eleventh-largest private company:** For a company overview, see "Love's

Travel Stops & Country Stores," *Forbes*, n.d. https://www.forbes.com/companies/loves-travel-stops-country-stores/.

52 **largest food redistributor:** Deanna Toncray, "Remembering Dot's Co-Founder: 12 Funny, Heartfelt Stories from His Children," Dotfoods.com, August 7, 2019. https://www.dotfoods.com/newsroom/dot-foods-news/remembering-dots-co-founder-12-funny-heartfelt-stories-from-his-children/. See also Aaron Keeports, "How a $7B Food Redistributor Meets Customers' Evolving Data Demands," *Cleo*, n.d. https://www.cleo.com/blog/dot-foods-food-redistributor.

52 **nation's forty-second-largest company:** See the *Forbes* profile: "Dot Foods," *Forbes*, n.d. https://www.forbes.com/companies/dot-foods/. The *Forbes* ranked list of largest private companies is available here: https://www.forbes.com/lists/top-private-companies/.

53 **Tracys added more:** Deanne Stone, "Big Family, Big Business," *Family Business*, November 4, 2013. https://familybusinessmagazine.com/ownership/legal/big-family-big-business-1/.

53 **grandchildren:** "Dot Foods History," Dot Foods, 2024. https://www.dotfoods.com/about/dot-foods-history/.

54 **Piggly Wiggly:** "Who Is Mr. George?" Publix Super Markets, August 2, 2016. https://corporate.publix.com/newsroom/news-stories/the-history-of-publix-founder-mr-george.

54 **Enter Publix:** "George W. Jenkins," Horatio Alger Association of Distinguished Americans, March 4, 2024. https://horatioalger.org/members/detail/george-w-jenkins/.

54 **Publix operates:** For more on the company, see "Publix Super Markets," *Forbes*, n.d. https://www.forbes.com/companies/publix-super-markets/. For more on the Jenkins family, see "Jenkins Family," *Forbes*, 2024. https://www.forbes.com/profile/jenkins/.

55 **one grocery store:** "Celebrating a 75-Year Legacy in Kansas City: Cosentino's Food Stores," *KC Yesterday*, May 17, 2023. https://kcyesterday.com/articles/cosentinos-food-stores.

55 **mostly in northeast Ohio:** Jane Kaufman, "Heinen's Fine Foods Celebrates 90 Years," *Cleveland Jewish News*, April 22, 2019. https://www.clevelandjewishnews.com/news/local_news/heinen-s-fine-foods-celebrates-90-years/article_1f382bd0-6502-11e9-800b-b7f815e0b397.html.

55 **prominent examples:** See the *Forbes* pages for these businesses (2023).

55 **Charles Butt:** See the *Forbes* profiles on H-E-B and Charles Butt: "H-E-B Grocery Company," *Forbes*, n.d. https://www.forbes.com/companies/h-e-b/; and "Charles Butt," *Forbes*, n.d. https://www.forbes.com/profile/charles-butt/.

56 **Wendy Award:** "Schmidt Family Restaurant Group," Schmidt Family, 2015. https://schmidtgroup.us/our-story/.

56 **franchise-owned:** The Wendy's Company 2025 Form 10-K. https://www

.sec.gov/Archives/edgar/data/30697/000003069725000003/wen-20241229.htm.

56 **Bridgeman built a $1.4 billion fortune:** Jabari Young, "How This Legendary NBA Sixth Man Became a Billionaire," *Forbes*, March 25, 2025. https://www.forbes.com/sites/jabariyoung/2025/02/13/former-nba-sixth-man-junior-bridgeman-billionaire/.

56 **son of a steelworker:** Richard Sandomir, "Junior Bridgeman, N.B.A. Player Turned Mogul, Dies at 71," *New York Times*, March 15, 2025. https://www.nytimes.com/2025/03/15/sports/basketball/junior-bridgeman-dead.html.

56 **Sidney Moncrief:** Baxter Holmes, "How an NBA Sixth Man Built a $600M Empire," ESPN, September 26, 2024. https://www.espn.com/nba/story/_/id/40625836/how-nba-sixth-man-built-600m-empire.

56 **10 percent stake:** Jim Owczarski, "Junior Bridgeman's Family Talks About the Future of Its Milwaukee Bucks Ownership Stake," *Milwaukee Journal Sentinel*, July 10, 2025.

56 **Larry Fleming:** Melinda Schnyder, "Wichita Business Hall of Fame | Larry Fleming," *Wichita Business Magazine*, March 1, 2023. https://wichitabusinessmagazine.com/wichita-business-hall-of-fame-larry-fleming/.

56 **businesses generated:** Sherry Graham, "Early Years in the Corporate World Gave Larry Fleming the Courage to Go Solo," *Wichita Business Journal*, December 6, 2002. https://wichitabusinessmagazine.com/wichita-business-hall-of-fame-larry-fleming/.

56 **sold his Wendy's franchises:** Carrie Rengers, "Longtime Wendy's Franchisee Larry Fleming Sells 38 Restaurants," *Wichita Eagle*, March 13, 2017. https://www.kansas.com/news/business/biz-columns-blogs/carrie-rengers/article138305698.html.

57 **John Paterakis:** "John Paterakis," American Society of Baking, 2019. https://asbe.org/bhof-2007-jpaterakis/; and "H&S Bakery at 70," *Baltimore*, July 2013. https://www.baltimoremagazine.com/section/community/h-s-bakery-at-70/.

57 **"big fish":** Carrie Wells and Jacques Kelly, "John Paterakis, Multimillionaire Baker and Baltimore Developer, Dies," *Baltimore Sun*, October 16, 2016. https://www.baltimoresun.com/2016/10/16/john-paterakis-multimillionaire-baker-and-baltimore-developer-dies/.

57 **serve around nine thousand:** "Louis Kuchuris," American Society of Baking, April 7, 2009. https://asbe.org/wp-content/uploads/2019/05/ASB-HOF-plaque-Kuchuris-01.pdf.

57 **East Balt:** Eric Schroeder, "Grupo Bimbo to Acquire East Balt Bakeries," *Baking Business*, July 21, 2017. https://www.bakingbusiness.com/articles/32403-grupo-bimbo-to-acquire-east-balt-bakeries.

58 **Grendys amassed:** "Joseph Grendys," *Forbes*, n.d. https://www.forbes.com/profile/joseph-grendys/.

58 **Tyson Foods:** Monica Watrous, "Tyson Foods to Acquire American Proteins and AMPRO Products Assets," *Food Business News*, May 15, 2018. https://www.foodbusinessnews.net/articles/11824-tyson-foods-to-acquire-american-proteins-and-ampro-products-assets.

58 **Pizza Hut opened:** Quote from: Chloe Sorvino, "This Secretive Billionaire Makes the Cheese for Pizza Hut, Domino's and Papa John's," *Forbes*, June 28, 2021. https://www.forbes.com/sites/chloesorvino/2017/05/23/james-leprino-exclusive-mozzarella-billionaire-cheese-pizza-hut-dominos-papa-johns/.

59 **"all-time monopolists":** See Sorvino, "This Secretive Billionaire Makes the Cheese."

60 **Heritage Bag:** Kaleem Khan, "Carl Allen Net Worth and Biography," *Impact Wealth*, December 11, 2024. https://impactwealth.org/carl-allen-net-worth-and-biography-2025/.

60 **literal treasure hunt:** Lee Cowan, "Hunting Sunken Treasure from a Legendary Shipwreck," CBS News, April 16, 2023. https://www.cbsnews.com/news/carl-allen-hunting-sunken-treasure-at-walkers-cay-in-the-bahamas/.

61 **Jeep:** "Lakes and Rivers: A Middle Class Task Force Visit to the Chrysler Toledo Assembly Complex," White House, August 23, 2010. https://obamawhitehouse.archives.gov/realitycheck/blog/2010/08/23/lakes-and-rivers-a-middle-class-task-force-visit-chrysler-toledo-assembly-complex-1.

61 **Twitter ever did:** For Twitter, the estimate is 7,500 before Musk purchased the company, according to Faiz Siddiqui and Jeremy B. Merrill, "Musk Issues Ultimatum to Staff: Commit to 'Hardcore' Twitter or Take Severance," *Washington Post*, November 16, 2022. https://www.washingtonpost.com/technology/2022/11/16/musk-twitter-email-ultimatum-termination/. For ADAC, Andy Balaskovitz lists 14,500 in: Andy Balaskovitz, "Family-Owned Supplier ADAC Automotive Taps Outsider as New President and CEO," *Crain's Grand Rapids Business*, August 23, 2022.

61 **account for around half:** This estimate is based on "Table F. Distribution of Private Sector Employment by Firm Size Class, Not Seasonally Adjusted," U.S. Bureau of Labor Statistics, Business Employment Dynamics, 2025. https://www.bls.gov/web/cewbd/table_f.txt; similar estimates for 2021 can also be found in the Statistics of U.S. Businesses (SUSB) data: "2021 SUSB Annual Data Tables by Establishment Industry," Census, December 2023. https://www.census.gov/data/tables/2021/econ/susb/2021-susb-annual.html.

62 **Tocqueville:** Alexis de Tocqueville, *Democracy in America*, ed. Phillips Bradley, trans. Henry Reeve (Vintage Books, 1945).

CHAPTER 4: THE TYPICAL TOP EARNER

63 **have needed $60 million:** Based on authors' analysis of 2022 SCF.

63 **your wage:** March 2024 data update to Thomas Piketty and Emmanuel Saez, "Income Inequality in the United States, 1913–1998," *Quarterly Journal of Economics* 118, no. 1 (February 2003): 1–41. https://eml.berkeley.edu/~saez/TabFig2022.xlsx. Assumed annual hours equal to 2,000.

64 **Taxpayers who earn more:** Joint Committee on Taxation, "Present Law and Background on the Income Taxation of High Income and High Wealth Taxpayers (JCX-51-23)," November 7, 2023. https://www.jct.gov/getattachment/b2168cb1-1026-4e58-9f62-65802dddfa79/x-51-23.pdf; Tax Extension, "Comparing State Tax Rates Across the US," Tax Extension, February 4, 2025. https://www.taxextension.com/resources/comparing-state-tax-rates-across-the-us/.

64 **federal-state income tax:** Joint Committee on Taxation, "Present Law and Background on the Income Taxation of High Income and High Wealth Taxpayers."

64 **typical household:** Jon Kamp and Paul Overberg, "U.S. Median Income Rose to $80,610 in 2023, Census Bureau Says," *Wall Street Journal*, September 10, 2024. https://www.wsj.com/economy/consumers/household-income-2023-census-report-38b7d21d.

64 **wakes up every morning:** Katie Warren, "A Day in the Life of the Top Real-Estate Broker in the US, Who Sold $2.2 Billion Worth of Homes in 2018, Wakes Up at 5 A.M. Every Day, and Works Out with a Personal Trainer 3 Times a Week," *Business Insider*, January 3, 2020. https://www.businessinsider.com/top-real-estate-broker-usa-daily-routine-ben-caballero-2019-3.

65 **worth an estimated $3.7 billion:** The Power Is Now, "The 20 Richest Real Estate Agents in the U.S. in 2022—Moneyinc," Internet Archive, August 17, 2022. https://web.archive.org/web/20250513073348/https://www.thepowerisnow.com/the-20-richest-real-estate-agents-in-the-u-s-in-2022-moneyinc/.

65 **serve in the Air Force:** Ben Caballero, "Ben Caballero Real Estate Agent Series: Part 1—How Ben Became #1," podcast, HomesUSA.com, November 26, 2010. https://podcasts.apple.com/us/podcast/ben-caballero-real-estate-agent-series-and-builder/id1444134076?i=1000424296947.

66 **more than sixty years:** Caballero, "Ben Caballero Real Estate Agent Series: Part 1."

66 **explained on his podcast:** Caballero, "Ben Caballero Real Estate Agent Series: Part 1."

66 **built custom homes for eighteen years:** Michele Lerner, "Meet a Record-Setting Real Estate Agent," *Washington Post*, June 5, 2018. https://www.washingtonpost.com/news/where-we-live/wp/2018/06/05/meet-a-record-setting-real-estate-agent/.

66 **funnel new homes:** HomesUSA, "Who Are We?" November 26, 2024. https://homesusa.com/who_are_we/; HomesUSA, "Who Are You?" July 22, 2025. https://homesusa.com/who_are_you/; "HomesUSA," n.d. https://homesusa.com/.

66 **$1 billion in home sales:** HomesUSA.com, "Ben Caballero Crushes the World Record for Annual US Home Sales," *Cision PR Newswire*, April 30, 2024. https://www.prnewswire.com/news-releases/ben-caballero-crushes-the-world-record-for-annual-us-home-sales-302131533.html.

67 **sold 7,012 homes:** "Ben Caballero—Business Leader, Real Estate Broker, Innovator," 2024. https://bencaballero.com; Jael Batty, "How Much Commission Does a Real Estate Broker Receive?" *HomeLight* (blog), February 28, 2025. https://www.homelight.com/blog/average-broker-commission/.

67 **almost twice what the typical agent sells:** Derek Macy, "How Many Homes Does the Average Realtor Sell in a Year?" Accessed August 21, 2025. https://thinkrealstate.com/how-many-homes-does-the-average-realtor-sell-in-a-year/.

67 **still the one making presentations:** HomesUSA, "An Unstoppable Legend: Ben Caballero Remains America's Top-Performing Real Estate Agent-HomesUSA," May 13, 2024. https://homesusa.com/2024/05/13/an-unstoppable-legend-ben-caballero-remains-americas-top-performing-real-estate-agent/.

67 **one to two times its revenue:** Matthew Smith, Owen Zidar, and Eric Zwick, "Top Wealth in America: New Estimates Under Heterogeneous Returns," *Quarterly Journal of Economics* 138, no. 1 (February 2023): 515–73.

68 **termination payment and retirement benefits:** Lucian Bebchuk and Jesse Fried, "Executive Compensation as an Agency Problem," *Journal of Economic Perspectives* 17, no. 3 (Summer 2003): 71–92.

68 **business owners are married:** Based on authors' analysis of 2022 SCF.

68 **car wash in Milwaukee:** Alex Groth, "'This Is Giving Us the Muscle to Expand': Jilly's Car Wash Four Locations Sell to Private Firm for $19 Million," Yahoo! News, *Milwaukee Journal Sentinel*, August 30, 2022. https://www.yahoo.com/news/giving-us-muscle-expand-jillys-153416402.html.

68 **everyone with at least:** Based on authors' analysis of 2022 SCF.

69 **younger than forty:** Based on authors' analysis of 2022 SCF.

70 **each hold around:** Board of Governors of the Federal Reserve System, Distributional Financial Accounts, 2025:Q1 data. Accessed August 22, 2025. https://www.federalreserve.gov/releases/z1/dataviz/dfa/distribute/chart/#quarter:142;series:Private%20businesses;demographic:generation;population:1,3,5,7;units:shares.

70 **40 percent have a postgraduate degree:** Based on authors' analysis of 2022 SCF.

70 **don't own businesses:** Based on authors' analysis of 2022 SCF.

70 **beyond one location:** Based on authors' analysis of the Census's 2021 County Business Patterns data.

71 **"still doing the same thing":** Devin Sean Martin, "The Car Dealership Billionaire No One Knows," *Forbes*, January 15, 2024. https://www.forbes.com/sites/devinseanmartin/2024/01/15/the-car-dealership-billionaire-no-one-knows/.

71 **dedicated to the business:** Carrie Wells and Jacques Kelly, "John Paterakis, Multimillionaire Baker and Baltimore Developer, Dies," *Baltimore Sun*, October 16, 2016. https://www.baltimoresun.com/2016/10/16/john-paterakis-multimillionaire-baker-and-baltimore-developer-dies/.

71 **twenty-hour days:** Wells and Kelly, "John Paterakis, Multimillionaire Baker and Baltimore Developer, Dies."

73 **gathering of entrepreneurship students:** Technion, "John Osher—Lollipops and Toothbrushes Technion Lecture," YouTube, June 2, 2015. https://www.youtube.com/watch?v=MTQc_f9bt4o.

73 **worked for about five years:** "Toys and Spinning Brushes: How John Osher Found His Way to Profits," *Knowledge at Wharton*, November 19, 2003. https://knowledge.wharton.upenn.edu/article/toys-and-spinning-brushes-how-john-osher-found-his-way-to-profits/.

73 **product designer:** William A. Sahlman, "Dr. John's Products, Ltd.—Case—Faculty & Research," Harvard Business School, July 2009. https://www.hbs.edu/faculty/Pages/item.aspx?num=29341.

73 **"vice president in charge of nothing":** "Toys and Spinning Brushes."

74 **company was going broke:** Technion, "John Osher—Lollipops and Toothbrushes Technion Lecture."

74 **developed in the late 1970s:** Brian VanHooker, "An Oral History of Stretch Armstrong's Delightful Destructibility," *MEL* magazine, December 4, 2021. https://melmagazine.com/en-us/story/stretch-armstrong.

75 **SpinPop was designed:** "Kids Are Suckers for Lollipop That Spins Around and Costs $4," *Deseret News*, July 10, 1994. https://www.deseret.com/1994/7/10/19119134/kids-are-suckers-for-lollipop-that-spins-around-and-costs-4/.

75 **acquired the rights to both:** "Toys and Spinning Brushes."

75 **eventually selling one hundred million:** William A. Sahlman, "Opportunity Recognition and Leveraging One's Experience," Stanford ECorner, Stanford Technology Ventures Program, May 1, 2007. https://stvp.stanford.edu/videos/opportunity-recognition-and-leveraging-ones-experience/.

75 **cost only 80 cents:** Technion, "John Osher—Lollipops and Toothbrushes Technion Lecture"; Mark Frauenfelder, "Gross National Product," *Wired*, June 1, 1999. https://www.wired.com/1999/06/candy/.

75 **Hasbro bought CAP:** "Toys and Spinning Brushes."

75 **pursued the top three:** Technion, "John Osher—Lollipops and Toothbrushes Technion Lecture."

75 **sell it for $5 at Walmart:** Technion, "John Osher—Lollipops and Toothbrushes Technion Lecture."

76 **Osher was selling six thousand a day:** William A. Sahlman, "Dr. John's Products, Ltd.," Harvard Business School Case 803-063, October 2002 (revised July 2009). https://store.hbr.org/product/dr-john-s-products-ltd/803063.

76 **helped boost sales:** Robert Berner, "Case Study—SpinBrush: Why Procter & Gamble Smile Is So Bright," *Businessweek*, August 12, 2002. https://www.bloomberg.com/news/articles/2002-08-11/why-p-and-gs-smile-is-so-bright.

76 **agreed to stay on with the company:** Technion, "John Osher—Lollipops and Toothbrushes Technion Lecture."

76 **electric toothbrush market:** *Procter & Gamble Co.—Annual Report, 2002.* 2002. Kuching: Acquisdata Pty Ltd. https://www.proquest.com/reports/procter-amp-gamble-co-annual-report-2002/docview/1793820338/se-2.

76 **P&G bought out:** Berner, "Case Study—SpinBrush."

76 **covers of business magazines:** Gregory Heisler, "Jeff Bezos—Person of the Year," *Time*, December 27, 1999. https://content.time.com/time/covers/0%2C16641%2C1101991227%2C00.html; Nina Munk and Sam Jones, "The Taking of Time Warner," *Vanity Fair*, January 2004. https://www.vanityfair.com/news/2004/01/time-warner200401.

76 **dozens of patents:** Justia.com, "John D. Osher Inventions, Patents and Patent Applications—Justia Patents Search," 2020. https://patents.justia.com/inventor/john-d-osher; Justia.com, "John Osher Inventions, Patents and Patent Application—Justia Patents Search," 2016. https://patents.justia.com/inventor/john-osher.

77 **around thirty workers:** Raj Chetty, Gaia Dossi, Matt Smith, John Van Reenen, Owen Zidar, and Eric Zwick, "Creating New Businesses in America: The Determinants of and Returns to Entrepreneurship," Working Paper, 2025.

78 **grew his father-in-law's business:** Lynne R. Zacharias, "A Driven Life—a Man with More Than Business on His Mind," Corpmagazine.com, September 2009. https://www.corpmagazine.com/uncategorized/a-driven-life-a-man-with-more-than-business-on-his-mind/.

78 **sold it for $65 million:** "Aspen Mansion Sells for $65 Million," *Aspen Daily News*, May 24, 2023. https://www.aspendailynews.com/news/aspen-mansion-sells-for-65-million/article_d337973c-fa19-11ed-81d2-9bd7c86c2066.html.

78 **this one for $76 million:** E. B. Solomont, "Florida Car Dealership Owner Pays $76 Million for Aspen's Most Expensive Home," *Wall Street Journal*, September 6, 2023. https://www.wsj.com/real-estate/luxury-homes/florida-car-dealership-owner-pays-76-million-for-aspens-most-expensive-home-cb2f13fd.

78 **source told *Forbes*:** Martin, "The Car Dealership Billionaire No One Knows."

78 **lists come from public registrations:** Jetnet, "Aircraft Transaction History," n.d. https://www.jetnet.com/data/transaction-history/; "SuperYacht Owners Database—2023 Edition," n.d. https://www.superyachtfan.com/yacht-owners/.

79 **owns multiple yachts:** "SuperYacht Owners Database—2023 Edition."

CHAPTER 5: WHERE DO ENTREPRENEURS COME FROM?

83 **"The American Dream":** James Truslow Adams. *The Epic of America* (Little, Brown, 1931).

83 **He had no franchises:** Dick Portillo and Don Yaeger, *Out of the Dog House: Turning a $1,100 Investment into a Billion-Dollar Profit* (Triumph Books, 2018).

83 **Chicago-area mansion:** Authors' analysis of Jetnet data. Accessed May 15, 2024, at https://www.jetnet.com/.

83 **130-foot Westport yacht:** Authors' analysis of SuperYacht Fan data. Accessed May 15, 2024, at https://www.superyachtfan.com/.

83 **expanded into multiple states:** Authors' interview with Karen Bentlage, October 10, 2024.

84 **daunting poverty to spectacular wealth:** This profile draws from interviews with Portillo and his associates, and also fills in substantial detail from his memoir, *Out of the Dog House.*

85 **"good people and raised on hard work":** See Portillo and Yaeger, *Out of the Dog House.*

85 **"scariest places in urban America":** Ben Austen, "The Towers Came Down, and with Them the Promise of Public Housing," *New York Times*, February 6, 2018. https://www.nytimes.com/2018/02/06/magazine/the-towers-came-down-and-with-them-the-promise-of-public-housing.html.

85 **personality traits as youths:** Ross Levine and Yona Rubinstein, "Smart and Illicit: Who Becomes an Entrepreneur and Do They Earn More?" *Quarterly Journal of Economics* 132, no. 2 (May 2017): 963–1018. https://doi.org/10.1093/qje/qjw044.

86 **far from the only troublemaker:** See Levine and Rubinstein, "Smart and Illicit."

86 **"career of odd jobs":** See Portillo and Yaeger, *Out of the Dog House.*

86 **strong problem-solving skills:** See Levine and Rubinstein, "Smart and Illicit."

86 **Test scores strongly predict future income:** Raj Chetty, Gaia Dossi, Matthew Smith, John Van Reenen, Owen Zidar, and Eric Zwick, "Creating New Businesses in America: The Determinants of and Returns to Entrepreneurship," 2025. Figure: Entrepreneurship Rates, Income, and Patenting Rates by Standardized Test Score Percentiles. Based on authors' analysis of U.S. Treasury Department data.

87 **only 1.3 times as often:** See Chetty et al., "Creating New Businesses in

America," Figure: Entrepreneurship Rates, Income, and Patenting Rates by Standardized Test Score Percentiles. Based on authors' analysis of U.S. Treasury Department data.

87 **elite colleges don't play nearly as large a role:** See Chetty et al., "Creating New Businesses in America," Figure: Entrepreneurship and the American Dream.

90 **dishes home every night:** See Portillo and Yaeger, *Out of the Dog House.*

93 **"best moments of my life":** Authors' interview with Karen Bentlage.

94 **70 percent wound up earning more than their parents:** Raj Chetty, David Grusky, Maximilian Hell, Nathaniel Hendren, Robert Manduca, and Jimmy Narang, "The Fading American Dream: Trends in Absolute Income Mobility Since 1940," 2017. Online Data Table 6: Levels of Child and Parent Income in 2014 Dollars by Income Percentile and Child Birth Cohort. https://opportunityinsights.org/data/?geographic_level=0&topic=0&paper_id=546#resource-listing.

94 **More than 90 percent:** Raj Chetty, David Grusky, Maximilian Hell, Nathaniel Hendren, Robert Manduca, and Jimmy Narang, "The Fading American Dream: Trends in Absolute Income Mobility Since 1940," *Science* 356, no. 6336 (April 2017): 398–406. https://doi.org/10.1126/science.aal4617.

94 **American Dream is dying:** David Leonhardt, *Ours Was the Shining Future* (Random House, 2023).

94 **higher rates of upward mobility:** Ran Abramitzky, Leah Boustan, Elisa Jácome, and Santiago Pérez, "Intergenerational Mobility of Immigrants in the United States over Two Centuries," *American Economic Review* 111, no. 2 (February 2021): 580–608. https://doi.org/10.1257/aer.20191586.

95 **Entrepreneurs come from every socioeconomic class:** See Chetty et al., "Creating New Businesses in America," Table: Unique Founder Summary Statistics. Based on authors' analysis of U.S. Treasury Department data.

95 **families with two well-educated parents:** See Levine and Rubinstein, "Smart and Illicit."

95 **as likely to have founded a firm:** See Chetty et al., "Creating New Businesses in America." Based on authors' analysis of U.S. Treasury Department data.

95 **likelier to come from certain racial and gender groups:** Authors' calculations using the U.S. Census Bureau's 2023 Annual Business Survey (reference year 2022) and 2022 American Community Survey 1-Year Estimates (Table B03002).

95 **seven times likelier to found a superstar firm:** See Chetty et al., "Creating New Businesses in America," Figure: Entrepreneurship Rates by Parental Background, Geography, and Demographic Characteristics and authors' analysis of U.S. Treasury Department data.

95 **Racial gaps:** Authors' calculations using the U.S. Census Bureau's 2023 Annual Business Survey (reference year 2022) and 2022 American Community Survey 1-Year Estimates.

95 **Men are more than three times likelier:** See Chetty et al., "Creating New Businesses in America," Table: Differences in Characteristics and Outcomes (1980–1987 Cohorts) and authors' analysis of U.S. Treasury Department data.

96 **Even among star founders:** See Chetty et al., "Creating New Businesses in America." Based on authors' analysis of U.S. Treasury Department data.

97 **the most entrepreneurial cities:** See Chetty et al., "Creating New Businesses in America." Based on authors' analysis of U.S. Treasury Department data.

97 **not strongly associated with:** See Chetty et al., "Creating New Businesses in America." Based on authors' analysis of U.S. Treasury Department data.

97 **odds of rising from the bottom fifth to the top fifth:** Raj Chetty, Nathaniel Hendren, Patrick Kline, and Emmanuel Saez, "Where Is the Land of Opportunity? The Geography of Intergenerational Mobility in the United States," 2014. Online Data Table 6: Geography of Mobility: Commuting Zone Quintile-Quintile Transition Matrices. https://opportunityinsights.org/data/?geographic_level=0&topic=0&paper_id=592#resource-listing.

97 **develops sales skills:** Jackson Lears, "The Mormon Ethic and the Spirit of Capitalism," *New Republic*, October 19, 2012. https://newrepublic.com/article/108787/the-mormon-ethic-and-the-spirit-capitalism.

97 **five factors matter:** Raj Chetty, Nathaniel Hendren, Patrick Kline, and Emmanuel Saez, "Where Is the Land of Opportunity? The Geography of Intergenerational Mobility in the United States," *Quarterly Journal of Economics* 129, no. 4 (November 2014): 1553–623. https://doi.org/10.1093/qje/qju022.

98 **region is slightly more racially segregated and unequal than average:** Chetty et al., "Where Is the Land of Opportunity?" Online Data Table 6: Geography of Mobility: Commuting Zone Quintile-Quintile Transition Matrices and Online Data Table 8: Geography of Mobility: Commuting Zone Characteristics.

98 **top origins of star entrepreneurs:** See Chetty et al., "Creating New Businesses in America," Tables: Top CZs by Star Entrepreneurship Rate (Childhood Location) and Bottom CZs by Star Entrepreneurship Rate (Childhood Location).

100 **credits his time in the Marines:** See Portillo and Yaeger, *Out of the Dog House*.

100 **"And I ended up number three":** Authors' interview with Karen Bentlage.

CHAPTER 6: WHAT DO ENTREPRENEURS NEED?

101 **cofounder of Y Combinator:** "Paul Graham: 'The Component of Entrepreneurship That Really Matters Is Domain Expertise,'" www.youtube.com. Accessed August 13, 2025. https://www.youtube.com/shorts/-8KWDNBfayo.

101 **Marceau Michel:** Emily Flitter, "A Black Venture Capitalist Sees Challenges as an Investing Edge," *New York Times*, September 10, 2020. https://www.nytimes.com/2020/09/10/business/black-venture-capital.html.

101 **Black founders had to provide most:** Flitter, "A Black Venture Capitalist Sees Challenges as an Investing Edge."

101 **female and minority owners:** Susan Coleman and Alicia Robb, "A Comparison of New Firm Financing by Gender: Evidence from the Kauffman Firm Survey Data," *Small Business Economics* 33, no. 4 (December 2009): 397–411.

102 **start a star company:** See Raj Chetty, Gaia Dossi, Matthew Smith, John Van Reenen, Owen Zidar, and Eric Zwick, "Creating New Businesses in America," 2025. Table: Direct and Indirect Effects.

102 **gaps in business creation:** See Chetty et al., "Creating New Businesses in America," Figure: Gaps in Entrepreneurship Rates.

103 **changed her life:** Authors' interview with Karen Bentlage.

104 **Small Business Administration loan:** Donald P. Cushman and Sarah Sanderson King, *Continuously Improving an Organization's Performance* (State University of New York Press, 1997).

104 **more than enough money:** Brian Solomon, "Shahid Khan: The New Face of the NFL and the American Dream," *Forbes*, September 5, 2012. https://www.forbes.com/sites/briansolomon/2012/09/05/shahid-khan-the-new-face-of-the-nfl-and-the-american-dream/?sh=4ae71bf50d2c.

105 **industry that produces more entrepreneurs:** See Chetty et al., "Creating New Businesses in America," Figure: The Effect of Labor Market Experience on Entrepreneurship (First Job Design).

105 **industry that produces more entrepreneurs:** See Chetty et al., "Creating New Businesses in America," Table: The Effect of Early Labor Market Experience on Entrepreneurship (Cohort Design).

105 **gaps in business creation:** See Chetty et al., "Creating New Businesses in America," Figure: Gaps in Entrepreneurship Rates.

105 **start businesses at lower rates:** See Chetty et al., "Creating New Businesses in America," Table: Differences in Characteristics and Outcomes (1980–1987 Cohorts).

106 **what kind of businesses:** Collin West and Gopinath Sundaramurthy, "Startups with at Least 1 Female Founder Hire 2.5x More Women," *Kauffman Journal*, October 17, 2019. https://www.kauffmanfellows.org/journal/female-founders-hire-more-women.

106 **entrepreneurs earned on average:** See Chetty et al., "Creating New Businesses in America," Figure: The Returns to Entrepreneurship.

108 **outsource as little as possible:** See Dick Portillo and Don Yaeger, *Out of the Dog House* (Triumph Books, 2018).

111 **knowing where every penny went:** See Portillo and Yaeger, *Out of the Dog House.*

111 **"This is going down":** Authors' interview with Karen Bentlage.

112 **commission for each franchise it sold:** Joseph Golden and A. J. Wasserstein, "Yale Case: European Wax Center in Manhattan: Determining Where in a Franchise System to Build a Business," Yale School of Management, December 17, 2019. https://som.yale.edu/sites/default/files/2025-04/European%20Wax%20Center%20in%20Manhattan.pdf.

112 **"really pretty bulletproof":** Authors' interview with Karen Bentlage.

113 **suddenly and without warning:** See Golden and Wasserstein, "Yale Case."

114 **her region generated:** Authors' interview with Karen Bentlage.

115 **business coach:** Outpace Enterprises, "Karen Bentlage." https://outpaceenterprises.com/coaches/karen-bentlage/.

118 **"making more money than I ever thought imaginable":** See Portillo and Yaeger, *Out of the Dog House.*

CHAPTER 7: GROWING AND SLICING THE PIE

122 **overall economic pie:** Authors' calculations using data from the IRS (Statistics of Income Division) and the Bureau of Economic Analysis.

123 **doubled their profits:** Results are based on calculations in Matthew Smith, Danny Yagan, Owen Zidar, and Eric Zwick, "Capitalists in the Twenty-First Century," *Quarterly Journal of Economics* 134, no. 4 (November 2019): 1675–745. https://doi.org/10.1093/qje/qjz020.

123 **owners took $15,000:** Smith et al., "Capitalists in the Twenty-First Century."

124 **did not receive paychecks:** Thomas Breen, "2nd Retreat Behavioral Health Exec Dies; Employees, Patients Scrambling," *CT Mirror*, June 27, 2024. https://ctmirror.org/2024/06/27/retreat-behavioral-health-new-haven-ct/.

124 **if the owner had lived:** See Smith et al., "Capitalists in the Twenty-First Century."

128 **building supply industry:** On their website, they provide a list of closed acquisitions. "Acquisitions," SRS Distribution, n.d. https://www.srsdistribution.com/en/about/acquisitions.

128 **ambitious growth-by-acquisition strategy:** For their biographies, see "Ron Ross," SRS Distribution, 2018. https://web.archive.org/web/20250418163833/https://www.srsdistribution.com/en/about/leadership/ron-ross/; and "Dan Tinker," SRS Distribution, 2018. https://www.srsdistribution.com/en/about/leadership/dan-tinker/.

128 **payout of $250 million:** See the press release from SRS Distribution, "SRS Announces $250 Million Distribution to Employees," June 21, 2021. https://www.srsdistribution.com/en/news-and-events/news/srs-announces-%24250-million-distribution-to-employees.

128 **Home Depot acquired SRS:** Home Depot, "The Home Depot Announces Agreement to Acquire SRS Distribution, a Leading Specialty Trade Distrib-

utor Across Multiple Verticals; Expands Offering and Capabilities for Pro Customers; Increases Total Addressable Pro Market by Approximately $50 Billion," March 28, 2024. https://ir.homedepot.com/news-releases/2024/03-28-2024-100102814.

129 **built a dataset:** Patrick Kline, Neviana Petkova, Heidi Williams, and Owen Zidar, "Who Profits from Patents? Rent-Sharing at Innovative Firms," *Quarterly Journal of Economics* 134, no. 3 (August 2019): 1343–404.

129 **Higher wages lead:** George A. Akerlof and Janet L. Yellen, eds., *Efficiency Wage Models of the Labor Market* (Cambridge University Press, 1986). https://doi.org/10.1017/CBO9780511559594.

129 **job at Buc-ee's:** Annasofia Scheve, "Watch: As Mega Buc-ee's Opens Between San Antonio and Houston, Greg Abbott Flirts with Career Change," *San Antonio Express-News*, June 11, 2024. https://www.expressnews.com/lifestyle/article/greg-abbott-worlds-largest-bucees-luling-19508616.php.

130 **100 percent matching policy:** See Stuart Buck, "Texas Gas Stations, NIH-Sponsored Post-Docs, and the Foolishness of Artificially Subsidizing Demand," Substack.com, Good Science Project, January 1, 2024. https://goodscience.substack.com/p/texas-gas-stations-nih-sponsored.

130 **Buc-ee's sued her:** More details of the case are included in a law blog post by Christopher McKinney, "Buc-ee's Loses Texas Retention Agreement Case," McKinney Law Firm, P.C., January 11, 2018. https://www.themckinneylawfirm.com/texasemploymentlawblog/2018/1/11/buc-ees-loses-texas-retention-agreement-case.

130 **fell from 65 percent:** Authors' update of Matthew Smith, Danny Yagan, Owen Zidar, and Eric Zwick, "The Rise of Pass-Throughs and the Decline of the Labor Share," *American Economic Review: Insights* 4, no. 3 (2022): 323–40. https://zidar.princeton.edu/sites/g/files/toruqf3371/files/syzz2022.pdf.

131 **goes to firm owners:** U.S. national income refers to the sum of all wages, salaries, profits, rents, and other forms of income generated by economic activity. Note that this figure differs from the numbers before because it represents the whole economy and includes payments to capital beyond profits, such as interest.

131 **shrunk in half:** U.S. Bureau of Labor Statistics, "Union Members Summary," Bls.gov., January 23, 2024. https://www.bls.gov/news.release/union2.nr0.htm.

131 **last time Congress:** See "History of Changes to the Minimum Wage Law," U.S. Department of Labor (Dol.gov.), 2023. https://www.dol.gov/agencies/whd/minimum-wage/history.

132 **Jimmy John's dropped:** "A.G. Schneiderman Announces Settlement with Jimmy John's to Stop Including Non-Compete Agreements in Hiring Packets," New York State Attorney General, June 22, 2016. https://ag.ny.gov/press-release/2016/ag-schneiderman-announces-settlement-jimmy-johns-stop-including-non-compete.

132 **"no-poaching" clause:** See the following: Joe Halpern, "Peter Cancro Optimistic Blackstone Can More Than Double the Size of Jersey Mike's," Franchisetimes.com, April 2, 2025. https://www.franchisetimes.com/franchise_mergers_and_acquisitions/peter-cancro-optimistic-blackstone-can-more-than-double-the-size-of-jersey-mike-s/article_f2b98949-b486-4fe6-aacf-d5caf7251e47.html; and Alan B. Krueger and Orley Ashenfelter, "Theory and Evidence on Employer Collusion in the Franchise Sector," *Journal of Human Resources* 57, no. S (April 2022): S324–S348.

132 **Camp Bow Wow:** Spencer Woodman, "Exclusive: Amazon Makes Even Temporary Warehouse Workers Sign 18-Month Non-Competes," *The Verge*, March 26, 2015. https://www.theverge.com/2015/3/26/8280309/amazon-warehouse-jobs-exclusive-noncompete-contracts; and Dave Jamieson, "Doggy Day Care Chain Makes Pet Sitters Sign Noncompetes to Protect 'Trade Secrets,'" *HuffPost*, November 24, 2014. https://www.huffpost.com/entry/camp-bow-wow_n_6207544.

132 **noncompete to a janitorial worker:** Matt O'Brien, "Even Janitors Have Noncompetes Now. Nobody Is Safe," *Washington Post*, October 18, 2018. https://www.washingtonpost.com/business/2018/10/18/even-janitors-have-noncompetes-now-nobody-is-safe.

133 **18 percent of workers:** Evan P. Starr, James J. Prescott, and Norman D. Bishara, "Noncompete Agreements in the US Labor Force," *Journal of Law and Economics* 64, no. 1 (2021): 53–84.

133 **lower wage growth:** See analysis in *Non-Compete Contracts: Economic Effects and Policy Implications* (Office of Economic Policy, U.S. Department of the Treasury, March 2016). https://home.treasury.gov/system/files/226/Non_Compete_Contracts_Econimic_Effects_and_Policy_Implications_MAR2016.pdf.

133 **afford to hire lawyers:** See, for instance, Dave Roos, "Noncompete Agreements Target Janitors as Well as VPs, but Why?" HowStuffWorks, July 19, 2021. https://money.howstuffworks.com/noncompete-agreements-news.htm.

133 **Oregon banned noncompetes:** Michael Lipsitz and Evan Starr, "Low-Wage Workers and the Enforceability of Noncompete Agreements," *Management Science* 68, no. 1 (2022): 143–70.

134 **$300 billion more:** More information can be found in the FTC's press release. See "FTC Proposes Rule to Ban Noncompete Clauses, Which Hurt Workers and Harm Competition," Federal Trade Commission, January 5, 2023. https://www.ftc.gov/news-events/news/press-releases/2023/01/ftc-proposes-rule-ban-noncompete-clauses-which-hurt-workers-harm-competition.

134 **abandoned this Biden-era rule:** Mark Goldstein, "FTC's Abandonment of the Noncompete Rule Does Not Necessarily Spell End of Scrutiny for U.S. Businesses," *Employment Law Watch*, September 15, 2025. https://

www.employmentlawwatch.com/post/102lpcj/ftcs-abandonment-of-the-noncompete-rule-does-not-necessarily-spell-end-of-scruti.

134 **prohibited noncompetes:** Paul Starkman and Daniel Kinsella, "States Are Charting Their Own Course on Employment Noncompetes," @BLaw, April 24, 2024. https://news.bloomberglaw.com/antitrust/states-are-charting-their-own-course-on-employment-noncompetes.

134 **exempt from key labor protections:** Matt Bruenig makes the case that small businesses are overrated for this reason, as well as several others, in the following article: Matt Bruenig, "Small Businesses Are Overrated," *Jacobin*, January 16, 2018. https://jacobin.com/2018/01/small-businesses-workers-wages.

135 **20 percent of small businesses:** In 2023, 22.5 percent of small (fewer than ten employees) private-sector firms offered health insurance. See the Medical Expenditure Panel Survey (MEPS) Insurance Component (IC) data tool for more estimates. "MEPS-IC Data Tool," Agency for Healthcare Research and Quality, n.d. https://datatools.ahrq.gov/meps-ic.

135 **only applies to those:** Internal Revenue Service, "Employer Shared Responsibility Provisions," Irs.gov., 2025. https://www.irs.gov/affordable-care-act/employers/employer-shared-responsibility-provisions.

136 **avoid costly environmental controls:** Policies are outlined in the U.S. federal register: Environmental Protection Agency (EPA), Small Business Compliance Policy, April 11, 2000. https://www.govinfo.gov/content/pkg/FR-2000-04-11/pdf/00-8955.pdf.

136 **Kim Jordan gathered:** Rachel Zurer, "How Kim Jordan Created a Beloved Employee-Owned Brand," SOCAP Global, April 24, 2018. https://socap-global.com/2018/04/how-kim-jordan-created-a-beloved-employee-owned-brand/.

136 **workers would own:** Information is from the documentary *We the Owners: Employees Expanding the American Dream*. Rutgers.edu., 2025. https://smlr.rutgers.edu/we-the-owners.

136 **second mortgage:** The history of New Belgium Brewing is described at "We Were Born on a Bike. The Rest Is History," New Belgium Brewing, 2025. https://www.newbelgium.com/company/story; and in the following live podcast episode: Guy Raz, "New Belgium Brewing Company: Kim Jordan," How I Built This Podcast with Guy Raz, *Wondery*, September 9, 2018. https://wondery.com/shows/how-i-built-this/episode/10386-live-episode-new-belgium-brewing-company-kim-jordan/?queryID=d43594fdc14fef0c6598402746b4dab9.

136 **craft breweries were relatively rare:** Kristin Toussaint, "New Belgium at 30: How the Iconic Brewery Has Evolved, from Employee Ownership to Acquisition," *Fast Company*, December 23, 2021. https://www.fastcompany.com/90706317/new-belgium-at-30-how-the-iconic-brewery-has-evolved-from-employee-ownership-to-acquisition.

136 **"acknowledged to our workers":** See Toussaint, "New Belgium at 30."

137 **New Belgium established its ESOP:** Jacob Laxen, "New Belgium Founder Jeff Lebesch Shares Insights on Life After Beer," *Coloradoan*, March 22, 2018. https://www.coloradoan.com/story/life/food/beer/2018/03/22/new-belgium-founder-jeff-lebesch-shares-insights-life-after-beer/417819002/.

137 **covering nearly 10 percent:** National Center for Employee Ownership (NCEO), "22% Increase in Closely Held Company ESOP Participants in Most Recent Data," Nceo.org, February 12, 2024. https://www.nceo.org/employee-ownership-blog/22-increase-closely-held-company-esop-participants-most-recent-data.

137 **median ESOP company:** Estimates on the shares of ESOPs from various industries are available from the National Center for Employee Ownership (NCEO), "ESOP Breakdowns by Industry," Esop.org, 2025. https://www.esop.org/infographics/esops-by-industry-sector.php.

137 **"high involvement culture":** Michelle Goodman, "How to Build an Employee-Owned Business," *Entrepreneur*, February 23, 2015. https://www.entrepreneur.com/growing-a-business/how-to-build-an-employee-owned-business/241522.

138 **company offered benefits:** New Belgium's benefits package is further described on its website: "Do Right by People," New Belgium Brewing Company, 2025. https://www.newbelgium.com/company/mission/do-right-by-people.

138 **ESOP sold the company:** See Toussaint, "New Belgium at 30."

138 **Miller filed for several patents:** A list of patents filed by Willis Miller can be found by searching using Justia, "Patents Search," 2025. https://patents.justia.com/inventor/willis-d-miller.

138 **C.H.I. employed eight hundred people:** More information on the acquisition can be found in the following clip and publication: *60 Minutes*, "Private Equity Heavyweight Pushing Employee Ownership," YouTube, May 7, 2024. https://www.youtube.com/watch?v=S0yAK2kiW1M; and Alyssa Choi, "Private Equity: Ownership 2.0," *Ivey Business Review*, April 30, 2025. https://www.iveybusinessreview.ca/magazine/articles/pe-employee-equity.

138 **bought C.H.I. for $3 billion:** Robert Channick, "This Illinois Company Was Just Sold for $3 Billion, but Hundreds of Employees Are Getting a Cut. Some Will Get $800,000," *Chicago Tribune*, May 17, 2022. https://www.chicagotribune.com/2022/05/16/this-illinois-company-was-just-sold-for-3-billion-but-hundreds-of-employees-are-getting-a-cut-some-will-get-800000/.

138 **6.5 times their annual pay:** Debra Pressey, "Payouts for Arthur Company's Employee-Owners Will Impact Local Economy, Officials Say," *News-Gazette*, May 18, 2022. https://www.news-gazette.com/business/employment/payouts-for-arthur-companys-employee-owners-will-impact-local-economy-officials-say/article_c276ba87-f44b-5349-8aed-8040650ce625.html; and Leslie Picker

and Ritika Shah, "Garage-Door Maker Employees Get Cash Reward in Takeover as Private Equity Tests Ownership Model," CNBC, May 17, 2022. https://www.cnbc.com/2022/05/17/garage-door-maker-employees-get-cash-reward-in-takeover-as-private-equity-tests-ownership-model.html.

139 **taken a second job:** Jon Wertheim, "Private Equity's Unlikely Champion for Giving Workers a Leg Up with Employee Ownership," CBS News, August 11, 2024. https://www.cbsnews.com/news/private-equitys-unlikely-champion-for-giving-workers-a-leg-up-with-employee-ownership-60-minutes-transcript/?ftag=CNM-00-10aab5j&linkId=419852479.

139 **"Grown men were crying":** The sale of C.H.I. is further described in Channick, "This Illinois Company Was Just Sold for $3 Billion."

CHAPTER 8: THE SHORTCUT: INHERITANCE

140 **Tyson Foods:** David Barboza, "Why Is He on Top? He's a Tyson, for One," *New York Times*, March 4, 2001. https://www.nytimes.com/2001/03/04/business/business-why-is-he-on-top-he-s-a-tyson-for-one.html.

141 **firm wisely pivoted:** Authors' interview with Adam Karns.

141 **Great Wealth Transfer:** Talmon Joseph Smith and Karl Russell, "The Greatest Wealth Transfer in History Is Here, with Familiar (Rich) Winners," *New York Times*, May 14, 2023. https://www.nytimes.com/2023/05/14/business/economy/wealth-generations.html; Jessica Dickler, "Strategies to Navigate the $68 Trillion 'Great Wealth Transfer,' According to Top-Ranked Advisors," CNBC, October 17, 2022. https://www.cnbc.com/2022/10/17/how-to-navigate-the-great-wealth-transfer-according-to-top-advisors.html.

141 **older generations of Americans:** Board of Governors of the Federal Reserve System, "DFA: Distribution of Household Wealth in the U.S. Since 1989." Updated June 20, 2025. https://www.federalreserve.gov/releases/z1/dataviz/dfa/distribute/chart/#quarter:140;series:Private%20businesses;demographic:generation;population:1,3,5,7;units:levels.

141 **concentrated great wealth:** Richard Fry, "Millennials Overtake Baby Boomers as America's Largest Generation," Pew Research Center, April 28, 2020. https://www.pewresearch.org/short-reads/2020/04/28/millennials-overtake-baby-boomers-as-americas-largest-generation/.

144 **retained his power:** Authors' interview with Adam Karns.

144 **estates worth more:** Internal Revenue Service, "Estate Tax." Updated October 29, 2024. https://www.irs.gov/businesses/small-businesses-self-employed/estate-tax.

145 **"all the credit":** Authors' interview with Adam Karns.

146 **inherited *or* bought:** Authors' calculations using the 2007 Survey of Business Owners (SBO). To arrive at the figure in the text, we combine (1) the 7 percent who said they inherited them, (2) the 70 percent of the 14 percent who said they received them as gift or transfers (because 70 percent of the

gift and transfer category are family firms, while the other 30 percent were not), and (3) 20 percent of the 32 percent who said they purchased them (because 40 percent of the purchased category are family firms, and the ages of those family firms suggest that around half of them—thus, 20 percent—are old enough to be inherited).

146 **earn at least $1 million:** Based on authors' calculations using U.S. Treasury Department data.

147 **worth at least $5 million:** Based on authors' calculations using 2022 Survey of Consumer Finances.

147 **Inherited firms on average:** Authors' calculations using 2007 Survey of Business Owners (SBO).

148 **Millionaire heir who inherited:** Based on authors' calculations using 2022 Survey of Consumer Finances.

149 **almost as high:** For the 9 percent, see Raj Chetty, Gaia Dossi, Matthew Smith, John Van Reenen, Owen Zidar, and Eric Zwick, "Creating New Businesses in America: The Determinants of and Returns to Entrepreneurship," 2025. Table: Differences in Characteristics and Outcomes (1980–1987 Cohorts) and authors' analysis of U.S. Treasury Department data. We use the 2007 Survey of Business Owners (SBO) to estimate the probability of inheriting a business by combining the share reporting inheritance with an additional estimate of those who either were gifted or purchased a family firm following similar steps to the inherited *or* bought (note above) but for all firms rather than just those above $5 million.

150 **took over after Perrino died:** See, for instance, Mitchell Armentrout, "Home Run Inn Pizza's CEO Joe Perrino Dies at 64—Saw Chicago as 'Pizza Capital of the World,'" *Chicago Sun-Times*, July 21, 2018. https://chicago.suntimes.com/2018/7/20/18407444/home-run-inn-pizza-s-joe-perrino-dies-saw-city-as-pizza-capital-of-the-world; Tom Barnas, "The History of Chicago's Very Own Home Run Inn Pizza," WGN9, August 25, 2020. https://wgntv.com/morning-news/chicago-scene/the-history-of-chicagos-very-own-home-run-inn-pizza/; Robert Channick, "Home Run Inn Promotes Dan Costello to CEO of Family-Owned Chicago Pizza Empire," *Chicago Tribune*, August 29, 2018. https://www.chicagotribune.com/2018/08/29/home-run-inn-promotes-dan-costello-to-ceo-of-family-owned-chicago-pizza-empire/; "People, Purpose, and Passion: How Home Run Inn Provides Pizza Perfection," *FoodChain Magazine*, June 28, 2024. https://foodchainmagazine.com/news/people-purpose-and-passion-how-home-run-inn-provides-pizza-perfection/; and Adam Rubenfire, "B-Schools Take On the Family Business," *Wall Street Journal*, July 2, 2014. https://www.wsj.com/articles/b-schools-take-on-the-family-business-1404327573.

150 **climbing the corporate ladder:** See Channick, "Home Run Inn Promotes Dan Costello to CEO of Family-Owned Chicago Pizza Empire."

150 **leverage the lucky circumstances:** Raj Chetty, Nathaniel Hendren, John

Friedman, Maggie R. Jones, and Sonya R. Porter, "The Opportunity Atlas: Mapping the Childhood Roots of Social Mobility," Opportunity Insights, 2018. https://opportunityinsights.org/paper/the-opportunity-atlas/.

151 **sand and gravel business:** Facebook. Modified November 21, 2014. https://www.facebook.com/SuperYachtFan/photos/katy-perry-placed-a-photo-of-herself-online-on-board-the-yacht-sassy-the-yacht-w/758594344189720/.

151 **Biscuitville restaurant chain:** Eric Townsend, "Biscuitville CEO Shares Story for 'Legends of Business' Series," Today at Elon, October 5, 2010. https://www.elon.edu/u/news/2010/10/05/biscuitville-ceo-shares-story-for-legends-of-business-series/.

151 **family grocery store chain:** "Convenience Store News Hall of Fame Inducts Former Sheetz CEO," *Altoona Mirror*, December 14, 2023. https://www.altoonamirror.com/news/local-news/2023/12/convenience-store-news-hall-of-fame-inducts-former-sheetz-ceo/.

151 **net worth at $1.9 billion:** "Sheetz Says Forbes Got It Wrong," CSP Daily News, July 28, 2015. https://www.cspdailynews.com/company-news/sheetz-says-forbes-got-it-wrong.

151 **fourth-generation cooperage company:** ISC Barrels, "Rooted in Family and Tradition," n.d. https://www.iscbarrels.com/rooted-family-tradition/.

151 **nine sixth-generation family members:** Shia Kapos, "Klein Tools Hammers Out a New Leadership Team," *Crain's Chicago Business*, August 26, 2014. https://www.chicagobusiness.com/article/20140826/BLOGS03/140829908/klein-tools-in-lincolnshire-sees-leadership-transition-but-family-tradition-continues.

151 **Canandaigua Wine Company:** Noah Kirsch, "How Two Brothers Built Their Family Wine Business into a $40 Billion Alcohol Empire," *Forbes*, October 18, 2017. https://www.forbes.com/sites/noahkirsch/2017/10/18/how-two-brothers-built-their-family-wine-business-into-a-40-billion-alcohol-empire/.

151 **Georgia Crown Distributing:** Tina Hunsicker, "Third Most Expensive Home Sale in Atlanta in 2011—Habersham Road in Buckhead," Real Vinings | Buckhead, January 9, 2012. https://realviningsbuckhead.com/tag/donald-leebern-iii/.

151 **now does business in:** Georgia Crown Distributing Co., "About Us," July 2, 2025. https://www.georgiacrown.com/about-us/.

151 **drain their inheritances:** Arash Nekoei and David Seim, "How Do Inheritances Shape Wealth Inequality? Theory and Evidence from Sweden," *Review of Economic Studies* 90, no. 1 (January 2023): 463–98. https://doi.org/10.1093/restud/rdac016.

152 **more harm than good:** Andrew Carnegie, "The Gospel of Wealth," Carnegie Corporation of New York, June 1889. https://www.carnegie.org/about/our-history/gospelofwealth/.

152 **leave the labor force:** Douglas Holtz-Eakin, David Joulfaian, and Harvey S. Rosen, "The Carnegie Conjecture: Some Empirical Evidence," *Quarterly Journal of Economics* 108, no. 2 (May 1993): 413–35. https://doi.org/10.2307/2118337.

152 **perform worse in dynamic industries:** Morten Bennedsen, Kasper Meisner Nielsen, Francisco Pérez-González, and Daniel Wolfenzon, "Inside the Family Firm: The Role of Families in Succession Decisions and Performance," *Quarterly Journal of Economics* 122, no. 2 (May 2007): 647–91. https://doi.org/10.1162/qjec.122.2.647.

152 **when heirs do not attend:** Francisco Pérez-González, "Inherited Control and Firm Performance," *American Economic Review* 96, no. 5 (December 2006): 1559–88. https://doi.org/10.1257/aer.96.5.1559.

152 **"picking the eldest sons":** David Cay Johnston, "Dozens of Rich Americans Join in Fight to Retain the Estate Tax," *New York Times*, February 14, 2000. https://archive.nytimes.com/www.nytimes.com/library/financial/010214tax-news-estate.html.

153 **"given the choice":** Authors' interview with Annette Lareau.

158 **Miller had established himself:** Larry H. Miller and Doug Robinson, *Driven: An Autobiography* (Shadow Mountain Publishing, 2010).

159 **bought the dealerships:** Scott Pierce and Tony Semerad, "Larry H. Miller Group Sells Its Foundational Car Dealerships to Georgia Company for $3.2 Billion," *Salt Lake Tribune*, September 29, 2021. https://www.sltrib.com/news/business/2021/09/29/larry-h-miller-automotive/.

160 **strongest in part:** Chaire Entreprises Familiales, "Research Letter #1," Dauphine Fondation, Université Paris Dauphine-PSL, January 2024. https://dauphine.psl.eu/fileadmin/mediatheque/chaires/Entreprises_familiales/lettres_recherche/Chair_FF_Research_letter_Janv2024_ENG.pdf.

160 **20 percent of larger companies:** Gur Aminadav and Elias Papaioannou, "Corporate Control Around the World," *Journal of Finance* 75, no. 3 (June 2020): 1191–246. https://doi.org/10.1111/jofi.12889.

160 **heirs who run them:** See Pérez-González, "Inherited Control and Firm Performance."

160 **"non-blood heirs":** Vikas Mehrotra, Randall Morck, Jungwook Shim, and Yupana Wiwattanakantang, "Adoptive Expectations: Rising Sons in Japanese Family Firms," *Journal of Financial Economics* 108, no. 3 (June 2013): 840–54. https://doi.org/10.1016/j.jfineco.2013.01.011.

CHAPTER 9: CASHING OUT AND CASHING IN

162 **"prestigious private equity firm":** Matt Levine, "Money Stuff," NewsletterHunt. Accessed July 28, 2025. https://newsletterhunt.com/emails/65994.

162 **opened the first Outback Steakhouse:** Chris T. Sullivan, "A Stake in the Business," *Harvard Business Review*, September 2005. https://hbr.org/2005/09/a-stake-in-the-business.

163 **juicy $115 million:** Kris Hundley, "Outback Returns to Roots for $3.2B," *Tampa Bay Times*, November 7, 2006. https://www.tampabay.com/archive/2006/11/07/outback-returns-to-roots-for-3-2b/; and "EX-99.A.5," U.S. Securities and Exchange Commission, June 14, 2007. https://www.sec.gov/Archives/edgar/data/874691/000095012307008688/y36002a7exv99waw5.htm.

163 **60 percent of PE deals:** The share of private equity deals involving small, founder-owned firms was 61 percent in 2023. See Michael Sasso, "Why Private Equity Is Chasing Plumbers and Lumber Yards," Bloomberg, July 12, 2023. https://www.bloomberg.com/news/articles/2023-07-12/why-private-equity-is-chasing-plumbers-and-lumber-yards.

164 **Kodiak Building Partners:** See "About Kodiak Building Partners | Empowering Local Businesses," Kodiak Building Partners, Accessed July 9, 2025. https://kodiakbp.com/about/.

164 **PE sector has soared:** PE sector transaction volume is documented in Steven N. Kaplan and Per Strömberg, "Leveraged Buyouts and Private Equity," *Journal of Economic Perspectives* 23, no. 1 (Winter 2009): 121–46. https://doi.org/10.1257/jep.23.1.121; and total value is documented in Palash Ghosh, "North America Increasingly Dominates Global Private Assets Industry—Preqin Report," Pionline.com, March 20, 2024. https://www.pionline.com/alternatives/north-america-increasingly-dominates-global-private-assets-industry-preqin-report/.

165 **nearly half of Yale's:** Liese Klein, "Yale University to Sell Billions in Private Equity amid Challenges," *CT Insider*, April 23, 2025. https://www.ctinsider.com/business/article/ct-yale-university-endowment-private-equity-sale-20288542.php.

165 **Endowment distributions grew:** "'Self-Confident Yet Selfless': Yale's David Swensen Dies at 67," *YaleNews*, May 6, 2021. https://news.yale.edu/2021/05/06/self-confident-yet-selfless-yales-david-swensen-dies-67.

166 **San Francisco Sausage Company:** "Our History | Columbus Foods," Archive.org, 2016. https://web.archive.org/web/20160321040028/http://www.columbussalame.com/about-us/our-history/.

166 **Under Endeavour's ownership:** "Columbus Foods," Endeavour. Accessed April 27, 2023. https://endeavour.com/portfolio/columbus-foods/.

167 **Endeavour sold:** Steven N. Kaplan, Juan F. Hernandez, and Adam Lucas, "Columbus Manufacturing and Arbor Investments," Chicago Booth Case Study, 2018.

167 **attract strategic interest:** Reuters Staff, "Hormel to Buy Premium Deli Meat, Salami Maker for $850 Million," Reuters, October 31, 2017. https://www.reuters.com/article/world/europe/hormel-to-buy-premium-deli-meat-salami-maker-for-850-million-idUSKBN1D01EO/.

168 **Staples had grown:** Sam Roberts, "Thomas G. Stemberg, Who Joined a Rival to Found Staples, Dies at 66," *New York Times*, October 23, 2015. https://www.nytimes.com/2015/10/24/business/thomas-g-stemberg-co

-founder-of-staples-dies-at-66.html; and Scott Helman, Michael Kranish, and André Carrilho, "The Dark Side of Mitt Romney," *Vanity Fair*, January 4, 2012. https://www.vanityfair.com/news/politics/2012/02/mitt-romney-201202.

168 **"redeeming social value":** Bloomberg News, "Romney Backer, Tom Stemberg, Defends Bain's Private-Equity Role of Making Money," Boston.com, May 18, 2012. https://www.boston.com/uncategorized/noprimarytagmatch/2012/05/18/romney-backer-tom-stemberg-defends-bains-private-equity-role-of-making-money/.

168 **cut its employee rolls:** Steve Rockwell, "Private Equity Pros: No Bain, No Gain?" Nrn.com, June 25, 2012. https://www.nrn.com/restaurant-insights/private-equity-pros-no-bain-no-gain-?successfulPurchase=true.

168 **cut the state's minimum wage:** Zaid Jilani, "Outback Steakhouse Is Pushing Florida to Lower Its Minimum Wage for Servers to $2.13," Republic Report, February 8, 2012. https://www.republicreport.org/2012/outback-florida-minimum-wage.

168 **management forced employees:** "Lawsuit by Outback Steakhouse Waiters and Bartenders Allowed to Proceed as Both Class Action and Collective Action," Waiterpay.com, January 22, 2011. https://www.waiterpay.com/blog/lawsuit-by-outback-steakhouse-waiters-and-bartenders-allowed-to-proceed-as-both-class-action-and-collective-action.

168 **175 protesters gathered:** Bill Varian, "Protesters Descend on Tampa Restaurant Firm Controlled by Bain Capital," *Tampa Bay Times*, August 27, 2012. https://www.tampabay.com/news/publicsafety/protesters-descend-on-tampa-restaurant-firm-controlled-by-bain-capital/1248239/; and Kari Lydersen, "Romney's Bain in the Ass," *In These Times*, August 27, 2012. https://inthesetimes.com/article/romneys-bain-in-the-ass.

169 **Bain's cost-cutting measures:** Paul Gompers, Kristin Mugford, and J. Daniel Kim, "Bain Capital: Outback Steakhouse," HBS Case Study, 2012.

169 **profits had shrunk:** Associated Press, "Bloomin' Brands Files for IPO," Yahoo! Finance, April 6, 2012. https://finance.yahoo.com/news/bloomin-brands-files-ipo-201259867.html.

169 **PE's notorious reputation:** Jennifer Szalai, "Book Review: 'Plunder,' by Brendan Ballou; 'These Are the Plunderers,' by Gretchen Morgenson and Joshua Rosner," review of *These Are the Plunderers: How Private Equity Runs—and Wrecks—America* by Gretchen Morgenson and Joshua Rosner; *Plunder: Private Equity's Plan to Pillage America*, by Brendan Ballou, *New York Times*, July 4, 2023. https://www.nytimes.com/2023/06/21/books/review/plunder-brendan-ballou-these-are-the-plunderers-gretchen-morgenson-joshua-rosner.html.

171 **mortality rose by 11 percent:** Atul Gupta, Sabrina T. Howell, Constantine Yannelis, and Abhinav Gupta, "Owner Incentives and Performance in Healthcare: Private Equity Investment in Nursing Homes," *Review of*

Financial Studies 37, no. 4 (April 2024): 1029–77. https://doi.org/10.1093/rfs/hhad082.

172 **procedural specialties doctor:** In 2017, the average wage income of a procedural specialties doctor (aged forty to fifty-five) was $635,700, which translates into roughly $815,000 in 2024. The share of procedural specialists in the top 1 percent of income (2017) was 56 percent. See Joshua D. Gottlieb, Maria Polyakova, Kevin Rinz, Hugh Shiplett, and Victoria Udalova, *Who Values Human Capitalists' Human Capital? The Earnings and Labor Supply of US Physicians.* No. w31469. National Bureau of Economic Research, 2023.

172 **changes the employer-employee relationship:** Will Gornall, Oleg R. Gredil, Sabrina T. Howell, Xing Liu, and Jason Sockin, "Do Employees Cheer for Private Equity? The Heterogeneous Effects of Buyouts on Job Quality," *Management Science* 71, no. 5 (May 2025): 4287–317. https://doi.org/10.1287/mnsc.2022.00951.

173 **small declines in overall employment:** See Kaplan and Strömberg, "Leveraged Buyouts and Private Equity."

173 **Upper East Side:** Lauren Thomas, "Meet the Best Friends Who Are Private Equity's Newest Young Stars," *Wall Street Journal*, March 1, 2025. https://www.wsj.com/finance/investing/meet-the-best-friends-who-are-private-equitys-newest-young-stars-401214d5.

173 **PE at L Catterton:** Matthew Perelman, LinkedIn. https://www.linkedin.com/in/matthew-perelman-6b289148/.

173 **PE at Apollo:** Alex Sloane, LinkedIn. https://www.linkedin.com/in/alex-sloane-7105263/.

173 **grew the portfolio:** Sujeet Indap, "Harvard Burger School," *Financial Times*, July 13, 2020. https://www.ft.com/content/7b2146f7-f55f-41f2-b0a9-772a1a3c317a.

174 **"Harvard Burger School":** Indap, "Harvard Burger School."

174 **letter to Buffett:** Chip Cutter, "A Warren Buffett Protégée Is on the Hunt for Small Companies. She Now Has Millions More to Spend," *Wall Street Journal*, March 1, 2024. https://www.wsj.com/business/entrepreneurship/warren-buffett-tracy-britt-kanbrick-fb304a50.

174 **"the three T's":** Anupreeta Das, "A Warren Buffett Protégée Strikes Out on Her Own," *New York Times*, July 16, 2022. https://www.nytimes.com/2022/07/16/business/warren-buffett-tracy-britt-cool.html.

174 **reviving struggling businesses:** Das, "A Warren Buffett Protégée Strikes Out on Her Own."

174 **walked her down the aisle:** Das, "A Warren Buffett Protégée Strikes Out on Her Own."

175 **avoid chopping up companies:** Chip Cutter, "Warren Buffett's Protégé Is Building a Mini Berkshire," *Wall Street Journal*, April 9, 2022. https://www.wsj.com/business/entrepreneurship/warren-buffetts-protege-is-building-a-mini-berkshire-11649496605.

176 **astonishing returns:** Peter Kelly and Sara Heston,"2024 Search Fund Study," Stanford Graduate School of Business, 2024. https://www.gsb.stanford.edu/faculty-research/case-studies/2024-search-fund-study.

176 **five times the annual number:** Neil Gallogly, "Young Entrepreneurs Find a Way to Indulge Their C.E.O. Dreams," *New York Times*, March 15, 2024. https://www.nytimes.com/2024/03/15/business/entrepreneurs-startups-search-fund.html; Josh Dennis and Erick Laseca, "The Evolution of Entrepreneurship Through Acquisition," November 7, 2016. https://polsky.uchicago.edu/wp-content/uploads/2018/03/Booth-Research-Evolution-of-ETA_FA110716.pdf; and "2024 Search Fund Study."

177 **a bit of an outlier:** See results from the 2024 Search Fund Study. In 2023, the percentage of female searchers increased to 17 percent.

182 **Nobody was doing that:** In 2024, the estimate of average unit volume (AUV) of McDonald's was closer to $4M, and the AUV of Jack in the Box locations was around $2M. See Danny Klein, "McDonald's Made a Big Growth Push in 2024," *QSR Magazine*, April 18, 2025. https://www.qsrmagazine.com/story/mcdonalds-made-a-big-growth-push-in-2024/; Jack in the Box, "What's the Average Unit Volume (AUV) of Jack in the Box?" Jack in the Box Corporate, May 8, 2025. https://www.jackintheboxfranchising.com/blog/average-unit-volume-auv-jack-in-the-box; and Jennifer Williams, "Chicago Hot Dog Eatery Portillo's Slims Down Menus to Expand Nationally," *Wall Street Journal*, April 10, 2025. https://www.wsj.com/articles/chicago-hot-dog-eatery-portillos-slims-down-menus-to-expand-nationally-311be817?.

CHAPTER 10: STEALTHY POLITICS

187 **"we're governed by the rich":** Nicholas Carnes, "Which Millionaire Are You Voting For?" *New York Times*, October 13, 2012. https://www.nytimes.com/2012/10/14/opinion/sunday/which-millionaire-are-you-voting-for.html?_r=0.

187 **highest property tax rates:** "50-State Property Tax Comparison Study: For Taxes Paid in 2021," Lincoln Institute of Land Policy and Minnesota Center for Fiscal Excellence, July 2022. https://www.lincolninst.edu/app/uploads/legacy-files/pubfiles/50-state-property-tax-comparison-for-2021-exec-summary.pdf.

187 **no law firm won more:** Ray Long, "Madigan's Kind of Town," *Chicago Tribune*, August 23, 2021. https://www.chicagotribune.com/2010/01/24/madigans-kind-of-town/.

187 **"Madigan Political Industrial Complex":** James Ylisela Jr., "Michael Madigan Is the King of Illinois," *Chicago*, November 20, 2013. https://www.chicagomag.com/chicago-magazine/december-2013/michael-madigan/.

188 **"In a good year":** Bernie Becker, "Let's Make a Deal," *Politico*, November 28, 2017. https://www.politico.com/newsletters/morning-tax/2017/11/28/lets-make-a-deal-034608.

188 **"piss off the Speaker":** Long, "Madigan's Kind of Town."

188 **narrowed it considerably**: Jon Seidel and Dave McKinney, "Madigan, ComEd Bribery Cases Could Be Upended by U.S. Supreme Court Ruling, Defense Attorneys Say," *Chicago Sun Times*, June 26, 2024. https://chicago.suntimes.com/chicago-corruption-trials/2024/06/26/supreme-court-snyder-ruling-madigan-corruption.

188 **to appeal his conviction:** Jon Seidel, "Madigan Heading into Appeal with Lawyers Who Convinced Supreme Court to Narrow Bribery Law," August 1, 2025. https://www.wbez.org/government-politics/2025/08/01/madigan-heading-to-appeals-court-with-lawyers-who-convinced-supreme-court-to-narrow-bribery-law.

189 **seats in far higher percentages:** Authors' analysis of employer businesses in the Current Population Survey.

189 **mean wealth of a House:** "Personal Finances: Net Worth—2018," OpenSecrets, 2018. https://www.opensecrets.org/personal-finances/top-net-worth?display=B&year=2018.

189 **more than ten times as likely:** Based on authors' analysis of "Personal Finances: Net Worth—2018" and Board of Governors of the Federal Reserve System, *Survey of Consumer Finances, 2019* (Board of Governors of the Federal Reserve System, 2022). Dataset. Accessed August 17, 2025. https://www.federalreserve.gov/econres/scf_2019.htm.

189 **25 percent of federal lawmakers:** Based on authors' analysis of Nicholas Carnes, *Congressional Leadership and Social Status (CLASS) Dataset*, Version 1.9 (Duke University, 2016). Accessed April 14, 2023. http://www.duke.edu/~nwc8/class.html.

190 **data from Northwestern:** Raymond Fisman, Jetson Leder-Luis, Catherine M. O'Donnell, and Silvia Vannutelli, "Revolving Door Laws and Political Selection," NBER Working Paper 33626, March 2025. https://www.nber.org/papers/w33626.

191 **Vern Buchanan:** "Vernon Buchanan," OpenSecrets, 2018. https://www.opensecrets.org/personal-finances/vernon-buchanan/net-worth?cid=N00027626.

191 **Don Beyer:** "Don Beyer," OpenSecrets, 2018. https://www.opensecrets.org/personal-finances/don-beyer/net-worth?cid=N00036018.

191 **Kevin Hern:** "Kevin Hern," OpenSecrets, 2018. https://www.opensecrets.org/personal-finances/net-worth?cid=N00040829.

191 **Brad Schneider:** "Brad Schneider," OpenSecrets, 2018. https://www.opensecrets.org/personal-finances/brad-schneider/net-worth?cid=N00033101.

191 **Mike Kelly:** "Mike Kelly," OpenSecrets, 2018. https://www.opensecrets.org/personal-finances/mike-kelly/net-worth?cid=N00031647.

191 **David Kustoff:** "David Kustoff," OpenSecrets, 2018. https://www.opensecrets.org/personal-finances/david-kustoff/net-worth?cid=N00025445.

191 **Lloyd Smucker:** "Lloyd Smucker," OpenSecrets, 2018. https://www.opensecrets.org/personal-finances/lloyd-smucker/net-worth?cid=N00038781.

191 **had working-class backgrounds:** Nicholas Carnes, "Does the Numerical Underrepresentation of the Working Class in Congress Matter?" *Legislative Studies Quarterly* 37, no. 1 (January 2012): 5–34.

191 **40 percent of legislators:** Authors' analysis of the data from Nicholas Carnes and Eric R. Hansen, *The 2023–24 State Legislators Dataset*, Version 1.3 [dataset] (Duke University, 2024). Accessed August 1, 2025. http://www.duke.edu/~nwc8/stateleg.html.

191 **ten times as likely:** Of the 7,386 state legislators serving across America listed in the Nick Carnes 2023–4 State Legislators Dataset, 21 are current or former auto dealers—Matt Woods (AL), Robert Ingram (AL), Roger Niello (CA), Emanuel Jones (GA), Stacey Donato (IN), Jeff Longbine (KS), Elaine Bowers (KS), Thomas Huff (KY), Phillip E. Tarver (LA), Shelley Rudnicki (ME), Brenden H. Jones (NC), Don Vigesaa (ND), Joni Albrecht (NE), Donovan Fenton (NH), Bill Reineke (OH), Brandon C. Potter (RI), Mike Reichenbach (SC), Mike Sparks (TN), Sam E. Harless (TX), Nancy VanderMeer (WI), and Amy Whalen (WI)—while just 2 are factory workers: Morgan Rielly (ME) and Robert Wirch (WI).

191 **most comprehensive study ever:** The Mayoral Candidates Dataset of Patricia Kirkland's "Electing CEOs," which builds on the data in this paper: Patricia A. Kirkland, "Business Owners and Executives as Politicians: The Effect on Public Policy," *Journal of Politics* 83, no. 4 (October 2021): 1652–68. https://doi.org/10.1086/715067.

191 **32 percent of all candidates:** Kirkland, "Business Owners and Executives as Politicians."

192 **weeds out:** Andrew B. Hall, *Who Wants to Run? How the Devaluing of Political Office Drives Polarization* (University of Chicago Press, 2019). https://doi.org/10.7208/chicago/9780226609607.001.0001.

192 **base pay at $174,000:** Ida Brudnick, "Salaries of Members of Congress: Recent Actions and Historical Tables," Congress.gov, August 26, 2025. https://www.congress.gov/crs-product/97-1011.

192 **job was part-time:** Kirkland, "Business Owners and Executives."

193 **routinely cost more:** Amisa Ratliff, "The Congressional Fundraising Treadmill," *Issue One*, February 10, 2023. https://issueone.org/articles/the-congressional-fundraising-treadmill-2022-election; and McKayla Girardin, "How Much Does It Cost to Run for Office in 2025?" GoodParty.org, November 7, 2025. https://goodparty.org/blog/article/how-much-cost-run-for-office.

194 **When Bob Corker won:** "Bob Corker," OpenSecrets, 2015. https://www.opensecrets.org/personal-finances/bob-corker/net-worth?cid=N00027441.

194 **collected trash and bagged ice:** Carl Fussman, "What I've Learned: Senator

Bob Corker (R, Tenn.)," *Esquire*, October 18, 2010. https://www.esquire.com/news-politics/news/a8668/bob-corker-interview-1110/#ixzz22IyuuJe9.

194 **built projects in eighteen states:** Fussman, "What I've Learned."

194 **tenants included a law firm:** Will Tucker, "Corker's Top Contributors Are Tenants in Building He Owns," Campaign for Accountability, January 20, 2016. https://campaignforaccountability.org/corkers-top-contributors-are-tenants-in-building-he-owns/.

194 **primary campaign war chest:** Christine Buttorff, "Corker Tops Latest Fundraising Numbers with Own Donation," WPLN, July 21, 2006. https://wpln.org/post/corker-tops-latest-fundraising-numbers-with-own-donation/.

194 **won the nomination:** "Sabato's Crystal Ball: Tennessee Races," Center for Politics, 2006. https://centerforpolitics.org/crystalball/2006/senate/tn.

197 **start a family produce business:** "Othal Brand Obituary," Legacy.com, December 14, 2009. https://www.legacy.com/us/obituaries/caller/name/othal-brand-obituary?id=39429121.

197 **America's largest onion shipper:** Brent M. S. Campney, "'A Bunch of Tough Hombres': Police Brutality, Municipal Politics, and Racism in South Texas," *Journal of the Southwest* 60, no. 4 (Winter 2018): 787–825. https://www.jstor.org/stable/48564035.

198 **farmed 40,000 acres:** Campney, "'A Bunch of Tough Hombres'" and "Othal Brand Obituary."

198 **pack eighty thousand bags:** Pamela Morales, "Stories from the Rio Grande—Season One," Museum of South Texas History. Accessed August 3, 2025. https://mosthistory.org/stories-from-the-rio-grande-season-one.

198 **"largest single payrolls":** Roberto Hugo Gonzalez, "Anecdote: Othal E. Brand, a Life of Public Service and Independent Leadership," *Texas Border Business*, July 7, 2023. https://texasborderbusiness.com/anecdote-othal-e-brand-a-life-of-public-service-and-independent-leadership.

198 **"seed to shelf":** "Heritage Hall of Honor," State Fair of Texas. Accessed August 3, 2025. https://bigtex.com/supporting-texans/agriculture/hall-of-honor.

198 **an iron will:** Campney, "'A Bunch of Tough Hombres.'"

198 **"the necessary equipment":** Dan Balz, "Brutality Charges, Bitterness Haunt McAllen, Tex.," *Washington Post*, June 1, 1981. https://www.washingtonpost.com/archive/politics/1981/06/02/brutality-charges-bitterness-haunt-mcallen-tex/ddf97d23-83c9-4ca8-a6fa-296caadff557.

198 **feudal lord:** Campney, "'A Bunch of Tough Hombres.'"

199 **an effort to intimidate:** Balz, "Brutality Charges."

199 **dominated city politics:** Campney, "'A Bunch of Tough Hombres.'"

199 **bloated octopus:** Campney, "'A Bunch of Tough Hombres.'"

199 **"every key leadership role":** Benn Farrell, "Palmer Lake Mayor Glant Havenar Resigns After 12 Years of Public Service," *Colorado Springs Gazette*, June 5, 2025. https://gazette.com/thetribune/palmer-lake-mayor-glant

-havenar-resigns-after-12-years-of-public-service/article_64a1a9ca-db27-40f3-9d21-18a9914b5956.html.

199 **Palmer Lake Board of Trustees:** Benn Farrell, "Palmer Lake Mayor-Elect Glant Havenar Eager to Continue Serving the Town," *Colorado Springs Gazette*, December 6, 2022. https://gazette.com/thetribune/palmer-lake-mayor-elect-glant-havenar-eager-to-continue-serving-the-town/article_bd9afb5a-735d-11ed-919d-532c6b77d6bb.html.

200 **"on the outskirts":** Jim Carlton, "The 'Cable Cowboy' Battles a Giant Gas Station for the Soul of the West," *Wall Street Journal*, July 12, 2025. https://www.wsj.com/us-news/bucees-gas-station-malone-colorado-d0c2c131?st=7MJ3kz&reflink=desktopwebshare_permalink.

200 **Facing a firestorm:** Havenar never gave a reason for resigning and never admitted to any of the charges.

201 **project remains uncertain:** Briana Heaney, "In Debate over New Buc-ee's, Early Results Show Palmer Lake Residents Want a Public Vote and Recall of Two Trustees," Colorado Public Radio, September 10, 2025. https://www.cpr.org/2025/09/10/in-debate-over-new-buc-ees-early-results-show-palmer-lake-residents-want-a-public-vote-and-recall-of-two-trustees/.

201 **who donates to:** "House Ways and Means Committee—118th Congress (2022 Cycle)," OpenSecrets, 2022. https://www.opensecrets.org/cong-cmtes/industries?cmte=HWAY&cmtename=Ways+and+Means&cong=118&cycle=2022; and "Senate Finance Committee—118th Congress (2022 Cycle)," OpenSecrets, 2022. https://www.opensecrets.org/cong-cmtes/industries?cmte=SFIN&cmtename=Finance&cong=118&cycle=2022.

201 **state lobbying totals:** Sarah Moshary and Cailin Slattery, "Consolidation and Political Influence in the Auto Retail Industry," *SSRN Electronic Journal*, January 1, 2024. https://doi.org/10.2139/ssrn.4832068.

201 **top five industries:** Moshary and Slattery, "Consolidation and Political Influence in the Auto Retail Industry."

202 **supported right-wing causes:** Justin Elliott, Megan O'Matz, and Doris Burke, "That Cardboard Box in Your Home Is Fueling Election Denial," ProPublica, October 26, 2022. https://www.propublica.org/article/uline-uihlein-election-denial.

203 **spent more than $300 million:** Elliott et al., "That Cardboard Box."

203 **largest federal campaign donors:** Elliott et al., "That Cardboard Box."

203 **Club for Growth Action:** "Uihlein, Richard: Donor Detail," OpenSecrets, February 6, 2025. https://www.opensecrets.org/outside-spending/donor_detail/2024?id=U0000003690&name=Uihlein,+Richard+&+Elizabeth=&super_only=S&type=I.

203 **$43.5 million in tax savings:** Justin Elliott and Robert Faturechi, "Secret IRS Files Reveal How Much the Ultrawealthy Gained by Shaping Trump's 'Big, Beautiful Tax Cut,'" ProPublica, August 11, 2021. https://www.propublica

.org/article/secret-irs-files-reveal-how-much-the-ultrawealthy-gained-by-shaping-trumps-big-beautiful-tax-cut.

204 **"they have no choice":** Steve Volk, "George Norcross: The Man Who Destroyed Democracy," *Philadelphia*, March 29, 2013. https://www.phillymag.com/news/2013/03/29/george-norcross-man-destroyed-democracy/2/.

204 **"unless George is OK":** Steve Kornacki, "With Enemies Like These, Chris Christie Doesn't Need to Make Friends," *Politico*, July 5, 2011. https://www.politico.com/states/new-york/city-hall/story/2011/07/with-enemies-like-these-chris-christie-doesnt-need-to-make-friends-068865.

205 **entities tied to Norcross:** Nancy Solomon and Jeff Pillets, "How Companies and Allies of One Powerful Democrat Got $1.1 Billion in Tax Breaks," ProPublica, May 1, 2019. https://www.propublica.org/article/george-norcross-democratic-donor-tax-breaks.

205 **"boorish and indecorous":** Matt Friedman, "Corruption Indictment Against New Jersey Power Broker George Norcross Is Tossed," *Politico*, February 26, 2025. https://www.politico.com/news/2025/02/26/corruption-indictment-against-new-jersey-power-broker-george-norcross-is-tossed-00206192.

206 **"skeptical of government regulation":** Neil Malhotra, Yotam Margalit, and Saikun Shi, "The Politics of Small Business Owners," *British Journal of Political Science* 55, e94 (July 2025): 1–25.

206 **a large-scale 2024 survey:** Malhotra et al., "The Politics of Small Business Owners."

206 **most Republican leaning:** Authors' analysis of FEC donation data.

206 **Norcross-linked projects:** Nancy Solomon, WNYC, *Dead End: Crime and Politics* (Podcast), Season 1, Episode 6, "On the (Camden) Waterfront," May 24, 2022.

207 **Paycheck Protection Program:** João Granja, Christos Makridis, Constantine Yannelis, and Eric Zwick, "Did the Paycheck Protection Program Hit the Target?" *Journal of Financial Economics* 145, no. 3 (September 2022): 725–61. https://doi.org/10.1016/j.jfineco.2022.05.006; and David Autor, David Cho, Leland D. Crane, Mita Goldar, Byron Lutz, Joshua Montes, William B. Peterman, David Ratner, et al., "The $800 Billion Paycheck Protection Program: Where Did the Money Go and Why Did It Go There?" *Journal of Economic Perspectives* 36, no. 2 (Spring 2022): 55–80. https://doi.org/10.1257/jep.36.2.55.

207 **operated the same way:** Granja et al., "Did the Paycheck Protection Program Hit the Target?" and Autor et al., "The $800 Billion Paycheck Protection Program."

207 **twenty-eight members of Congress:** Jon Skolnik, "GOP Congressmen Reap Millions in Federal Loans for Personal Car Dealerships," *Salon*, September 25, 2021. https://www.salon.com/2021/09/25/congressmen-reap-millions-in-loans-for-personal-car-dealerships/; and Justin Glawe, "Members of

Congress Profited from COVID Bailout While Small Businesses Were Shut Out," *Sludge*, December 24, 2020. https://readsludge.com/2020/12/24/members-of-congress-profited-from-covid-bailout-while-small-businesses-were-shut-out/.

207 **Other PPP beneficiaries from Congress:** Skolnik, "GOP Congressmen Reap Millions in Federal Loans," and Glawe, "Members of Congress Profited from COVID Bailout."

208 **"a Large Order of PPP":** Timothy L. O'Brien, "'McCongressman' Gets a Large Order of PPP," Bloomberg, July 7, 2020. https://www.bloomberg.com/view/articles/2020-07-07/-mccongressman-kevin-hern-gets-a-large-order-of-ppp.

208 **broader social costs:** Jason Grotto, "An Unfair Burden," *Chicago Tribune*, June 10, 2017. https://apps.chicagotribune.com/news/watchdog/cook-county-property-tax-divide/assessments.html.

208 **tax reductions when they do:** Carlos Avenancio-Leon and Troup Howard, "The Assessment Gap: Racial Inequalities in Property Taxation," *Quarterly Journal of Economics* 137, no. 3 (August 2022): 1383–434.

CHAPTER 11: MARKET POWER IN A MILLION MARKETS

210 **James Willis Hensley:** Noam Scheiber, "Made Man: How Cindy Hensley Invented John McCain," *New Republic*, August 20, 2008. https://newrepublic.com/article/64809/made-man.

210 **net worth at $200 million:** John Dougherty and Amy Silverman, "Haunted by Spirits," *Phoenix New Times*, February 17, 2000. https://www.phoenixnewtimes.com/news/haunted-by-spirits-6438434.

210 **company revenues of $300 million:** David M. Halbfinger, "Beer Money: The McCains and the InBev, Anheuser-Busch Deal," *New York Times*, July 14, 2008. https://archive.nytimes.com/thecaucus.blogs.nytimes.com/2008/07/14/mccains-to-profit-from-inbev-anheuser-busch-deal/.

210 **eleven of their thirteen vehicles:** Jonathan Martin and Mike Allen, "McCain Unsure How Many Houses He Owns," *Business Insider*, August 21, 2008. https://www.businessinsider.com/2008/8/john-mccain-unsure-how-many-houses-he-owns; Keith Naughton, "All the Candidates' Cars," *Newsweek*, September 19, 2008. https://www.newsweek.com/all-candidates-cars-88579; and David M. Halbfinger, "For McCains, a Public Path but Private Wealth," *New York Times*, August 22, 2008. https://www.nytimes.com/2008/08/23/us/politics/23mccain.html.

211 **country's largest beer distributor:** Steven R. Strahler, "A Family Empire Built on Beer," *Crain's Chicago Business*, February 9, 2022. https://www.chicagobusiness.com/manufacturing/how-reyes-holdings-became-biggest-beer-distributor-us.

211 **each worth $12 billion:** "J. Christopher Reyes," *Forbes*. Accessed August

18, 2025. https://www.forbes.com/profile/j-christopher-reyes/; and "Jude Reyes," *Forbes*. Accessed August 18, 2025. https://www.forbes.com/profile/jude-reyes/.

211 **fifty-two facilities across eleven states:** Reyes Beverage Group. Accessed August 3, 2025. https://reyesbeveragegroup.com/.

211 **sixteen million cases' worth:** Kate Bernot, "Unstoppable Force—New Acquisitions Set Reyes on Path to Dominate U.S.'s Largest Beer Markets," *Good Beer Hunting*, October 17, 2022. https://www.goodbeerhunting.com/sightlines/2022/10/17/new-acquisitions-set-reyes-on-path-to-dominate-uss-largest-beer-markets.

213 **"first real beer is yours":** "Roosevelt Gets First Cases of Capital's 3.2 Beer; Gov. Lehman Will Serve the Brew at Albany," *New York Times*, April 7, 1933. https://timesmachine.nytimes.com/timesmachine/1933/04/07/issue.html.

213 **1935 federal anti-tied-house law:** Andrew J. Miller, "Crafting a Better Industry: Addressing Problems of Regulation in the Craft Beer Industry," *University of Illinois Law Review* 19, no. 4 (2019): 1353–84. https://illinoislawrev.web.illinois.edu/wp-content/uploads/2019/09/Miller.pdf.

214 **born the middle tier:** Marc Sorini, "Understanding the Three-Tier System: Its Impacts on U.S. Craft Beer and You," CraftBeer.com, March 6, 2017. https://www.craftbeer.com/craft-beer-muses/three-tier-system-impacts-craft-beer.

214 **"the opportunity to sell beer":** Harry Hurt III, "Muscling in on Texas Beer," *Texas Monthly*, March 1976. https://www.texasmonthly.com/food/muscling-in-on-texas-beer/.

214 **gobbled up regional players:** "Brewers Association Releases Annual Craft Brewing Industry Production Report and Top 50 Producing Craft Brewing Companies for 2023," Brewers Association, April 16, 2024. https://www.brewersassociation.org/association-news/brewers-association-releases-annual-craft-brewing-industry-production-report-and-top-50-producing-craft-brewing-companies-for-2023/.

215 **"distributors were fabulously rich":** Dan Baum, *Citizen Coors: A Grand Family Saga of Business, Politics, and Beer*. Illustrated reprint ed. (HarperCollins, 2001).

215 **"modest subdivision house":** Baum, *Citizen Coors*, 50.

215 **restricted brewers from canceling:** Jacob Burgdorf, *Franchise Termination Laws, Craft Brewery Entry and Growth*, Economic Analysis Group Discussion Paper EAG 21–3 (U.S. Department of Justice, November 2021). https://www.justice.gov/atr/page/file/1454331/dl.

215 **provide such franchise protection:** Marc E. Sorini, *Beer Franchise Law Summary*, Brewers Association, June 2014. https://www.brewersassociation.org/wp-content/uploads/2015/06/Beer-Franchise-Law-Summary.pdf.

215 **Wine and spirits distributors:** Ryan Malkin and Ashley Hanke, "How to

Do Business in a Franchise State," SevenFifty Daily, October 22, 2018. https://daily.sevenfifty.com/how-to-do-business-in-a-franchise-state/.

216 **thirty-six feature that stipulation:** Based on a review of a 2014 legal analysis by the Brewers Association.

216 **conference:** National Beer Wholesalers Association, "America's Beer Distributors Deliver Effective Advocacy at NBWA Legislative Conference," NBWA, April 17, 2024. https://nbwa.org/press-release/2024-legislative-conference/.

216 **Purser quarterbacked:** Jim Myers, "McCurdy, Inhofe Win," *Tulsa World*, August 24, 1994. https://tulsaworld.com/archive/mccurdy-inhofe-win/article_e5d12ddb-ae85-55f2-a0db-a0552f83736b.html.

216 **trade press:** According to *VinePair* reporter Dave Infante. Portions of this chapter on beer distributors draw on research that the authors commissioned from Infante.

216 **making over $1.5 million:** Oksana Davidyan, "National Beer Wholesalers Association Inc Nonprofit Explorer," ProPublica. Accessed August 3, 2025. https://projects.propublica.org/nonprofits/organizations/361521005.

217 **two other political action committees:** "Political Action Committees (PACs)," OpenSecrets, 2022. https://www.opensecrets.org/political-action-committees-pacs/2022.

217 **political power often shocks:** Liz Essley Whyte, "Alcohol Distributors Ply Statehouses to Keep Profits Flowing," *Time*, August 6, 2015. https://time.com/3986536/alcohol-distributors-lobbying/.

217 **Jeffrey Birnbaum:** Jeffrey Birnbaum, Tyler Maroney, and Dustin Smith, "The Influence Merchants," esp. inset "Hey, Beer Man!" *Fortune*, December 7, 1998, 132–52; see also Conor McGrath, "'Family Businesses Distributing America's Beverage': Managing Government Relations in the National Beer Wholesalers Association," *Journal of Public Affairs* 3, no. 3 (August 2003): 212–24.

217 **President Clinton:** Robin Toner, "Clinton's Health Plan; Smokers Will Pay, Drinkers Will Not," *New York Times*, September 25, 1993. https://www.nytimes.com/1993/09/25/us/clinton-s-health-plan-smokers-will-pay-drinkers-will-not.html.

217 **Anheuser-Busch:** Portions of this chapter on beer distributors draw on research that the authors commissioned from Infante, who subsequently published an article that drew on that same research: Dave Infante, "Beer Distributors Got Their Long-Coveted Tax Cut. Here's Why It Matters," *VinePair*, August 1, 2025.

217 **"1-800-BEER-TAX":** Clifford Krauss, "CLINTON'S HEALTH PLAN: Interest Groups; Lobbyists of Every Stripe Turning to the Grass Roots on Health Care," *New York Times*, September 24, 1993. https://www.nytimes.com/1993/09/24/us/clinton-s-health-plan-interest-groups-lobbyists-every-stripe-turning-grass-roots.html.

218 **anti-FET rally:** "Anheuser-Busch Distributor Launches National Con-

sumer Tax Alert," TaxNotes, February 10, 1993. https://www.taxnotes.com/research/federal/other-documents/washington-roundup/full-text-beer-tax-awareness-release/146pk.

218 **"letters and phone calls":** Conor McGrath, "Lobbying by US Beer Wholesalers," in *The Handbook of Public Affairs*, ed. Phil Harris and Craig S. Fleisher (SAGE Publications, 2005), 269–80. https://doi.org/10.4135/9781848608108.n17.

218 **"health care reform package":** McGrath, "Lobbying by US Beer Wholesalers."

218 **David Rehr:** Interview cited in McGrath, "Lobbying by US Beer Wholesalers."

218 **MADD:** Juliet Eilperin, "Beer Lobby Keeps Anti-Drug Drive Alcohol-Free," *Washington Post*, July 23, 1999. https://www.washingtonpost.com/archive/politics/1999/07/23/beer-lobby-keeps-anti-drug-drive-alcohol-free/3b866b94-aa89-4ee8-a127-2834af220ec3/.

218 **"as hard as any":** Eilperin, "Beer Lobby Keeps Anti-Drug Drive Alcohol-Free."

218 **PepsiCo:** For reporting on PepsiCo's Blue Cloud Distribution, the rollout of Hard Mtn Dew, and the opposition from beer wholesalers, see Dave Infante, "Big Soda's Alcohol Ambitions Ain't Over," *VinePair*, March 8, 2024. https://vinepair.com/articles/hop-take-big-soda-alcohol-ambitions. Portions of this chapter on beer distributors draw on research that the authors commissioned from Infante.

219 **Purser told:** Justin Kendall, Jessica Infante, and Zoe Licata, "NBWA Annual Convention Day 1: Craig Purser on Adaptability, Hard MTN Dew Distribution Blues," *Brewbound*, October 10, 2022. https://www.brewbound.com/news/nbwa-annual-convention-day-1-craig-purser-on-adaptability-hard-mtn-dew-distribution-blues/.

219 **confusion in the marketplace:** Kate Bernot, "Citation Needed—Despite Lack of Details, Trade Orgs Go on Offense, Claim Hard MTN DEW Distributor Targets Kids," *Good Beer Hunting*, November 7, 2022. https://www.goodbeerhunting.com/sightlines/2022/11/7/trade-orgs-claim-hard-mtn-dew-distributor-targets-kids.

219 **"couldn't beat the middle tier":** Sean O'Leary, "PepsiCo Calls It Quits on Blue Cloud Distribution," Irish Liquor Lawyer, February 27, 2024. https://irishliquorlawyer.com/liquor-case-discussion/pepsico-calls-it-quits-on-blue-cloud-distribution/.

220 **"'force' dealers to buy":** Tesla, Inc. v. The Delaware Division of Motor Vehicles, Delaware Courts (The Supreme Court of the State of Delaware, filed December 9, 2022). https://www.courts.delaware.gov/supreme/oralarguments/download.aspx?id=4404.

220 **soured manufacturer-dealer relations:** "The NADA Story," NADA. Accessed August 3, 2025. https://www.nada.org/nada/nada-story.

220 **"good faith" standard:** *United States Code*. Title 15, § 1222. Accessed August 1, 2025. https://www.law.cornell.edu/uscode/text/15/1222.

221 **pay those dealers:** Francine Lafontaine and Fiona Scott Morton, "Markets: State Franchise Laws, Dealer Terminations, and the Auto Crisis," *Journal of Economic Perspectives* 24, no. 3 (Summer 2010): 233–50. https://doi.org/10.1257/jep.24.3.233.

221 **seventeen thousand franchised dealerships:** Sarah Moshary and Cailin Slattery, "Consolidation and Political Influence in the Auto Retail Industry," *SSRN Electronic Journal*, January 1, 2024. https://doi.org/10.2139/ssrn.4832068.

221 **1.3 million people:** "Automotive Industry: Employment, Earnings, and Hours," U.S. Bureau of Labor Statistics, August 2025. https://www.bls.gov/iag/tgs/iagauto.htm.

221 **Jones quipped:** Christopher Kamrani and Brian Hamilton, "Thanks to NIL, Local Car Dealers Are Out of the Shadows and Landing Star College Athletes," *New York Times*, June 10, 2024. https://www.nytimes.com/athletic/5550463/2024/06/10/nil-car-dealers-college-athletes-ncaa/.

222 **close low-volume dealerships:** Lafontaine and Morton, "Markets: State Franchise Laws, Dealer Terminations, and the Auto Crisis."

222 **one thousand of its thirty-two hundred:** Soyoung Kim and John Crawley, "GM, Chrysler to Cut up to 3,000 Dealers: Sources," Reuters, May 13, 2009. https://www.reuters.com/article/world/us/gm-chrysler-to-cut-up-to-3000-dealers-sources-idUSTRE54C64K/.

222 **just twelve hundred dealers:** U.S. House of Representatives, *GM and Chrysler Dealership Closures and Restructuring: Hearing Before the Subcommittee on Oversight and Investigations of the Committee on Energy and Commerce, House of Representatives, One Hundred Eleventh Congress, First Session, June 12, 2009*. Serial No. 111–49 (U.S. Government Printing Office, 2012). https://www.govinfo.gov/content/pkg/CHRG-111hhrg73744/html/CHRG-111hhrg73744.htm.

222 **moving too fast:** Kim and Crawley, "GM, Chrysler to Cut up to 3,000 Dealers: Sources."

222 **special arbitration system:** David Phelps, "Final Score: 28 Franchise Dealers Reprieved, 24 Shut," *Minnesota Star Tribune*, July 8, 2010. https://www.startribune.com/final-score-28-franchise-dealers-reprieved-24-shut/98076299/.

222 **GM reversing a third:** John Crawley, "Watchdog Questions GM and Chrysler Dealer Closings," Reuters, July 18, 2010. https://www.reuters.com/article/us-gm-dealers-idUSTRE66H2HS20100718; and Lafontaine and Morton, "Markets: State Franchise Laws, Dealer Terminations, and the Auto Crisis."

222 **"might be difficulties":** Crawley, "Watchdog Questions GM and Chrysler Dealer Closings."

223 **Multiple Listing Service:** "Multiple Listing Service (MLS): What Is It,"

National Association of Realtors. Accessed August 3, 2025. https://www.nar.realtor/mls-online-listings/multiple-listing-service-mls-what-is-it.

223 **platforms restricted:** Maggie Severns and Byron Tau, "Realtors Partied, Spent Big and Lobbied Hard. Then It All Came Crashing Down," *NOTUS*, May 20, 2024. https://www.notus.org/money/national-realtors-lobbying-politics.

223 **two to three times higher:** Panle Jia Barwick and Maisy Wong, "Competition in the Real Estate Brokerage Industry: A Critical Review," Brookings Institution, December 2019. https://www.brookings.edu/wp-content/uploads/2019/12/ES-12.12.19-Barwick-Wong.pdf.

224 **"sending the message":** Debra Kamin, "Home Sellers Win $1.8 Billion After Jury Finds Conspiracy Among Realtors," *New York Times*, October 31, 2023. https://www.nytimes.com/2023/10/31/realestate/nar-antitrust-lawsuit.html?smid=url-share.

224 **powerful market mechanism:** Anne Marie Cushmac, W. Robert Majure, Matthew Magura, John R. Read, Nina B. Hale, Joyce L. Bartoo, Matthew J. Bester, William H. Jones II, et al., *Competition in the Real Estate Brokerage Industry: A Report by the Federal Trade Commission and the U.S. Department of Justice.* Federal Trade Commission, August 2007. https://www.ftc.gov/reports/competition-real-estate-brokerage-industry-report-federal-trade-commission-us-department-justice.

224 ***Burnett v. NAR*:** "National Association of REALTORS® Reaches Agreement to Resolve Nationwide Claims Brought by Home Sellers," National Association of Realtors, March 15, 2024. https://www.nar.realtor/newsroom/nar-reaches-agreement-to-resolve-nationwide-claims-brought-by-home-sellers.

224 **NAR's rule:** Andrea V. Brambila, "Read the Playbooks of NAR, Keller Williams Ahead of Sitzer | Burnett," Inman, October 17, 2023. https://www.inman.com/2023/10/17/read-the-playbooks-of-nar-keller-williams-ahead-of-sitzer-burnett/.

224 **deny "any wrongdoing":** "National Association of REALTORS® Reaches Agreement to Resolve Nationwide Claims Brought by Home Sellers."

224 **"cooperating compensation":** National Association of Realtors, *Kevin Sears Discusses Key Settlement Considerations and Ongoing Advocacy Efforts on the Road*. Video, 5:07. March 21, 2024. https://www.nar.realtor/videos/kevin-sears-discussing-key-settlement-considerations-and-ongoing-advocacy-efforts-on-the-road?cid=em_LR-016.

224 **$350 million in annual revenue:** Andrea Suozzo, Alec Glassford, Ash Ngu, and Brandon Roberts, "National Association of Realtors Nonprofit Explorer," ProPublica, June 30, 2025. https://projects.propublica.org/nonprofits/organizations/361520690; Andrea Suozzo, Alec Glassford, Ash Ngu, and Brandon Roberts, "Chamber of Commerce of the United States of America," ProPublica, June 30, 2025. https://projects.propublica.org/nonprofits

/organizations/530045720; and Andrea Suozzo, Alec Glassford, Ash Ngu, and Brandon Roberts, "Business Roundtable Inc," ProPublica, June 30, 2025. https://projects.propublica.org/nonprofits/organizations/237236607.

224 **spent more on federal lobbying:** Indy Scholtens, "Federal Lobbying Set New Record in 2024," OpenSecrets, February 11, 2025. https://www.opensecrets.org/news/2025/02/federal-lobbying-set-new-record-in-2024.

225 **strategically funded stealthily named groups:** See this report on the funding sources of Alliance for a Better Pennsylvania, which lists the National Association of Realtors—Federal as the only contributor. Accessed December 9, 2025. https://www.transparencyusa.org/pa/committee/alliance-for-a-bettr-pennsylvania-pac-20130096; See also Severns and Tau, "Realtors Partied, Spent Big and Lobbied Hard."

225 **"a million times easier":** Carolyn Schwaar, "How and Why to Get Members Elected," National Association of Realtors, January 1, 2011. https://www.nar.realtor/realtor-ae-magazine/how-and-why-to-get-members-elected.

225 **rent hike:** Severns and Tau, "Realtors Partied, Spent Big and Lobbied Hard."

225 **local rent control ordinances:** Christie Zizo, "Orange County Rent Control Case Turned Away by Florida Supreme Court," ClickOrlando, April 17, 2023. https://www.clickorlando.com/news/politics/2023/04/17/orange-county-rent-control-case-turned-away-by-florida-supreme-court.

225 **artificial constraints on the number of residency positions:** Nicole C. McCann and Rochelle Walensky, "The First Step to Addressing the Physician Shortage," STAT, January 15, 2025. https://www.statnews.com/2025/01/15/physician-shortage-gme-residency-specialties-setting-limitations/.

226 **1997 Balanced Budget Act:** Stephanie Mackiewicz, "How Underfunded Graduate Medical Education Programs May Affect Otolaryngology," *ENTtoday*, April 1, 2014. https://www.enttoday.org/article/how-underfunded-graduate-medical-education-programs-may-affect-otolaryngology/3/?singlepage=1.

226 **only by one thousand positions:** "CMS Awards Third Round of Medicare-Funded Residency Slots to Hospitals," American Hospital Association, November 22, 2024. https://www.aha.org/news/headline/2024-11-22-cms-awards-third-round-medicare-funded-residency-slots-hospitals.

226 **doctors per thousand people:** "Number of Practicing Physicians per 1,000 Population," Commonwealth Fund, 2017. https://www.commonwealthfund.org/international-health-policy-center/system-stats/practicing-physicians.

226 **"full practice authority":** Deborah L. Feinstein, Martin Gaynor, Michael J. Bloom, Mark N. Hertzendorf, Elizabeth R. Hilder, David R. Schmidt, and Patricia Schultheiss, "Policy Perspectives: Competition and the Regulation of Advanced Practice Nurses," Federal Trade Commission, March 2014. https://www.ftc.gov/reports/policy-perspectives-competition-regulation-advanced-practice-nurses.

226 **costs substantially less:** Perri A. Morgan, Valerie A. Smith, Theodore S. Z. Berkowitz, David Edelman, Courtney H. Van Houtven, Sandra L. Woolson, Cristina C. Hendrix, Christine M. Everett, et al., "Impact of Physicians, Nurse Practitioners, and Physician Assistants on Utilization and Costs for Complex Patients," *Health Affairs* 38, no. 6 (June 2019). https://www.healthaffairs.org/doi/10.1377/hlthaff.2019.00014.

226 **repeatedly warned:** See, for example, their March 2014 report, "Policy Perspectives: Competition and the Regulation of Advanced Practice Nurses."

226 **Only Colorado and Oregon:** "Dental Home," Colorado Department of Regulatory Agencies. Accessed August 3, 2025. https://dpo.colorado.gov/Dental.

227 **lower reimbursements:** Ed Kilgore, "Why Dentists Oppose Democrats' Plan to Add Dental Coverage to Medicare," *Intelligencer*, September 27, 2021. https://nymag.com/intelligencer/2021/09/why-dentists-oppose-plan-to-add-dental-coverage-to-medicare.html.

227 **Medicare Sustainable Growth Rate:** Keith Fontenot, Caitlin Brandt, and Mark B. McClellan, "A Primer on Medicare Physician Payment Reform and the SGR," Brookings Institution, February 2, 2015. https://www.brookings.edu/articles/a-primer-on-medicare-physician-payment-reform-and-the-sgr/.

228 **flooded congressional offices:** For example, the AMA Morning Rounds, "How You Can Tip the Balance for SGR Repeal," which has a grassroots hotline. https://www.arkmed.org/news/how-you-can-tip-the-balance-for-sgr-repeal.

228 **undercut the hefty prices:** Ethan W. Davis, Jan P. Levine, and Robin P. Summer, "The State Action Doctrine: Active Supervision Reigns Supreme," Troutman Pepper Locke, February 26, 2015. https://www.troutman.com/insights/the-state-action-doctrine-active-supervision-reigns-supreme.html.

228 **forty-two cease-and-desist letters:** "Administrative Law Judge Concludes That North Carolina Dental Board Illegally Blocked Non-Dentists from Providing Teeth Whitening Services," Federal Trade Commission, July 19, 2011. https://www.ftc.gov/news-events/news/press-releases/2011/07/administrative-law-judge-concludes-north-carolina-dental-board-illegally-blocked-non-dentists.

228 **sued the board:** Alexandra Sifferlin, "Supreme Court Says Dentists Can't Decide Who Gets to Whiten Your Teeth," *Time*, February 25, 2015. https://time.com/3722756/supreme-court-teeth-whitening/.

229 **"online with a fixed price":** Austin Jenkins, "As EVs Disrupt Auto Sales, Courts and Legislators Step In to Referee," *Pluribus News*, June 28, 2023. https://pluribusnews.com/news-and-events/as-evs-disrupt-auto-sales-courts-and-legislators-step-in-to-referee/.

229 **"future of ICE [internal combustion engines] and EVs":** "Outgoing 2022 NADA Chairman Mike Alford Underscores Dealer Commitment to Evolving Business Model," NADA, January 27, 2023. https://www.nada.org/nada

/press-releases/outgoing-2022-nada-chairman-mike-alford-underscores-dealer-commitment-evolving.

229 **"maintain a certain number":** Kristy Hartman and Laura Shields, *State Laws on Direct Sales* (National Conference of State Legislatures, August 2021). https://www.wispolitics.com/wp-content/uploads/2021/08/State-Laws-on-Direct-Sales.pdf.

229 **escape public or regulatory scrutiny:** Thomas G. Wollmann, "Stealth Consolidation: Evidence from an Amendment to the Hart-Scott-Rodino Act," *American Economic Review: Insights* 1, no. 1 (June 2019): 77–94. https://doi.org/10.1257/aeri.20180137.

230 **consolidation of anesthesiology:** Aslihan Asil, Paulo Ramos, Amanda Starc, and Thomas G. Wollmann, "Painful Bargaining: Evidence from Anesthesia Rollups," NBER Working Paper No. 33217, November 2024, revised April 2025. https://doi.org/10.3386/w33217.

230 **consolidation in dialysis:** Thomas G. Wollmann, "How to Get Away with Merger: Stealth Consolidation and Its Effects on US Healthcare," NBER Working Paper No. 27274, May 2020, revised March 2024. http://www.nber.org/papers/w27274.

CHAPTER 12: THE LOOPHOLE LOBBY

232 **"in my heart a real affinity":** Jim Tankersley, "Why a Firm Believer in Tax Cuts Could Derail the Senate Tax Cut Plan," *New York Times*, November 18, 2017. https://www.nytimes.com/2017/11/18/us/politics/ron-johnson-senate-tax-cut.html.

232 **"biggest, sweetest, juiciest" peaches:** Weatherford Chamber of Commerce. Accessed August 26, 2025. https://www.experienceweatherford.com/p/about/peach-capital-of-texas.

233 **most of his $85 million:** "Roger Williams," OpenSecrets, 2018. https://www.opensecrets.org/personal-finances/roger-williams/net-worth?cid=N00030602.

233 **"nearly lose a family business":** Roger Williams, "It's Time for Tax Reform," Legistorm, April 3, 2017. https://www.legistorm.com/stormfeed/view_rss/1062808/member/2894/title/it039s-time-for-tax-reform.html.

235 **fewer than one in five hundred:** "U.S. Department of the Treasury, IRS Announce New Initiative to Close Loopholes, Ensure Wealthiest Taxpayers Pay What They Owe," U.S. Department of the Treasury, June 17, 2024. https://home.treasury.gov/news/press-releases/jy2408; and Shannon Najmabadi, "Richest Americans, Big Businesses Might Welcome IRS Cuts, Officials Say," *Washington Post*, March 13, 2025. https://www.washingtonpost.com/business/2025/03/12/irs-staff-cuts-audits-delayed/.

235 **accounted for 44 percent:** "IRS: The Tax Gap," Internal Revenue Service, 2022. https://www.irs.gov/statistics/irs-the-tax-gap; and Samantha Jacoby, "Policy-

makers Should Ensure Pass-Throughs Pay More of Taxes They Owe," Center on Budget and Policy Priorities, November 22, 2019. https://www.cbpp.org/blog/policy-makers-should-ensure-pass-throughs-pay-more-of-taxes-they-owe.

236 **much more generous for mid-market companies:** Section 179 Deduction Limits—Historical Yearly Data, "Historical Section 179 Deduction Limits & Tax Year Archive." https://www.section179.org/previous_years_section_179_expense_deduction/.

236 **boosted it:** Note that the One Big Beautiful Bill Act (OBBBA) ultimately made full expensing à la Section 179 permanent and available to all businesses, though Section 179 covers a slightly broader set of investments.

236 **prohibited business deductions for cars:** David Zipper, "The Reckless Policies That Helped Fill Our Streets with Ridiculously Large Cars," *Vox*, April 28, 2024. https://www.vox.com/future-perfect/24139147/suvs-trucks-popularity-federal-policy-pollution.

236 **"best tax deal in America":** Mitchell Baldridge (@baldridgecpa), "Owning a small business is the best tax deal in America. Whether it's a $10k side hustle or a $10MM business, earning business income opens up amazing opportunities for tax savings and wealth creation. Let's walk through how it works," Twitter, August 25, 2024. https://x.com/baldridgecpa/status/1827704994113454229.

237 **rates reaching as high as 77 percent:** Darien B. Jacobson, Brian G. Raub, and Barry W. Johnson, "The Estate Tax: Ninety Years and Counting," *Statistics of Income Bulletin* 27, no. 1 (Summer 2007): 118–28. https://www.irs.gov/pub/irs-soi/ninetyestate.pdf.

237 **fundamentally transformed public perceptions:** Conor Kenny, Taylor Lincoln, Chuck Collins, and Lee Farris, *Spending Millions to Save Billions: The Campaign of the Super Wealthy to Kill the Estate Tax* (Public Citizen and United for a Fair Economy, April 2006). https://www.citizen.org/wp-content/uploads/estatetaxfinal.pdf.

237 **intergenerational wealth concentration:** Michael Graetz, "'Death Tax' Politics," *Boston College Law Review* 57, no. 3 (2016): 801–14.

237 **campaign proved remarkably effective:** Michael J. Graetz and Ian Shapiro, *Death by a Thousand Cuts: The Fight over Taxing Inherited Wealth*, rev. ed. (Princeton University Press, 2011).

237 **without paying a penny:** David Kocieniewski, "Legacy for One Billionaire: Death, but No Taxes," *New York Times*, June 8, 2010. https://www.nytimes.com/2010/06/09/business/09estate.html.

237 **avoiding or minimizing taxes:** For discussions of strategies used to reduce estate and gift tax liability, see Daniel J. Hemel and Robert Lord, "Closing Gaps in the Estate and Gift Tax Base," *University of Chicago Law School Coase-Sandor Working Paper Series in Law and Economics*, Research Paper No. 937, August 16, 2021. https://chicagounbound.uchicago.edu/cgi/viewcontent.cgi?article=2629&context=law_and_economics. For discussions

of GRATs (grantor retained annuity trusts), IDGTs (intentionally defective grantor trusts), valuation discounts, and dynasty trusts, see Hemel and Lord, "Closing Gaps in the Estate and Gift Tax Base." See also Jesse Drucker, "How One of the World's Richest Men Is Avoiding $8 Billion in Taxes," *New York Times*, December 5, 2024. https://www.nytimes.com/2024/12/05/business/nvidia-jensen-huang-estate-taxes.html.

238 **about 0.1 percent of all estates:** "How Many People Pay the Estate Tax?" Tax Policy Center, January 2024. https://taxpolicycenter.org/briefing-book/how-many-people-pay-estate-tax.

238 **Trump's top economic adviser:** Julie Hirschfeld Davis and Kate Kelly, "Two Bankers Are Selling Trump's Tax Plan. Is Congress Buying?" *New York Times*, August 28, 2017. https://www.nytimes.com/2017/08/28/us/politics/trump-tax-plan-cohn-mnuchin.html.

238 **complex web of trusts:** Shandra Martinez, "Exclusive Interview: Sons Detail Lessons, Moves Fred Meijer Made to Help Company Flourish After His Death," MLive, February 19, 2012. https://www.mlive.com/business/2012/02/fred_meijers_sons_give_first_i.html.

238 **the business as a whole:** Zachary Mider, "How Wal-Mart's Waltons Keep the Tax Man at Bay," *Dallas News*, September 14, 2013. https://www.dallasnews.com/business/retail/2013/09/14/how-wal-marts-waltons-keep-the-tax-man-at-bay/.

238 **watching those assets appreciate in value:** Darren T. Case, "Understanding the Step-Up in Basis Rules upon Death," *Forbes*, October 1, 2024. https://www.forbes.com/sites/darrencase/2024/09/30/understanding-the-step-up-in-basis-rules-upon-death/.

238 **two-thirds of unrealized capital gains:** Emmanuel Saez, Danny Yagan, and Gabriel Zucman, "Capital Gains Withholding," UC Berkeley Working Paper, 2021, Table 1. https://eml.berkeley.edu/~yagan/CapitalGainsWithholding.pdf.

238 **pass on around $200 billion:** Jesse Drucker, "Death and Taxes," *New York Times*, December 5, 2024. https://www.nytimes.com/2024/12/05/briefing/estate-taxes.html.

239 **tax expert Jack Bogdanski observes:** Drucker, "How One of the World's Richest Men Is Avoiding $8 Billion in Taxes."

239 **corporate income above $5,000:** "Corporation Income Tax Brackets and Rates, 1909–2002," Internal Revenue Service. Accessed August 1, 2025. https://www.irs.gov/pub/irs-soi/02corate.pdf; and "Corporate Top Tax Rate and Bracket," Tax Policy Center, January 29, 2024. https://taxpolicycenter.org/statistics/corporate-top-tax-rate-and-bracket.

239 **a quarter of federal revenues:** "What Are the Sources of Revenue for the Federal Government?" Tax Policy Center, January 2024. https://taxpolicycenter.org/briefing-book/what-are-sources-revenue-federal-government.

240 **pass-throughs reap millions:** Bernie Becker, "Let's Make a Deal," *Politico*,

November 28, 2017. https://www.politico.com/newsletters/morning-tax/2017/11/28/lets-make-a-deal-034608.

240 **we spoke about our findings:** National Bureau of Economic Research, *Business in the United States: Who Owns It and How Much Tax They Pay*, 30th Annual Conference on Tax Policy and the Economy, National Press Club, September 24, 2015. https://www.youtube.com/watch?v=qUgDpLNzaNA.

240 **that government reform:** "General Explanations of the Administration's Fiscal Year 2016 Revenue Proposals," Department of the Treasury, February 2015. https://home.treasury.gov/system/files/131/General-Explanations-FY2016.pdf.

243 **70 cents of every dollar:** Matthew Knittel, Susan Nelson, Jason DeBacker, John Kitchen, James Pearce, and Richard Prisinzano, "Methodology to Identify Small Businesses and Their Owners," U.S. Department of the Treasury, Technical Paper 4, August 2011. https://home.treasury.gov/system/files/131/TP-4.pdf; and Eric Zwick, Michael Cooper, John McClelland, James Pearce, Richard Prisinzano, Joseph Sullivan, Danny Yagan, and Owen Zidar, "Business in the United States: Who Owns It and How Much Tax Do They Pay?" *Tax Policy and the Economy* 30, no. 1 (2016): 91–128.

243 **Senate Republicans unveiled their version:** Siobhan Hughes, "Republican Sen. Ron Johnson Opposes GOP Senate Tax Package," *Wall Street Journal*, November 15, 2017. https://www.wsj.com/articles/republican-sen-ron-johnson-opposes-gop-senate-tax-package-1510777290.

244 **same year he married:** "Ron Johnson," *Encyclopedia Britannica*, June 28, 2025. https://www.britannica.com/biography/Ron-Johnson-United-States-Senator.

244 **polyester plastics company:** Tom Kertscher, "The Incomplete Claim That Sen. Ron Johnson 'Started' Pacur, His Plastics Manufacturing Company," PolitiFact, May 4, 2016. https://www.politifact.com/factchecks/2016/may/04/ron-johnson/incomplete-claim-sen-ron-johnson-started-pacur-his/.

244 **Bemis was Pacur's only customer:** Jud Lounsbury, "Senate Historian Removes Ron Johnson's Big Lie from Official Bio," *Progressive Magazine*, May 19, 2016. https://progressive.org/latest/senate-historian-removes-ron-johnson-s-big-lie-official-bio/.

244 **"came along for the ride":** Kertscher, "Incomplete Claim That Sen. Ron Johnson 'Started' Pacur."

244 **retained Johnson as chief executive:** "Ron Johnson," *Encyclopedia Britannica*.

244 **"had Obamacare not been passed":** "CNS News: Sen. Johnson: Health Care Freedom Saved My Daughter's Life—Obamacare Will 'Lead to Rationing,'" Ron Johnson, U.S. Senator for Wisconsin, March 29, 2012. https://www.ronjohnson.senate.gov/2012/3/cns-news-sen-johnson-health-care-freedom-saved-my-daughter-s-life-obamacare-will-lead-to-rationing.

245 **stifle the innovation:** "CNS News: Sen. Johnson: Health Care Freedom

Saved My Daughter's Life"; and Ron Johnson, "Chairman Ron Johnson Opening Statement 'Connecting Patients to New and Potential Life Saving Treatments,'" Committee on Homeland Security & Governmental Affairs, February 25, 2016. https://www.hsgac.senate.gov/media/reps/chairman-ron-johnson-opening-statement-connecting-patients-to-new-and-potential-life-saving-treatments/.

245 **resonated with audiences:** "Ron Johnson," *Encyclopedia Britannica.*

245 **could run for office:** Clare Goldsberry, "Plastics Today: Mr. Johnson, Plastics Processor," *Plastics Today*, March 3, 2011. https://www.plasticstoday.com/plastics-processing/mr-johnson-plastics-processor-goes-to-washington.

245 **the Senate's sixth-richest member:** "Ron Johnson," OpenSecrets, 2018. https://www.opensecrets.org/personal-finances/ron-johnson/net-worth?cid=N00032546&year=2018.

245 **million to pro-Johnson groups:** Justin Elliott and Robert Faturechi, "Secret IRS Files Reveal How Much the Ultrawealthy Gained by Shaping Trump's 'Big, Beautiful Tax Cut,'" ProPublica, August 11, 2021. https://www.propublica.org/article/secret-irs-files-reveal-how-much-the-ultrawealthy-gained-by-shaping-trumps-big-beautiful-tax-cut.

246 **"Koch brothers of Wisconsin politics":** Daniel Bice, "Uihleins Spend Big to Help Ron Johnson Defend Senate Seat from Russ Feingold," *Milwaukee Journal Sentinel*, October 4, 2015. https://web.archive.org/web/20151106194532/http://www.jsonline.com/watchdog/noquarter/uihleins-spend-big-to-help-ron-johnson-defend-senate-seat-from-russ-feingold-b99589973z1-330585321.html.

246 **around $12 million to committees:** Elliott and Faturechi, "Secret IRS Files Reveal How Much the Ultrawealthy Gained."

246 **acted as a conduit:** The primary source for the information in this paragraph comes from Elliott and Faturechi, "Secret IRS Files Revealed How Much the Ultrawealthy Gained by Shaping Trump's 'Big, Beautiful Tax Cut.'" who obtained these emails via a FOIA request.

246 **"especially for private real estate pass-through entities":** Ted Kellner, Letter to Ron Johnson, "Ron Johnson et al. TCJA Correspondence," 2017. https://www.documentcloud.org/documents/20744688-ron-johnson-et-al-tcja-correspondence/#document/p2/a2050053, cited in Elliott and Faturechi, "Secret IRS Files Reveal How Much the Ultrawealthy Gained by Shaping Trump's 'Big, Beautiful Tax Cut.'"

246 **"disparate, grossly unfair" treatment:** Ron Johnson, Letter to Thomas Barthold, Mark Prater, Justin Muzinich, David Kautter, Drew Maloney, George Callas, Victoria Glover, et al., "Ron Johnson et al. TCJA Correspondence," 2017. https://www.documentcloud.org/documents/20744688-ron-johnson-et-al-tcja-correspondence/#document/p2/a2050053, cited in Elliott and Faturechi, "Secret IRS Files Reveal How Much the Ultrawealthy Gained by Shaping Trump's 'Big, Beautiful Tax Cut.'"

246 **"improve the pass-through provisions":** Kevin Brady, Letter to Ron, "Ron Johnson et al. TCJA Correspondence," 2017. https://www.documentcloud.org/documents/20744688-ron-johnson-et-al-tcja-correspondence/#document/p2/a2050053, cited in Elliott and Faturechi, "Secret IRS Files Reveal How Much the Ultrawealthy Gained by Shaping Trump's 'Big, Beautiful Tax Cut.'"

247 **"smaller pass-throughs got a tax cut":** Ron Johnson, remarks at Politico Playbook The First 100 Days: Tax Reform Event," YouTube, January 22, 2025. https://www.youtube.com/live/qNNsKZoejmU.

247 **a Treasury study found:** Lucas Goodman, Katherine Lim, Bruce Sacerdote, and Andrew Whitten, "How Do Business Owners Respond to a Tax Cut? Examining the 199A Deduction for Pass-Through Firms," *Journal of Public Economics* 242 (February 2025): 105293. https://doi.org/10.1016/j.jpubeco.2024.105293. In 2018, taxpayers deducted $154 billion due to Section 199A (Table C2). Those earning more than $1 million in annual income accounted for $54.2 billion.

247 **Uline generated nearly $1 billion:** Elliott and Faturechi, "Secret IRS Files Reveal How Much the Ultrawealthy Gained by Shaping Trump's 'Big, Beautiful Tax Cut.'"

247 **reduced their taxes:** Elliott and Faturechi, "Secret IRS Files Reveal How Much the Ultrawealthy Gained by Shaping Trump's 'Big, Beautiful Tax Cut.'"

247 **saving $36 million in taxes:** Elliott and Faturechi, "Secret IRS Files Reveal How Much the Ultrawealthy Gained by Shaping Trump's 'Big, Beautiful Tax Cut.'"

247 **walked away with tax savings:** Elliott and Faturechi, "Secret IRS Files Reveal How Much the Ultrawealthy Gained by Shaping Trump's 'Big, Beautiful Tax Cut.'"

247 **special tax break:** Josh Keefe, David Sirota, and Alex Kotch, "Last-Minute Real Estate Tax Break in GOP Bill Will Benefit Trump," *International Business Times*, December 16, 2017. https://www.ibtimes.com/political-capital/last-minute-real-estate-tax-break-gop-bill-will-benefit-trump-2629381.

248 **rental income from real estate–related LLCs:** Keefe, Sirota, and Kotch, "Last-Minute Real Estate Tax Break."

248 **"is our country better with this":** Seung Min Kim, "Why Corker Flipped on the Tax Bill," *Politico*, December 18, 2017. https://www.politico.com/story/2017/12/18/bob-corker-tax-bill-kickback-republicans-respond-302482.

248 **"Corker kickback":** Kim, "Why Corker Flipped on the Tax Bill."

248 **a Montana Republican:** Igor Derysh, "Steve Daines Backed Policies That Benefited Himself and GOP Pal Greg Gianforte," *Salon*, October 8, 2020. https://www.salon.com/2020/10/08/montana-sen-steve-daines-backed-policies-that-benefited-him-and-gop-pal-rep-greg-gianforte/; and Brian Faler, "What You Need to Know About the Senate's Pass-Through Tax Debate," *Politico*, November 28, 2017. https://www.politico.com/story/2017/11/28/what-is-pass-through-tax-debate-senate-192470.

248 **Medicare payroll taxes withheld:** Tax Policy Center, "Payroll Tax Rates: 1937 to 2024," January 29, 2024. https://taxpolicycenter.org/statistics/payroll-tax-rates.

249 **saving him an estimated $69,000:** Seth Hanlon, "Closing Tax Loophole to Pay for Student Loan Bill Is Simply Common Sense," Center for American Progress, May 7, 2012. https://www.americanprogress.org/article/closing-tax-loophole-to-pay-for-student-loan-bill-is-simply-common-sense/.

249 **paid himself only $360,000:** Hanlon, "Closing Tax Loophole to Pay for Student Loan Bill Is Simply Common Sense."

249 **saving around $600,000:** Seth Hanlon, "Center for American Progress Supports S Corp Provision in Senate Student Loan Bill," *Tax Notes*, May 7, 2012. https://www.taxnotes.com/research/federal/other-documents/washington-roundup/center-american-progress-releases-plan-reform-tax-system-reduce-deficit/vm5x.

249 **Social Security or Medicare taxes:** Pamela S. Gardiner, "Actions Are Needed to Eliminate Inequities in the Employment Tax Liabilities of Sole Proprietorships and Single-Shareholder S Corporations," Memorandum for Deputy Commissioner for Services and Enforcement, U.S. Department of the Treasury, May 20, 2005. https://www.finance.senate.gov/imo/media/doc/rgtestrpt052505.pdf.

250 **launched an aggressive counterattack:** Paul Kiel, "How a Decades-Old Loophole Lets Billionaires Avoid Medicare Taxes," ProPublica, December 11, 2024. https://www.propublica.org/article/medicare-tax-loophole-steve-cohen?utm_source=sailthru&utm_medium=email&utm_campaign=majorinvestigations&utm_content=feature.

250 **ran radio ads to pressure:** NFIB Media, "NFIB West Virginia Radio Ad—No New Taxes on Small Business," July 18, 2022. https://www.youtube.com/watch?v=9usR6VigvV4.

250 **lawmakers deferred to business owners:** Kiel, "How a Decades-Old Loophole Lets Billionaires Avoid Medicare Taxes."

250 **pioneering an approach:** William Gorrod, Renn Neilson, Matthew Larsen, Jon Feldhammer, and Ali Foyt, "SALT Cap Workaround: Pass-Through Entity Tax Update, Part I," Bloomberg Tax, February 8, 2022. https://news.bloombergtax.com/tax-insights-and-commentary/salt-cap-workaround-pass-through-entity-tax-update-part-i.

251 **would cost the federal government:** Richard Rubin, "The SALT Cap Has a $20 Billion Hole," *Wall Street Journal*, August 27, 2023. https://www.wsj.com/politics/the-salt-cap-has-a-20-billion-hole-a0cd2db.

251 **two Illinois anesthesiologists:** Joshua D. Gottlieb, Maria Polyakova, Kevin Rinz, Hugh Shiplett, and Victoria Udalova, "The Earnings and Labor Supply of U.S. Physicians," *Quarterly Journal of Economics* 140, no. 2 (May 2025): 1243–98. https://doi.org/10.1093/qje/qjaf001.

252 **individual income tax cuts:** Alicia Parlapiano, Margot Sanger-Katz, Aatish Bhatia, and Josh Katz, "Everything in Trump's Big Tax and Spending Law, and How Much It Will Cost or Save," *New York Times*, July 22, 2025. https://www.nytimes.com/interactive/2025/06/30/upshot/senate-republican-megabill.html; and "Breaking Down the One Big Beautiful Bill," Committee for a Responsible Federal Budget, June 4, 2025. https://www.crfb.org/blogs/breaking-down-one-big-beautiful-bill.

252 **"employees at certain Alaskan":** Brian Faler, "GOP Megabill Littered with Special Tax Breaks," *Politico*, July 4, 2025. https://www.politico.com/news/2025/07/04/from-rum-to-gun-silencers-tailored-tax-breaks-add-billions-to-megabill-00438962?utm_medium=news-DD&utm_source=urban_newsletters&utm_term=TPC.

253 **"many of them are small business owners":** *Meet the Press*, "June 1, 2025: Full Transcript of NBC's 'Meet the Press,'" NBC News, June 1, 2025. https://www.nbcnews.com/meet-the-press/june-1-2025-n1312211.

253 **"I'm a man of modest means":** "Mike Johnson's Net Worth in 2025 and Why the Speaker of the House Says He's Essentially Living Paycheck to Paycheck," *Parade*, November 6, 2025. https://parade.com/celebrities/mike-johnson-net-worth.

253 **Republican donor from Nashville:** Joshua Kaplan, Justin Elliott, and Alex Mierjeski, "Speaker Mike Johnson Is Living in a D.C. House That Is the Center of a Pastor's Secretive Influence Campaign," ProPublica, February 28, 2025. https://www.propublica.org/article/mike-johnson-evangelical-pastor-steve-berger-roommates.

EPILOGUE

255 **a series of essays:** David Remnick, ed., *The New Gilded Age: "The New Yorker" Looks at the Culture of Affluence* (Random House, 2000).

255 ***Unequal Democracy*:** Larry M. Bartels, *Unequal Democracy: The Political Economy of the New Gilded Age* (Princeton University Press, 2008).

255 **"Sound familiar?":** Edward T. O'Donnell, "Are We Living in the Gilded Age 2.0?" History.com, February 12, 2025. https://www.history.com/news/second-gilded-age-income-inequality.

255 **"second Gilded Age":** Paul Krugman, "Why We're in a New Gilded Age," *New York Review of Books*, May 8, 2014. https://www.nybooks.com/articles/2014/05/08/thomas-piketty-new-gilded-age/; and Joshua Zeitz, "The Gilded Age Is Back—and That Should Worry Conservatives," *Politico*, March 2, 2025. https://www.politico.com/news/magazine/2025/03/02/trump-musk-bezos-gilded-age-corporations-economy-00205454.

255 **2025 essay:** Paul Krugman, "Understanding Inequality, Part I," Substack, June 1, 2025. https://open.substack.com/pub/paulkrugman/p/understanding-inequality-part-i?

257 **Rockefeller's wealth:** Ron Chernow, *Titan: The Life of John D. Rockefeller, Sr.* (Vintage Press, 2004).

258 **Rockefeller and Vanderbilt:** "Half a Billion Back of McKinley," *New York Journal*, August 3, 1896. https://www.loc.gov/resource/sn84024350/1896-08-03/ed-1/?sp=2&r=0.33,0.09,1.741,0.762,0.

258 **from New York City:** Herbert Croly, *Marcus Alonzo Hanna: His Life and Work* (Macmillan, 1912).

259 **more than 80 percent:** Authors' update of Francisco J. Buera and Joseph P. Kaboski, "The Rise of the Service Economy," *American Economic Review* 102, no. 6 (October 2012): 2540–69. https://doi.org/10.1257/aer.102.6.2540, using National Income and Produce Accounts (NIPA) data.

259 **President Ford reportedly hoarded:** "Coors," Encyclopedia.com. Accessed August 28, 2025. https://www.encyclopedia.com/media/encyclopedias-almanacs-transcripts-and-maps/coors.

259 **contraband east of the Mississippi:** Emily Bell, "The True Coors Bootlegging Story Behind Smokey and the Bandit," *VinePair*, March 29, 2016. https://vinepair.com/wine-blog/smokey-and-the-bandit-and-coors/.

260 **60 percent of Americans:** "What Percentage of Americans Own Stock?" Gallup, May 5, 2025. https://news.gallup.com/poll/266807/percentage-americans-owns-stock.aspx.

260 **double the share of 1989:** Matt Phillips, "A Record Share of U.S. Households Now Own Stocks," *Axios*, October 18, 2023. https://www.axios.com/2023/10/18/percentage-americans-own-stock-market-investing.

260 **"biggest economic misunderstanding":** Z Fellows (@zfellows), "Sam Altman: 'The Biggest Economic Misunderstanding of My Childhood Was That People Got Rich from High Salaries,'" X, March 6, 2024. https://x.com/ZFellows_/status/1765329892659409323.

261 **interest rates since 1980:** Daniel L. Greenwald, Matteo Leombroni, Hanno Lustig, and Stijn Van Nieuwerburgh, "Financial and Total Wealth Inequality with Declining Interest Rates," September 2, 2023. https://www.dlgreenwald.com/uploads/4/5/2/8/45280895/totalwealthinequality_08312023.pdf.

262 **Roark Capital:** Ben Cohen, "America's Hottest Chicken Chain Started with $900—and Just Sold for $1 Billion," *Wall Street Journal*, June 6, 2025. https://www.wsj.com/business/hospitality/daves-hot-chicken-deal-roark-bac46ced.

263 **Clayton Act of 1914:** "The Antitrust Laws," U.S. Department of Justice, December 20, 2023. https://www.justice.gov/atr/antitrust-laws-and-you.

264 **half as likely:** Ran Abramitzky, Leah Boustan, and Owen Zidar, "The Class Ceiling," Princeton Working Paper, 2025.

265 **chance of making it:** Opportunity Insights replication files.

265 **fifty hours per week:** Valerie Ramey and Neville Francis, "A Century of Work and Leisure," *American Economic Journal: Macroeconomics* 1, no. 2 (2009): 189–224. https://econweb.ucsd.edu/~vramey/research/Century_Published.pdf.

265 **a third of entrepreneurs:** Raj Chetty, Gaia Dossi, Matt Smith, John Van Reenen, Owen Zidar, and Eric Zwick, "Creating New Businesses in America," Working Paper, 2025.

265 **non-white business owners:** Authors' analysis of the SCF (Survey of Consumer Finances).

265 **better opportunities for talented individuals:** Chang-Tai Hsieh, Erik Hurst, Charles I. Jones, and Peter J. Klenow, "The Allocation of Talent and U.S. Economic Growth," *Econometrica* 87, no. 5 (September 2019): 1439–74.

267 **outperformed their non-entrepreneurial counterparts:** Chetty et al., "Creating New Businesses in America."

268 **account for around one-third:** Table F of "Business Employment Dynamics Data by Firm Size Class," U.S. Bureau of Labor Statistics. Accessed August 26, 2025. https://www.bls.gov/bdm/bdmfirmsize.htm#SIZE1.

268 **through their employers:** About 60 percent of Americans before the age of sixty-five—165 million people—had employer-provided insurance in 2023. Gary Claxton, Matthew Rae, and Aubrey Winger, "Employer-Sponsored Health Insurance 101," KFF, October 8, 2025. https://www.kff.org/health-costs/health-policy-101-employer-sponsored-health-insurance/?entry=table-of-contents-introduction.

268 **boost wages:** Amy Finkelstein, Casey McQuillan, Owen Zidar, and Eric Zwick, "The Health Wedge and Labor Market Inequality," Brookings Institution, March 29, 2023. https://www.brookings.edu/articles/the-health-wedge-and-labor-market-inequality/.

268 **many times since then:** "History of Federal Minimum Wage Rates Under the Fair Labor Standards Act, 1938–2009," U.S. Department of Labor. Accessed August 26, 2025. https://www.dol.gov/agencies/whd/minimum-wage/history/chart.

268 **reducing income inequality:** Ben Harris and Melissa S. Kearney, "The 'Ripple Effect' of a Minimum Wage Increase on American Workers," Brookings Institution, July 10, 2014. https://www.brookings.edu/articles/the-ripple-effect-of-a-minimum-wage-increase-on-american-workers/.

268 **minimum wage increases:** Nirupama Rao and Max Risch, "Who's Afraid of the Minimum Wage? Measuring the Impacts on Independent Businesses Using Matched U.S. Tax Returns," *Quarterly Journal of Economics* 141, no. 1 (February 2026): 373–427. https://doi.org/10.1093/qje/qjaf053.

269 **no federal income tax:** Jesse Eisinger, Jeff Ernsthausen, and Paul Kiel, "The Secret IRS Files: Trove of Never-Before-Seen Records Reveal How the Wealthiest Avoid Income Tax," ProPublica, June 8, 2021. https://www.propublica.org/article/the-secret-irs-files-trove-of-never-before-seen-records-reveal-how-the-wealthiest-avoid-income-tax.

271 **Bill Ussery:** Lusiana Suegart, "Luxe Speed Ahead," *Key Biscayne Magazine*, July 12, 2018. https://keybiscaynemag.com/luxe-speed-ahead/.

271 **a second site:** Denie Harris, "Mercedes-Benz of Cutler Bay Celebrating

Decade in Business," *Miami's Community News*, September 11, 2018. https://communitynewspapers.com/cutler-bay/mercedes-benz-of-cutler-bay-celebrating-decade-in-business/?utm_source=chatgpt.com.

271 **more than $650 million:** Jaelyn Campbell, "Mercedes-Benz Dealerships Owned by Bill Ussery Sell for $150 Million," CBT News, August 10, 2023. https://www.cbtnews.com/mercedes-benz-dealerships-owned-by-bill-ussery-gets-sold-for-150-million/.

271 **Nick Saban:** Campbell, "Mercedes-Benz Dealerships Owned by Bill Ussery Sell for $150 Million."

ACKNOWLEDGMENTS

This book builds on a decade of research during which we learned from many stellar coauthors including (in reverse alphabetical order): Constantine Yannelis, Danny Yagan, Heidi Williams, John Van Reenen, Joseph Sullivan, Matt Smith, Rich Prisinzano, Neviana Petkova, James Pearce, Christos Makridis, John McClelland, Casey McQuillan, Pat Kline, João Granja, Amy Finkelstein, Gaia Dossi, Michael Cooper, and Raj Chetty. We are grateful for the support of those in the Department of the Treasury and the IRS who made the research underlying this book possible.

Many people made material contributions to the book, especially Larry Haas, who helped turn our economistic jargon into plain language and made every chapter better with his sharp editing. It is interesting to note that we never had a major disagreement with Larry. Karen Alexander helped us interview and profile several of the Main Street Millionaires in the book. Drawing from rich institutional knowledge, Dave Infante helped us craft the story of beverage distributors. Rina Torchinsky helped draw together secondary materials on two other characters in the book. Our agent, Rafe Sagalyn, was instrumental in taking our rough first draft proposal and shaping it into the perfect road map for the final book. Tim Duggan and the team at Holt provided helpful guidance and editing throughout the project. Chad Zimmerman gave us an early nudge to consider writing for a popular audience.

We are grateful for supplementary data from Adam Bonica, the

National Establishment Time Series dataset, Chenoa Yorgason's local election data, Trish Kirkland's mayoral data, and Silvia Vannutelli and Nick Carnes's biographical information on state legislators.

We thank Isaias Nazareno Vilato, Nathan Reiser, Malcolm McCormick, Walker Lewis, Ruben Hernandez, Danika Grieser, Molly Cook, Anna Chernesky, and Kevin Cao for excellent research assistance. We acknowledge and greatly appreciate financial support from Princeton's Industrial Relation Section and the Booth School of Business at the University of Chicago.

We also want to thank the participants at our book conference, whose reactions to an early draft made the book even better. We thank Stan Veuger, Evan Soltas, Nolan McCarty, Annette Lareau, Ilyana Kuziemko, Henrik Kleven, Trish Kirkland, Sabrina Howell, Andy Hall, John Friedman, Jesse Eisinger, and Leah Boustan. We also thank Indy Parisi and the Industrial Relations Section for helping make the conference possible. Several other colleagues gave terrific comments on the book and championed the underlying research, including Richard Thaler, Nikita Taniparti, Larry Summers, Amir Sufi, Seth Stephens-Davidowitz, Isaac Solotaroff, Andrei Shleifer, Jim Poterba, Jordan Padnuk, Atif Mian, Travis McKee, Dylan Matthews, Dave Kushner, James Knight, Steve Kaplan, Michael Graetz, Nick Epley, Angus Deaton, Colleen Curry, and Jediphi Cabal.

Hillary and Holly, thank you for all your patience and wisdom, for tolerating the many coauthor phone calls that don't respect work hours, and for sanity checking so many silly ideas. Writing this book would not have been possible without the love and support of our families, several members of whom arrived just in time for the book's release (ahem, Leo and Emma). Zwick thanks Janet and Danny for accommodating with generous spirits his many unannounced extended visits to D.C. Major contributions of putting-it-all-into-perspective also came from Little O and Jamie.

INDEX

Note: Page numbers in *italics* indicate figures, and references following "n" refer to the notes.

ABOUT THE AUTHORS

OWEN ZIDAR is a professor of economics and public affairs at Princeton University. Zidar earned a PhD in economics from the University of California, Berkeley, and a BA from Dartmouth College. He lives in Princeton, New Jersey, with his wife and three children.

ERIC ZWICK is the Joel F. Gemunder Professor of Economics and Finance at the University of Chicago Booth School of Business. Zwick earned a PhD in business economics from Harvard University and a BA from Swarthmore College. He lives in Chicago, Illinois, with his wife and son.